M000159966

POLITICAL PHYSICS

Deleuze, Derrida and the Body Politic

JOHN PROTEVI

THE ATHLONE PRESS
LONDON and NEW YORK

First published in 2001 by
THE ATHLONE PRESS
A Continuum imprint
The Tower Building, 11 York Road, London SE1 7NX
370 Lexington Avenue, New York, NY10017-6503

British Library Cataloguing in Publication Data
*A catalogue record for this book is available
from the British Library*

ISBN 0 485 00426 7 HB
0 485 00619 7 PB

Library of Congress Cataloging-in-Publication Data
A catalog record for this book is available from the Library of Congress

Typeset by CentraServe, Saffron Walden, Essex
Printed and bound in Great Britain by
MPG Books Ltd, Bodmin, Cornwall

Contents

Acknowledgements

This book began with the 'phase transition' I underwent during my stay as Leverhulme Research Fellow in the Philosophy Department at University of Warwick in 1995–96. I encountered there a group of energetic, friendly and open-minded philosophers who engaged in what seemed to me at the time to be the most astonishingly interdisciplinary philosophical discussions, bringing together phenomenology, deconstruction, analytic philosophy of mind and philosophy of science, complexity theory, and Deleuze and Guattari. My colleagues there changed my style of thinking deeply and permanently, and their friendship made that year the best of my academic career. They included Miguel de Beistegui, without whose friendship and indeed faith in me I would never have been awarded the Leverhulme Fellowship; Nick Land, whose seminar provided a fascinating introduction to the 'twisted materialism' of Deleuze and Guattari; Alistair Welchman, who taught me everything I know about hylomorphism and who has since then graciously submitted to endless phone calls in which I go on and on about my latest attempts at working through what he already knows about biology and non-linear dynamics; Judith Norman, who helped me adjust to life in England by pointing out all the good balti shops in Leamington; Stephen Houlgate and Christine Battersby, whose comments on chapter drafts helped my understanding of Hegel and Kant, respectively, and whose exceptional friendship and generosity made my stay there a real pleasure; Andrew Benjamin, who graciously provided his office while on leave and who upon his return shared many a lunch with good conversation and good cheer; David Miller and Greg Hunt, who welcomed me to their seminar on philosophy of science and proved exceedingly gracious hosts, genuinely interested in the interchange of 'continental' and 'analytic' viewpoints; Martin Warner, whose open door and bibliographic and administrative skills as well as linguistic and philosophic knowledge solved many a problem; and Keith Ansell Pearson, whose subsequent work as editor on this book has been patient, sharp and insightful, and who, along with Jonathan Dronsfield, stoked my interest in English football, much to the chagrin of Simon Sparks, who would have preferred I follow cricket.

All in all Warwick was a heady brew for me, and after several years of catch-up reading, I began serious work on this book with the encouragement of Keith Ansell Pearson and Tristan Palmer at Athlone Press, who have been ideal editors, encouraging, supportive, and at the same time rigorous. I also thank the anonymous reviewer of the manuscript, who provided a careful and thorough reading which helped me focus the argument in many places. Here in the States, my work has been supported materially and emotionally by my colleagues at Louisiana State University, including Greg Stone, Greg Schufreider, Charles Bigger, Vladimir Djokic, Ken Zagacki, Peter Sutherland, Gail Sutherland, Ann Holmes, Lenny Stanton, Dena Goodman, Margaret Parker, Jill Suitor, Michelle Massé, Karl Roider and above all Jeff Humphries, who saved my career by arranging a variety of posts for me, and who has become a real friend in the process of our working together in the LSU Department of French Studies. In writing the book I was reminded once again, sentence by sentence, in detail and in depth, of all that I've learned from my teachers, colleagues, and students, only a few of whom I can name here: Joseph Kockelmans, John Sallis, Tom Sheehan, Jeff Nealon, George Matthews, Robert Bernasconi, Len Lawlor, Kevin Thompson, Walter Brogan, Kevin Miles, Keith Peterson, Dan Conway, Francisco Varela, Brian Rotman, Paul Patton, Dan Smith, Richard Beardsworth and Robert Rose.

Some sections of this book are based on previously published material. Grateful acknowledgment is made for permission to use revised versions of the following: DePaul University, 'Egyptian priests and German professors: on the alleged difficulty of philosophy', *Philosophy Today* 41.1 (Spring 1997), 181–8; Kluwer Academic Publishers, '*Given Time* and the gift of life', *Man and World* 30.1 (Jan 1997), 65–82; SUNY Press, 'Derrida's political physics', in *Phenomenology, Interpretation, and Community*, edited by Lenore Langsdorf and Stephen H. Watson (Albany: SUNY Press, 1996), 221–35; 'Violence and authority in Kant', *Epoché* 2 (1994), 65–89; 'Derrida and Hegel:

Différance and *Unterschied'*, *International Studies in Philosophy* 25.3 (1993), 59–74.

I dedicate this book to my wife, Kate Jensen, for our love, our years together and our years to come.

Note on texts and references: I use two abbreviations throughout: 'ATP' for Deleuze and Guattari's *A Thousand Plateaus* and 'ITOG' for Derrida's *Introduction to Husserl's Origin of Geometry*. Page references cite the original French or German first, followed by the translation. I used the Oxford Classical Text editions for the Greek texts of Plato and Aristotle.

Introduction

Overview
Forceful bodies politic
Derrida, Deleuze and science
Hylomorphism and material self-ordering
Comparative and synthetic aspects
Preview of chapters

OVERVIEW

Although Jacques Derrida and Gilles Deleuze are the leading philosophers of French post-structuralism, very little has been done to
compare their work on common issues or to produce new work using
a synthesis of their approaches.[1] In *Political Physics* I do both, focusing
on their respective approaches to the question of the body politic[2] and
combining Derridean deconstructive close readings of the history of
philosophy and Deleuzean conceptual creation in dialogue with the
contemporary science popularly known as 'complexity theory'.[3] *Political Physics* is thus doubly transversal: crossing the transversal of Derrida
and Deleuze with that of philosophy and science.

An additional transversality comes about as the text consists of two
different types of readings of classic texts that are themselves transversals. In Part I, I produce readings of Derrida's relation to Husserl,
Hegel, the gift of life, and AIDS that highlight the 'forceful body
politic' inhabiting a 'general text' of force and signification, crossing
that reading of the Derridean concern with metaphysics with the
Deleuzean critique of 'hylomorphism' (the doctrine that production is
the imposition of formal order on chaotic or passive matter); Part II
presents Derridean-style close readings of the Deleuzean theme of the
implicit hylomorphism of the 'organ-ized body politic' in Plato,
Aristotle, Heidegger and Kant.

The underlying principle of the book is as follows: although the work of Jacques Derrida is a magnificent achievement and a lasting contribution to the tradition of post-phenomenological European philosophy, it is, while still necessary to any progressive philosophical and political practice, primarily of propaedeutic value in the reflection on and intervention into the convergent fields assuming the highest importance in the material structuring of the current global system of bodies politic: recombinant genetics, cognitive science, dynamical systems theory and others. Derrida's work, though destroying the self-evidence of the various identification machines at work today – the naturalized self-images of nations, races, genders, subjects and so on – by inscribing the production of meaning in a world of 'force and signification', can only prepare the way for the radicality of Deleuzean historical–libidinal materialism: the principles guiding the empirical study of forceful bodies politic in their material production.

In other words, in moving the concept of the transcendental from that of the conditions of possibility of experience to that of the quasi-transcendental conditions of impossibility, the aporias, of experience,[4] Derrida performs the labour necessary to shake free of millennia of philosophical idealism, thus moving us from the pretensions of the cultural stratum to the point where a Deleuzean investigation of the material forces of all strata can begin.[5] Thus a Derridean deconstructive reading will move us from the pretensions of metaphysics or phenomenology as the self-grounding of a rational, meaningful sign system – the book of nature – to the inscription of marks in a world of force and signification – the 'general text'.[6] At that point the Deleuzean injunction takes hold: conduct a material analysis of forceful bodies politic.[7] Deleuze's own shifting of the transcendental from the conditions of possibility investigated by phenomenology – and from the conditions of impossibility, the aporias investigated by deconstruction – to the virtual realm,[8] the patterns and triggers of actual bodies, thus implicitly articulates a research programme for the investigation of forceful bodies politic: he bids us investigate their virtual space to find their triggers ('singularities'), and their patterns of self-ordering ('abstract machines' linked together to form a 'machinic phylum'), in a 'micropolitics' (hence Deleuze's well-known affinity with Foucault).[9] We thus are confronted, in Deleuze's works, with a radically materialist philosophy that engages all the powers of contemporary physics and biology to analyse and intervene in those sectors of the contemporary global system which gleefully embrace difference and flow; with Derrida, on the other hand, we must remain content with the deconstruction of idealist philosophy and the consequent shaking of those political structures still reliant on identity – a necessary and not inconsiderable achievement, to be sure.

FORCEFUL BODIES POLITIC

The three key notions of *Political Physics*, the common content linking the chapters, are the Deleuzean–Nietzschean notion of forceful bodies politic, and what I take to be the major philosophic implications of complexity theory, a notion of material self-ordering and the critique of hylomorphism it makes possible. In describing Nietzsche's ontology of force in *Nietzsche and Philosophy* (1983), Deleuze describes the production of forceful bodies: 'Every relationship of forces constitutes a body – whether it is chemical, biological, social, or political' (45/40). The study of forceful bodies requires a political physics: both a politicized physics (paying attention to the political ground of such basic physics terms as 'law') and a physicalized politics (paying attention to the physical ground of such basic political terms as 'force') are needed in order to understand politics as the forceful organ-ization of bodies.[10] As the Deleuzean–Nietzschean notion of bodies allows us to think bodies in various registers, we have the conceptual license to divest politics of its restricted state-orientation, so that the constitution of physical, chemical, biological and social bodies can be thought politically (in terms of the law of their ordering of force relations), while the constitution of political bodies can be thought physically, chemically, biologically or socially (in terms of the forces involved in their ordering of laws). Forceful bodies (persons, families, groups, parties, gangs, corporations, races, sects, nations, worlds) are thus particular force-arrangements of chemical, biological and social bodies, themselves force-arrangements: they are forceful bodies politic. In its most radical Deleuzean moment, political physics, in thinking forceful bodies politic, thus moves both 'above' and 'below' the level of the individual as classically conceived in liberal humanism, opening ways

3

to investigate both 'social machines' (inter alia, tribalism, monarchism, liberalism, fascism, and the experimental immanent self-orderings Deleuze and Guattari call 'war machines') and the 'molecular flows' of matter (somatic fluids, of course – milk, sweat, sperm, urine, blood – but also steel, electricity, concrete) they order into forceful bodies politic. The classical modern notion of life, restricted to the organic individual or perhaps the species as collection of individuals, is thus too restricted for the scope of political physics.[11]

While to my knowledge Derrida does not use the term 'forceful body', he thematizes force in every discussion of politics, as I detail in Chapter 2.[12] Derrida's deconstructive approach to the question of the forceful body focuses on the undecidable role played by force in legitimating a body politic. In deconstructing the social contract, Derrida shows that the 'mystical force of authority', as he calls it, is unthinkable in the history of Western philosophy due to the allegiance to presence constitutive of the text of Western metaphysics. After the ground-clearing work of deconstruction's 'negative' moment, Derrida's 'positive' thought of the body politic conceives it as a 'general text' of 'force and signification'. For Derrida, however, force, while marking the breaking point for consciousness, its point of inscription in a world of force that robs it of its pretensions to self-mastery ('one would seek in vain a concept in phenomenology which would permit the thinking of intensity or force'; Derrida, *Writing and Difference*, 1978, 46/27; translation modified), remains an inarticulate ('mystical') other, even as the disruption of consciousness by force is affirmed in welcoming the other. Thus while deconstruction can dismantle the presence–form nexus at the heart of the metaphysical representation of the production of forceful bodies politic (the site for our transverse reading of a Derridean critique of hylomorphism) and move us onto a general text whose thought of the interlacing of force and signification exposes us to the disruption of the same by the other in the 'democracy to come', it can't offer us an empirical research programme for exploring that text and the material bodies formed therein. In other words, the powerful and to-be-prized effect of deconstruction – the opening out of phenomenological interiority in the form of consciousness to a world of 'force and signification' – is only the highlighting of the dismantling effects of such a world on pretensions to natural or rational identity and stability; deconstruction is unable to articulate the material processes of production of forceful bodies in the general text upon whose effects it lives. In a word, deconstruction is top-down: starting with claims of bodies politic to natural and simple identity it shows *différance* or its cousins worrying and shaking those pretensions and thus opening those inhabiting that body to the critical claims of the call of the other in the democracy to come. On the other hand Deleuzean historical–libidinal materialism is bottom-up: starting with a virtual differential field it investigates the triggers and patterns of the production of bodies politic and thus offers avenues for nuanced pragmatic intervention and experimental production of immanent and democratic bodies politic, which he calls 'war machines', 'planes of immanence', or 'full Bodies without Organs'.

DERRIDA, DELEUZE AND SCIENCE

This inability to grapple with material production is part and parcel of the (non-)relation of Derrida's work to science – or at least more modestly, to contemporary complexity theory.[13] For a long time people argued whether Derrida's work was philosophical or not. The principal objection seemed to be that it blurred the disciplinary boundaries between philosophy and literature or philosophy and rhetoric. By now, most people seem to have accepted an operational definition: as long as there are people in university philosophy departments who say they read Derrida or that they deconstruct texts, then Derridean deconstruction is as philosophical as anything else currently going on there. Thus it is that Derrida, after having been accused of blurring the disciplinary border of philosophy, gained its very protection in the latest round of 'Science Wars'.[14] Witness the way Alan Sokal and Jean Bricmont, in their recent polemic *Fashionable Nonsense*, absolve Derrida of most of the culpability in overstepping the philosophy/science border they impute to others: 'since there is no systematic misuse of (or indeed attention to) science in Derrida's work, there is no chapter on Derrida in this book'.[15]

But Derrida's virtue in Sokal and Bricmont's eyes is precisely his limitation in the eyes of others: his relative inattention to science. Now a limitation is not a vice: I do not *fault* Derrida for not engaging in a direct and sustained encounter with complexity theory (indeed the very genre of polemic, of inquisition, of fault-finding in Sokal and Bricmont borders on the grotesque).[16] No one can do everything, and we must let Derrida set his own agenda, define his own limits. Nonetheless, it is Derrida's post-phenomenological orientation (granting the point that he shows how phenomenology breaks down), his point of departure from the nexus philosophy–literature–rhetoric (granting the point that he wants to work on, not 'blur', their borders), his very *culture* (granting the point that he shows how culture breaks down in the face of 'force'), that limits his engagement with complexity theory and therefore limits contemporary interest in his work. In the final analysis, then, to consider one of our motifs in this work, for Derrida 'matter' is a concept to be read in metaphysical texts (as that which is resistant to form), or more precisely a marker or trace within metaphysics of a 'radical alterity' that cannot be conceptualized. Although this stance toward matter allows Derrida's thought to be articulated with the paradoxes of quantum mechanics, as Arkady Plotnitsky shows,[17] Derrida remains unable to engage the positive notion of material self-ordering as productive of the real, which, as we will see shortly, is proposed by Deleuze and Guattari in their engagement with complexity theory. Despite these content limits though, Derrida's method remains important and to an extent unsurpassable. A fantastic reader of the history of philosophy, a master at showing the breakdown of philosophy's pretensions to self-grounding, Derrida's post-phenomenological orientation might prevent the direct articulation of his work with contemporary complexity theory, but his reading techniques, his scrupulous attention to detail, are a welcome addition to any philosopher's toolkit: these cannot be forgotten and retain their usefulness in many, but not all, contexts.

Conversely, it's the very willingness of Deleuze to articulate his work with contemporary science that drives much of the current interest in his work. Although post-modern appropriations of science – to say nothing of critiques – have been the focus of much negative attention lately in the post-Sokal era, there does seem to be good cause to take seriously the work of Deleuze.[18] It's not too much, in my view, to say that Deleuze is our Kant.[19] Just as Kant's *Critiques* were (roughly speaking) the epistemology, metaphysics, ethics and aesthetics of a world of Euclidean space, Aristotelian time and Newtonian physics – and just as they (perhaps inadvertently) pinpointed biology as the key science that did not fit that world – Deleuze works to provide the philosophical concepts that make sense of our world of fractal geometry, anticipatory effects and non-linear dynamics – and to highlight biology as the key science of our time. In other words, Deleuze directly tackles the question of complexity theory, the study of the self-ordering and emergent properties of material systems in widely differing registers: the physical, chemical, biological, neural and social bodies politic. The best works in identifying Deleuze's interest in this field are Brian Massumi's *A User's Guide to Capitalism and Schizophrenia*[20] and Manuel DeLanda's 'Non-organic life'.[21] We will present a brief overview of Deleuze and complexity theory below in order to set up the themes of hylomorphism and material self-ordering we pursue in Chapters 5–7.

HYLOMORPHISM AND MATERIAL SELF-ORDERING

The second and third of the key concepts of this book, after that of the forceful body politic, are hylomorphism and material self-ordering. These concepts are created through the articulation of the philosophical significance of Deleuze and Guattari's elucidation of complexity theory, which allows us a way to think the self-ordering potentials of matter itself. This forces us to rethink the concept of production as the transcendent imposition of the architect's vision of form on chaotic matter, which Deleuze and Guattari call 'hylomorphism', following the work of Gilbert Simondon.[22] For Deleuze and Guattari, Simondon's work implies that we must add new concepts to the matter–form pair. First, we must see that matter-movement carries *singularities* as 'implicit forms'; in our terms, 'implicit forms' are potentials for material self-ordering with which the artisan negotiates, as in the case of woodworking: 'the variable undulations and torsions of the fibers guiding the operation of splitting wood' (ATP, 508/408). On the other hand, the form must be seen as suggested by the matter rather than as the pure product of the mind of the architect. In other words, forms are not pure but already laden with 'variable intensive affects' and thus tied to 'material traits of expression', that is, actual properties linked with

7

virtual potentials or singularities suggesting ways of working with and transforming the material (such potential transformations are what Deleuze means by 'affects': what the body can undergo; ATP, 508/ 408). Thus forms are developed out of these suggested potentials of the matter rather than being dreamed up and then imposed on a passive matter. In artisanal production, the artisan must therefore 'surrender' to matter, that is, follow its singularities by attending to its traits, and then devise operations that bring forth those potentials to actualize the desired properties. It is this link of singularities and traits via operations that distinguish weapons as belonging to different 'assemblages' or 'machinic phyla', as with the sabre and the sword (ATP, 506/406).

The architect[23] is blind to such traits and despises 'surrender' to matter; he only sees and commands. The link of complexity theory and the body politic found in the social and military resonances of 'surrender' and 'command' is grounded in Simondon's critique of hylomorphism as a socially conditioned doctrine. As Simondon puts it: 'the hylomorphic schema corresponds to the knowledge [*connaissance*] of someone who stays outside the workshop and only considers what goes in and comes out of it' (Simondon, *L'individu*, 1964, 40). Simondon refines his analysis of the social conditions of hylomorphism by showing that it is fundamentally not just the viewpoint of the observer outside the workshop, but that of the master commanding slave labour: 'What the hylomorphic schema reflects in the first place is a socialized representation of work . . . The technical operation which imposes a form on a passive and indeterminate matter is . . . essentially the operation commanded by the free man and executed by the slave . . .' (48–9).

Hylomorphism is thus the doctrine that production is the result of an (architectural) imposition of a transcendent form on a chaotic and/ or passive matter. This arche-thinking – that a simple unchanging commanding origin is responsible for change in others – is one of the fundamental philosophical issues of the West (we will see it take shape in the Platonic context in Chapter 5). It can be opposed to a thought of multiplicity, in which changes in a field are attributed to changes in the arrangement of its immanent elements. (It should be obvious how much of the basic Western philosophical vocabulary – One and Many, transcendence and immanence – expresses this same distinction.) In a formula that expresses the basic perspective of this book, we can say that Derrida works out the post-phenomenological consequences of the conflict of arche- and multiplicity thinking, while Deleuze works out the materialist consequences.

A hylomorphic representation of a body politic thus resonates with fascist desire: the leader comes from on high to rescue the chaos of the people by his imposition of order, the soul rules the body from on high, the will whips the body into shape, and so on.[24] The key to moving to a notion of production on an immanent plane of the force of material motion is the counter-concept to hylomorphism, material self-ordering. Such non-hylomorphic production can be seen as the artisanal coaxing forth of material self-ordering by moving a physical system toward one of its 'singularities' — one of its thresholds beyond which a process of self-ordering occurs.[25] A self-ordered and non-organismic body politic would be a 'full Body without Organs' in Deleuze's terms or 'radical democracy' in the terms of Antonio Negri and Michael Hardt.[26] (NB: This tentative identification of democracy and material self-ordering should not be taken to endorse a facile identification of 'the market' as a 'natural' force.[27])

As we will see in Chapter 1, while Derrida implicitly critiques the Husserlian production of meaning as a hylomorphic imposition of conceptual form on the stratum of sense, there is no counterpart to the notion of material self-ordering in his work. The closest we come is the notion of 'making sense' as the non-hylomorphic production of meaning in the general text, as I show in Chapter 2. It's precisely the Derridean concern with the (breakdown of the) production of meaning that isolates his work on the uppermost strata of the material world conceived by Deleuze, while it's Deleuze's materialism that enables him to articulate his thought with that of contemporary science in such a fruitful manner. This is not to say that Derridean political intervention is useless — far from it; I attempt to demonstrate the philosophical and political utility of work inspired, however fallibly, by my reading of Derrida in Chapters 3 and 4. Nonetheless, it is important to demonstrate where Derrida can help us and where he cannot, and I propose that he cannot help us in engaging with complexity theory; such engagement is the province of Deleuze and Guattari.

In the terms of traditional philosophy, Deleuze and Guattari offer us in their work on complexity theory a consistent materialism that avoids the opposition of mechanism and vitalism, coupled with a immanent and univocal ontology of becoming.[28] To think the former, a consistent materialism without mechanistic reductionism or vitalist reification, we must avoid attributing self-ordering to the components of actual physical systems (mechanism) while at the same time maintaining a distinction between virtual singularities and the actual system. But as Deleuze insists on the univocity of being and hence on the reality of the virtual, he avoids a hypostasized spiritual agent of change (vitalism). In other words, Deleuze exorcises the ghost in the machine, but in doing so leaves us with a different notion of machine, that of a concrete assemblage of heterogenous elements set to work by the potentials of self-ordering inherent in the virtual singularities of the actual system.

To think Deleuze's second contribution, the immanent and univocal ontology of becoming, the key is the time-scale of change. One could say that current mathematical modelling helps us manipulate the time-frames for the appearance of material systems beyond those to which our senses are attuned, so that we can determine the existence-span of any one configuration, whether that be astronomically or merely geologically long or sub-atomically short. With this time-manipulation granting us the ability to think an ontology of becoming, rather than a fixation on a being determined as presence, one can now access at any point the flux of matter and energy pulsing through – and in the 'crystallization' into a sensibly accessible pattern, forming – the sensibly accessible bodies on which a substantialist ontology is founded.[29]

To summarize then, Deleuze and Guattari's work on complexity theory highlights the way that the flux of matter and energy is self-ordering at various singularities or triggers – thresholds of tempera-ture, pressure, velocity, density, connectivity, etc. – giving rise to patterns of self-ordering such as crystallization, turbulence, autocataly-sis and so on. Unable to conceptualize self-ordering, hylomorphic 'State philosophy' displays the basic oscillation between chaotic matter and organizing spirit that organizes much of Western culture; Deleuze and Guattari challenge us to see that the self-ordering properties of matter itself have been 'vampirized' and put into a spirit that must return to organize a chaotic matter.

Let me be clear at this point. Although this work is prompted by the recognition of the philosophical importance of complexity theory – it shows what happens to the history of philosophy when it is re-read from a perspective transversally informed by contemporary science – I do not offer here a straightforward book on 'continental philosophy and science', for several reasons. First of all, to evaluate critically the scientific work involved in complexity theory is quite beyond any one person's competence, for drawing forth the full implications of a new scientific paradigm is the communal project of all those who have been at work in this field for several decades now. Second, such a book would also entail a comparison of the 'philosophy of science' that can be drawn from the work of Derrida and Deleuze, another major undertaking. Instead, I offer in *Political Physics* a demonstration of the powerful effects of using the theme of material self-ordering in tracing political physics in the history of Western philosophy. In other words, I test the results of using the search for hylomorphic and self-ordering models of the body politic as a reading machine for the history of Western philosophy. Thus *Political Physics* is the record of researches toward tracking down in Western philosophy the road not taken of the immanent self-ordering of a multiplicitous field (the radical democratic body politic) and the supplementary arche-thought of the transcendent formal imposition of order on chaos (the organ-ization of fascist bodies politic).

COMPARATIVE AND SYNTHETIC ASPECTS

The comparative aspect of *Political Physics* is thus concerned with the questions of the forceful body politic, hylomorphism, and material self-ordering: let us say this is the common content of the two thinkers for the purposes of this book. The synthetic aspect of this work lies in combining Derrida's slow reading and Deleuze's conceptual creativity. Perhaps as a result of a desire to arrive at new conceptual creations in articulation with contemporary science, Deleuze – at least in his work with Guattari in *Capitalism and Schizophrenia* – is notorious for his haste, his ransacking of libraries. In these volumes, Deleuze and Guattari are not in the slightest interested in what authors mean, and they especially aren't interested in a patient deconstruction that shows how texts are refractory to the intentions of their authors. (However, in his early work on the history of philosophy, Deleuze patiently, if a bit idiosyncratically, re-constructed philosophers in his own image), approaching them 'from behind', as he said, to beget 'monstrous offspring' with them.[30])

Overall then, we can say that, Deleuze and Derrida have different reading methods: rather than a work on the borders of philosophy, showing the breakdown of conceptuality in the face of force, as Derrida would have it, Deleuze and Guattari define philosophy as the creation of concepts as multiplicities that select from the 'chaos' of the virtual.[31] Thus for Deleuze the history of philosophy (and science and literature) becomes a resource for such creation, rather than a historical structure whose tricky borders must be negotiated with. When we go to read the history of philosophy in terms of hylomorphism and material self-ordering, however, we must slow down the hectic pace of Deleuze's reading in *Capitalism and Schizophrenia*. Only a Derridean close reading can reveal the investments of classic philosophers in hylomorphism, their desire for organismic ordering of bodies and their attendant allergy to material self-ordering and Bodies without Organs. In this way, the book strives for a transversal between Derridean method and Deleuzean content, a patient deconstruction aiming not at 'presence' but at hylomorphism.

PREVIEW OF CHAPTERS

In Part I, 'Derrida: deconstruction and forceful bodies', I first detail the critical and positive moments of Derrida's thought on forceful bodies, drawing on his readings of Husserl and Hegel. In Chapter 1, 'Forcing open consciousness' I show how Derrida implicitly includes force among the denigrated series of opposed terms that structure Husserl's work. The opposition around which *Speech and Phenomena* pivots — that of indication and expression — is the attempt to exile indication as a forced movement of thought to empirical psychology in order to leave a free space for voluntary expression. However, 'Form and meaning' shows Derrida locating an inner force of thought in the 'limiting power of form' that drives Husserl's hylomorphic conception of the production of meaning. Force is thus shown as the limits of Husserlian consciousness, the ruling agent in the 'conscious body politic'.

Moving to the positive moment of Derrida's thought of forceful bodies, in Chapters 2 and 3 I develop the consequences of his notion of a general text of force and signification. In Chapter 2, 'Force and signification in the general text', I examine Derrida's explicit examination of Hegel's thought of force, to which he contrasts his own notion of a general text of force and signification. Derrida's political physics is then articulated by the notion of 'making sense', a non-hylomorphic conception in which meaning arises from the forceful interaction of vectors in a field of force and signification. This general text of force and signification is the site of struggle for the 'democracy to come'.

In Chapter 3, '*Given Time* and the gift of life', I sketch a Derridean reading of the 'teleological semenology' of the basically Aristotelian patriarchal conception of maternal bodies as mere matter for the reproduction of male form in species reproduction. Aristotle's hylomorphism is countered by the force of maternity in giving life, which ruptures the circle of the species to allow us to think the gift of life as a non-hylomorphic production of another, a production that allows a politics of 'differantial species-being' in both the vital and civic bodies politic.

In Chapter 4, 'Economies of AIDS', I depart from a strict analysis of Derridean texts to examine the production of the forceful bodies politic produced by mainstream AIDS discourse. In so doing I examine the economy of truth in the scientific body politic, the economy of the borders of the somatic body politic, the economy of identity in the sexual body politic, and the economy of meaning in the academic body politic. I trace the disruption of those bodies politic by the thought of the general economy, a key Derridean notion that demonstrates the threatening power of AIDS, a call to struggle in the general text of force and signification. The disruption of mainstream AIDS discourse by the thought of the general text – Derrida's call for a defeat of hylomorphic arche-thinking – still does not enable us to positively think production as material self-ordering; Chapter 4 thus serves as the segue to Part II, an examination of Deleuze's historical–libidinal materialist approach to the study of the production of forceful bodies politic.

In Part 2, 'Deleuze: historical–libidinal materialism and organized bodies', I provide close readings, in the Derridean style, of the hylomorphic representations of the production of bodies politic found in Plato, Aristotle, Heidegger and Kant. In Chapter 5, 'Master and slave in the Platonic body politic' I examine the way in which, for Plato, soul, man, household, city and cosmos are all isomorphic because they all are (or should be) technically produced organic unities. However, the Platonic notion of techne, while it pretends to cover artisanal production, is in fact completely oriented to the perspective of the architect, as I show in a detailed reading of the political physics inherent in the cosmology of the *Timaeus*.

In Chapter 6, 'Philosophy and leisure: the social force of necessity', I examine the denigration of artisanship found in Aristotle's *Metaphysics* and in Heidegger's commentary on it in his 1924–5 lectures, *Plato's Sophist*. I then contrast Aristotle's economic account of the production of the surplus time necessary for the leisured bodies of philosophers with Heidegger's focus on individual temporalities. We also find here a force of necessity, but social rather than natural, a force that produces the forced bodies of workers and the leisured bodies of theoreticians. Heidegger's focus on temporality rather than surplus time reveals an elision of forceful bodies emblematic of his thought.

Finally, in Chapter 7, 'Force, violence and authority in the Kantian body politic', I present a reading of Kant's use of the term *Gewalt*, detailing the Kantian body politic in its cognitive, moral, aesthetic and civic registers, and showing that the resultant economy of force, violence and authority pivots on the undecidable term 'coercion'. I then present a reading of the *Critique of Judgment* that shows the way Kant flees the revolutionary potential of what he calls 'hylozoism' or 'living matter', to embrace a hylomorphic practical supplement of a divine architect or 'moral author' of the world. Thus rather than focusing on the architect's vision and the denigration of aesthetic sensitivity, as we did in Chapters 5 and 6, here we focus on the force used in the transcendent organ-ization of the contractual body politic, and on the concomitant rejection of the notion of material self-ordering.

In the Afterword I briefly consider the contemporary implications of the relations among hylomorphism, metaphysics and fascism, trying to pinpoint the relevance of the struggle against them in a 'New World Order' of global differential self-ordering capitalism.

PART 1

Derrida: Deconstruction and Forceful Bodies

CHAPTER 1

Forcing Open Consciousness

> I then find my *animate organism* as *uniquely* singled out –
> namely as . . . the only Object 'in' which I *'rule and govern'*
> *immediately* . . . (Husserl, 1950, *Cartesian Meditations*)

Introduction
The Basic Problem of Deconstruction
Indication: The Forcing of Thought
The Force of Form
Trace and Matter
Conclusion

INTRODUCTION

We begin Part 1 with an examination of the way Derrida's deconstruction of Husserl's early phenomenology reveals 'force' as the
other at the limit of consciousness. We will see how the Husserlian
opposition privileging expression as the free motion of thought over
indication as the forced motion of mediated thought is deconstructed,
just as are the parallel cases of identity over difference, time over
space, and interiority over exteriority. For the early Husserl, as
Derrida reads him, expression is the purely voluntary and rational
production of meaning reproducing the level of sense produced in the
living present, while indication is a motivation of belief relying upon
involuntary empirical association.[1] In pursuing the transversal communication of Derrida and Deleuze that is our guideline in this book,
we will show that Derrida's deconstruction of the allegiance to presence (the relation to 'metaphysics') in the Husserlian text also highlights the resources for revealing the Deleuzean theme of the implicit
hylomorphism of the organ-ized body politic. Indeed, despite appearances, the political stakes are high in this seemingly esoteric debate,

for 'contaminating' expression with indication, that is, freedom with forced motion, is tantamount to 'contaminating' the royal court, since, as the epigraph to this chapter shows, for Husserl self-conscious interiority and rationally legitimated rule are linked – the 'animate organism' is what we can call a 'conscious body politic' in which an 'I' rules from above, 'immediately'. As we will show in Chapter 5, variants on such a claim are the foundation of Plato's political philosophy, which is to say they are the foundation of most of Western political philosophy. Thus the Derridean deconstruction of phenomenological texts brings with it the opportunity to intervene in the hylomorphic representation of the foundation of the organ-ized body politic. After this treatment of the 'negative' moment of deconstruction, we will then be in a position to examine in Chapter 2 Derrida's treatment of Hegel and his 'positive' notion of democratic action in the body politic as 'making sense' in a 'general text' of 'force and signification'.

In two 1967 works, *Speech and Phenomena* and 'Form and meaning', Derrida focuses on Husserl's desire to safeguard a free zone of expression re-producing a sense transparently open to the living present – a zone created by exiling the force of thought named 'indication' to the world of empirical psychology with its causal associations. In *Speech and Phenomena*, Derrida attacks the opposition desired by Husserl of free meaning and forced indication by showing how Husserl himself describes a force internal to transcendental consciousness, the 'force of repetition of the living present' (Derrida, *Speech and Phenomena*, 1973, 116/103; translation modified); I will show that this 'force of repetition' is allied with the force Derrida reveals in 'Form and meaning' as the hylomorphic channelling of sense into the form of meaning.[2] We can thus read 'forcing' – the force of repetition of the living present and the force of form molding sense – as the pivot of a deconstruction that, by frustrating Husserl's desire for a free, unforced and self-present donation of sense, opens consciousness out onto a world of forces, a general text whose positive articulation by Derrida occurs in his confrontation with Hegel, which I sketch in Chapter 2. However, we must note that, while Derrida's readings in 'Form and meaning' allows us to thematize Husserl's hylomorphism, they do so only on the level of the deconstruction of phenomenology, without any notion of a positive engagement with the productive powers of matter. The general text, as we will see, while inextricably binding force and signification in 'making sense', is not an engagement with matter itself; such an engagement is impossible for deconstruction, for which 'matter' remains a concept, a philosopheme to be read in the text of metaphysics, or functions as a marker of a radical alterity outside the oppositions that make up the text of metaphysics.

THE BASIC PROBLEM OF DECONSTRUCTION

Although Derrida began his career as a Husserl scholar, in the 1968 essay in which Derrida sums up his thinking to date (*'Différance'*), the name Husserl rarely appears, and then only as an instance of the metaphysics of presence to be overcome, even as Saussure, Hegel, Levinas, Freud, Heidegger and a certain Deleuzean Nietzsche are introduced as forerunners to the thought of *différance*. To judge from this essay, it is as if reading Husserl was unproductive for Derrida, as if it only provided him with a target. Yet we know this cannot be the case, for the very word 'différance' first appeared in a 1959 text devoted to Husserl, '"Genesis and Structure" and phenomenology' (reprinted in *Writing and Difference*).

Whatever Derrida's motivation in casting the *'Différance'* essay as he did – and a simple desire to distance himself from the label of 'Husserl scholar' after an extended apprenticeship (1952–67) should not be overlooked – it was precisely Derrida's Husserl work that allowed him to formulate not only *différance* as his 'key concept',[3] but also what we could call 'the basic problem of deconstruction'.[4] As Derrida puts it in the first interview in *Positions*, conducted in December 1967:

[*Speech and Phenomena*] pose[s], at a point which appears juridically decisive . . . the question of the privilege of the <u>voice and of phonetic writing</u> in their relationship to the entire history of the West, such as this history can be represented by the history of metaphysics, and metaphysics in its most modern, critical, and vigilant form: Husserl's transcendental phenomenology. (Derrida, *Speech and Phenomena*, 1973, 13/5)

The basic problem of deconstruction is the relation of the privilege of presence in the entire history of the West to the representation of that history by the history of metaphysics. As we will see in detail in Chapter 2, Derrida thinks this relation in terms of the irreducibility of force that skews the putative oppositions of metaphysics into the hierarchies of social scripts patterning the body politic, even as those oppositions justify the enforcement of hierarchies. In other words, the basic problem of deconstruction is to articulate and intervene in the ways presence (identity, purity, nature, reason) serves as the focal point for hierarchical social scripts of civic and corporeal bodies politic whose enforcement is facilitated and defended by metaphysical schemes: identity of the nation, purity of the people, naturality of patriarchy, rationality of capitalism and so on. Since, for Derrida, Husserl's work is the 'most modern, critical, and vigilant' form of metaphysics, Derrida pursues in his Husserl works the point at which consciousness and its phenomenological articulation in what we call the 'conscious body politic' opens out onto a world of force.

That the basic problem of deconstruction, even in Derrida's technically detailed readings of phenomenology, is thus basically political is clear: the names of philosophers as signatories are indices of texts which are indices of real history. The role of presence in the West is the target; philosophy texts are only a path to this target. The long-debated relation of philosophy and politics, the difference between the history of the West and the history of metaphysics, is thought by Derrida under the rubric of 'force'.

Two thinkers of the left articulate this orientation to force as the linchpin of the relation between metaphysics and 'history'. Although Derrida's relation to Marxist academia is notoriously strained,[5] the notion of force allows us a possible point of contact. Marx's sarcasm in his critique of bourgeois history and political economy is never so bitter as in the analysis of the standard treatments of primitive accumulation:

This primitive accumulation plays in political economy about the same part as original sin in theology. . . . Such insipid childishness is every day preached to us in defense of property . . . In actual history it is notorious that conquest, enslavement, robbery, murder, briefly force [*Gewalt*], play the great part. (Marx, *Capital*, 1967, Volume 1, Chapter 26)

The difference between a 'theological' (in Derridean terms, a 'metaphysical') political economy, and 'actual history' is the recognition of the role of force in history; any writing that hopes not merely to interpret the world but to change it, to use its rhetorical force to unleash a political force for change in bodies politic, needs to take account of force.

Tran Duc Thao, in his 1951 *Phenomenology and Dialectical Materialism*, also thought through this basic problem of history, metaphysics and force. His themes will help us focus on the role force plays in opening subjectivity to the forces of the world, an opening that subsumes and vitiates the tracing of the constitution of the meaning of the world back to subjectivity. Tran Duc Thao claimed that genetic phenomenology, the study of the history of acts and objects making up the capabilities of the subject lived in the life world, must be supplemented by a historical materialist science, since the constitution of objects in consciousness is only a 'symbolic transposition'. Objects are first produced in the world by material labouring creativity and their meaning is then read off the world as if it were the result of originally subjective constitutive acts: 'The realizing of meaning is precisely nothing but the symbolic transposition of material operations of production into a series of intentional operations in which the subject appropriates the object ideally by reproducing it in his own consciousness' (Tran Duc Thao, *Phenomenology and Dialectical Materialism*, 1951, xxvi). In other words, I see a table not merely because I have picked up the habit of constituting it as such from a cultural background, but primarily because it was produced in the world as a table by real creative labour. The table, produced by the forced body of the worker, is merely re-produced in consciousness. For Tran Duc Thao, consciousness exploits the productivity of real labour by an ideal re-productive appropriation of meaning; consciousness, like capital, is a vampire, forcefully appropriating the production of labour in the mode of meaning.

Now as we will see in Chapter 2's analysis of 'making sense', Derrida will not follow the details of Tran Duc Thao's path in his work. In fact, Derrida's rejection of Tran Duc Thao's dialectical materialist reduction of phenomenology – along with the parallel rejection of Jean Cavaillès' dialectical formalist reduction – structures Derrida's *Le Problème de la genèse*, as he notes in the 'Avertissement' added for the 1990 edition (vii).[6] Nonetheless, Tran Duc Thao's formulation can help us think the basic problem of deconstruction posed in Derrida's Husserl works: how can consciousness and thus phenomenology be opened out onto a world of force producing the real?

INDICATION: THE FORCING OF THOUGHT

Speech and Phenomena was one of the three books published in Derrida's *annus mirabilis*, 1967, and, with 'Form and meaning', concludes the series of Derrida's explicit writings on Husserl. A certain 'economy of exteriority' forms the basic framework of the text, so that by focusing on the various registers of exteriority structuring his text we can see Derrida's articulation of the common differantial structure of the logical, temporal and liminological fields.[7] In *Speech and Phenomena*, the privileging of identity, time and interiority over difference, space and exteriority is deconstructed so that the formerly opposed terms are inscribed in a general economy governed by a third term ('*différance*', 'spacing' or 'exteriority in general') provisionally named by the formerly denigrated term. As in all such deconstructions, this third term is not however inscribed in a spiritual pedagogy, a form of writing Derrida learned to avoid through his reading of Hegel, as we will see in Chapter 2, but in a 'general text' or 'general economy' subtending both of the supposedly opposed terms.

Let us now see how 'force' takes its place as one of these 'others' Husserl wants to exile from the supposedly free inner life of the living present, and thus how 'forcing' can function as a 'third term'. Although relatively implicit in *Speech and Phenomena*, we can thematize the way in which force operates in Derrida's treatment of the movement of thought in indication as opposed to the voluntary nature of expression. Derrida begins Chapter 2 of *Speech and Phenomena*, 'The reduction of indication', by suggesting the vast scope of the problem facing Husserl in his desire to separate indicative and expressive sign-functions. The reduction of indication is necessary, yet infinite; indication would be threatening to the entire project of phenomenology if it were to be irreducible (Derrida, *Speech and Phenomena*, 1973, 28/27). After a consideration of Husserl's examples, both natural and artificial, of indicative signs, Derrida moves to consider the unity of the indicative function, which Husserl describes as the 'motivation' of the passage of thought, the linking of actual knowledge with nonactual (30/29). In Derrida's treatment of Husserl's notion of the motivated passage of thought, we see him implicitly calling attention to a force of connection between thoughts, a charge of psychic energy named 'motivation'. Indicative signs accomplish their task by forcing thought to move; indication is an unfree, a forced, movement of thought Husserl wishes to exile to empiricity in order to protect the pure freedom of the life of transcendental consciousness that rules in the conscious body politic. In a passage from the first *Logical Investigation* on the workings of association, the root of indication, which Derrida does not cite, Husserl makes clear the forceful nature of indication and motivation: 'If A summons B into consciousness, we are not merely simultaneously or successively conscious of both A and B, but we usually feel their connection forcing itself [*sich aufzudrängen*] upon us. . . .' (Husserl, *Logical Investigations*, 1970, Chapter 1, section 4). Indication: the force of thought, or perhaps better, the forcing of thought.

According to Derrida, Husserl's language suggests indication is a very broad category, including any object, ideal as well as real. Thus we reach the notion of a simple 'because' that propels the movement of thought; this 'because' covers *Hinweis* (= indicative allusion), as well as *Beweis* (= apodictic demonstration). The consequence of this distinction is that the act of linking A and B with even the highest probability falls under the scope of indication. Thus while indication, involving the psychological motivation of belief, propels the linking of *acts* grasping idealities, the linking of the *contents* of ideal objects in demonstration is not indication (Derrida, *Speech and Phenomena*, 1973, 30–31/29). Again we note Derrida's calling attention to the desire by Husserl to exile forced movements of thought, to protect an inner freedom of thought, the free movement of demonstration, from that mechanically conceived forcing of thought he names indication.

At this point in his treatment Derrida broaches the question of showing (*Weisen*) in general, prior to the distinction of manifestation and demonstration, a question which sharpens the larger question of the interweaving of indication and expression (31/29). The whole of psychic experience in signification is indicative, Derrida concludes; the exteriority of indication is reached and confirmed through the eidetic and transcendental reductions. Its origin in the empirical psychological law of association now revealed, the question of indication thus covers empiricity and, indeed, whatever will be excluded in reductions (32/30).[8]

Derrida now shows how the problematic of reductions is forecast in the distinction of sign functions, for the reduction of fact to reach essence, or of empiricity to reach transcendentality, depends upon the distinction between indication and expression, the markers of the two realms. In other words, we only know that we have reduced empiricity when we have isolated and excluded the forced movements of indication, just as we only know we have secured a transcendental realm when we can identify the pure freedom of expression. To accomplish this protective cordoning off of an unfree forcing of thought, the marking of the borders of the conscious body politic, Husserl will try to separate signification from the self-presence of transcendental life, first in isolating pre-indicative pure expression, and then in isolating pre-expressive pure sense (Derrida, *Speech and Phenomena*, 1973, 32–3/30–31).

Derrida objects that if we allow a linguistic distinction – that between the two types of sign function, indication and expression – to ground the reductions, then the protective isolation of indication that is the heart of the reduction is at work in any unthematized expressive act, prior to the reductions being made a method, the conscious and even ethical decision to leave the natural attitude. But if the reduction is essentially the ability to distinguish between linguistic functions, at work prior to its methodological thematization even in 'the most spontaneous act of spoken discourse' (Derrida, *Speech and Phenomena*, 1973, 32/31), then Derrida locates two contradictions with Husserl's 'express intention'. First, if a linguistic distinction goes all the way down to the heart of transcendental life, then Husserl's plan to isolate a pre-expressive and prelinguistic level of sense is jeopardized. Second,

24

the possibility of the entirety of speech being caught up in an 'indicative web' is raised, for if the marker of empiricity is indication, and if all language is to be excluded in order to isolate sense as the level of transcendental life free of empiricity, then Husserl risks consigning all language to indication and its forcing of thought (33/31).

In Chapter 3 of *Speech and Phenomena*, 'Meaning as soliloquy', Derrida shows Husserl's converse commitment; after the forcing of thought that is indication, we see the freedom of thought that is expression. First Derrida emphasizes the forcing of thought in indication: 'The effectiveness, the totality of the events of discourse, is indicative, not only because it is in the world, but also because it retains in itself something of the nature of an *involuntary* association' (Derrida, *Speech and Phenomena*, 1973, 36–7/34). This link of indication with the involuntary allows Derrida to focus upon the voluntary nature of expression. Expression lives in a free inner zone of intentionality, a realm whose voluntary nature perhaps entails an inextricable link to metaphysics, despite Husserl's later investigations in genetic phenomenology:

> For if intentionality never simply meant will, it certainly does seem that in the order of expressive experiences (supposing it to be limited) Husserl regards intentional consciousness and voluntary consciousness to be synonymous. And if we should come to think – as Husserl will authorize us to do in *Ideas I* – that every intentional lived experience may in principle be taken up again in an expressive experience, we would perhaps have to conclude that, in spite of all the themes of receptive or intuitive intentionality and passive genesis, the concept of intentionality remains caught up in the tradition of a voluntaristic metaphysics – that is, perhaps, in metaphysics *as such*. (Derrida, *Speech and Phenomena*, 1973, 37/34)

Derrida here demonstrates Husserl's desire to protect a space in which thought is not forced to move against its will, where will and thought are synonymous, protected in an inner space from which forced movements have been exiled, a living, consciously ruled, body politic in which an 'I' rules and governs. But we will see in our analysis of 'Form and meaning' how this free realm is constituted by a force of thought, a channelling of sense into an expressible form Derrida calls 'the limiting power of form'. But Husserl will not think 'forcing' as this inner, constitutive force of thought; he will only seek to exile force as the indicative forcing of thought through his attempted reductions of indication from expression and expression from sense.

The rest of *Speech and Phenomena* shows that the attempted reductions fail. Indication is the irresistible leading edge of the world, of space, difference and force; such forcing will not stay on the outside, because it was always already there constituting the inside. The freedom of the interior thus finds a force haunting it, the 'force of repetition of the living present' (Derrida, *Speech and Phenomena*, 1973, 116/103; translation modified). The second 'of' is a subjective genitive, designating the disconcerting 'empirical' force that constitutes the 'transcendental' living present and thus inscribes it in an impersonal general text in which supposedly self-ruling consciousness is interwoven – following the mediations of the 'economy of exteriority' – with mundane forces. As we will see in our reading of 'Form and meaning', expressive, volitional consciousness is forced open, is opened out to force by its own very workings, by the force of form, which is complicitous with a social force of identification, the reduction of difference to the same, the identity-machine of metaphysical conceptuality producing the phantasms of gendered, racial and natural identity which claim to qualify some as the 'rulers' of bodies politic.

The alignment of force with indication, with motivation, with empirical psychological causal association, is thus one key to Derrida's reading of Husserl and by extension to his deconstruction of the phenomenological/metaphysical representation of the body politic. Indications cause one thought to follow another; they have a certain force of connection. Husserl wants to keep expression and hence transcendentality free of this force, wants precisely to keep the living present 'free' in the sense of self-mastery. Now this desire to protect a free zone of thought is precisely the point of Husserl's audacious gambit of the 'voice'. The voice is the last hope for Husserl in establishing a free zone, a royal court in which consciousness can rule. Derrida's recourse to political language in his description of the voice makes clear the stakes:

The voice is the being close to itself [*auprès de soi*] in the form of universality, as con-sciousness. The voice *is* consciousness. . . . [The] possibility of reproduction [inherent in the hearing of the voice by another] . . . *gives itself out* as the phenomenon of a mastery or limitless power over the signifier. (Derrida, *Speech and Phenomena*, 1973, 88–9/80; translation modified)

The living voice is the mastery of the sign which otherwise promises powerlessness and death.

For Husserl, the masterful interiority of the voice implies the autonomy of the ego ruling in a body politic, as he writes in no. 44 of the fifth *Cartesian Meditation*: 'I then find my *animate organism* as *uniquely singled out* – namely as . . . the only Object "in" which I *"rule and govern" immediately* . . .'[9] Since ruling acts, like all others, are temporally constituted acts, 'spacing' would then be the mediation in this rule that desires to be immediate, the site for the forcing of thought. Thus spacing is also a 'forcing' which disrupts any free interiority, bringing the outside inside, letting the force of indicative motivation Husserl wished to exile infect the freedom of expression, the purity of sense and the transcendentality of the living present.

In other words, *Speech and Phenomena* is the forcing open of phenomenology, as the following passage from its penultimate page shows:

We no longer know whether the force of the *Vergegenwärtigung*, in which the *Gegenwärtigung* is de-presented so as to be re-presented as such, whether the force of repetition of the living present, which is re-presented in a *supplement*, because it has never been present to itself, or whether what we call with the old names of force and *différance*[,] is not more 'ancient' than what is primordial. (Derrida, *Speech and Phenomena*, 1973, 116/103; translation modified)

All the formerly denigrated terms: sign, writing, space, death, world, are here said to bear a force disruptive of presence. The force of thought, which Husserl wished to exile to empiricity as the mere forcing of thought's movement by the associational motivation of indication, disrupts the desired interior freedom of transcendental thought, the pure life of the living present, the royal court of the conscious body politic. 'Forcing' is thus a 'third term'. Contrary to Husserl's desire, there is an inner force of thought; forcing is the site of the opening of consciousness onto an impersonal general text of force and signification, the site of the disruption of the body politic as 'animate organism' in which an ego '"rules and governs" immediately'.

Thus what Derrida writes about *différance* in the essay of that name applies here as well to forcing:

> It governs nothing, reigns over nothing, and nowhere exercises any authority. It is not announced by any capital letter. Not only is there no kingdom of [forcing], but [forcing] instigates the subversion of every kingdom. Which makes it obviously threatening and infallibly dreaded by everything within us that desires a kingdom, the past or future presence of a kingdom. (Derrida, *Margins*, 1982, 22/22)

As this quotation shows, the radical alterity of differential forcing calls us to rethink property and power, the command and control centres of the phenomenological/metaphysical body politic, as turned inside out and distributed across an economy of exteriority. After deconstruction, the topology of the body politic cannot be metaphysically represented as pure self-presence; we are called upon instead to think a differantially structured body politic in which a force of the outside is insinuated into the space of interior self-control so that consciousness is an effect in a general text of force and signification.[10]

To sum up, in *Speech and Phenomena* Derrida decodes, overturns and reinscribes the essential distinctions Husserl establishes in phenomenology's 'germinal structure' (Derrida, *Speech and Phenomena*, 1973, 1/1), Chapter 1 of the first *Logical Investigation*. He thus shows the marginal economy of phenomenology's relation to the metaphysics of presence, its radical rupture and its sustained allegiance. The main accomplishment is the forcing open of phenomenology to show a supposedly exiled absence, delay, relay, sign, difference, space, death or force at the heart of the self-identity of the temporal form guaranteeing the consciousness-structure of transcendental constitution, thus contaminating, with their 'others', presence, immediacy, proximity, identity, time, life and freedom.

Let us now move to consider 'Form and meaning', where we can see forcing as the force of thought as the 'limiting power of form'.

THE FORCE OF FORM

The structure of 'Form and meaning' is straightforward: an epigraph, followed by an untitled introductory section, then four titled sections: 'Meaning in the text', 'Mirror-writing', 'The limiting power of form', and 'Form "is" – its ellipse'. The strategy of the essay as whole is equally straightforward: in it, Derrida shows phenomenology's complicity with the metaphysics of presence by using 'form' as his leading thread to investigate Husserl's contention in section 124 of *Ideas I* that sense and expression are separate levels, with sense as a silent, pre-expressive stratum and expression as non-productive conceptualization. After a close reading of Husserl's metaphors of expression as writing and as mirror, Derrida shows how sense is preformed by expression: for all experience to be able to be conceptualized – for all sense to be able to be expressed – there must be a core of sense preformed to accept the predicative meaning form of 'S is P'.[11] This leads Derrida to question the metaphysical character of the circular relation of form and the sense of Being as presence as it appears in Husserl's text, and to propose that a thought of the trace might deform that circle into an ellipse, that is, indicate a way to think metaphysics, not from outside – which would be impossible – but from its margin.

Where Derrida sees metaphysical entanglement in the circle of form and the sense of Being as presence, we see two Deleuzean materialist themes, transversal to Derrida's Heideggerian concern with metaphysics. First, we can thematize, across the grain of Derrida's reading, a hylomorphic production of meaning in Husserl: the conceptual form of meaning forcefully channels sense into the direction of possible intuition, that which can be presented to the vision of consciousness in the form of the living present. This force of form is complicitous with a social force of identification, the hylomorphic production of an organized body politic. Second, in the conclusion of the essay, where Derrida sets the link of form and the sense of Being as presence over against the notion of trace, which he claims is refractory to any philosophic concept of form or matter, we see an important clue for us in determining the limits of a deconstructive engagement with the revolutionary implications of complexity theory's notion of material self-ordering.

Let us now proceed with a brief treatment of each section of 'Form and meaning'. Derrida begins the introductory section, which concerns the overall relation of phenomenology to metaphysics, as thematized by Husserl himself, by claiming that phenomenology sees itself as a purifying critique of metaphysics. Derrida then proposes 'form' as his leading thread to investigate a more intricate complicity of phenomenology and metaphysics conceived as the allegiance to presence (Derrida, 'Form and meaning', 1982, 187/157). As Derrida puts it, Husserl tries to awaken an original sense of form that was nonetheless perverted from the start; however, his recall rests on metaphysical resources, for 'form' relies on the 'evidence of a certain source [foyer] of sense' (Derrida, 'Form and meaning', 1982, 188/157; translation modified).[12] Again, as in Speech and Phenomena, presence is the key to the Derridean investigation of Husserl, who is said to want sense to be present to the act in the donative self-presence of the living present, a self-presence free of the alterity of 'force'. (As we recall, Husserl wished to exile forced movements of thought to indicative mediation, while Derrida showed the constitutive role of the 'force of repetition of the living present'.)

For Derrida, the inescapable bind of sense and form is seen in considering the finite system of metaphysical oppositions carried in metaphysical language. Despite Husserl's work in reworking Platonic and Aristotelian conceptuality, Derrida continues, form is linked to presence in general, as we see in Husserl's casting of the living present as the form of transcendental experience (Derrida, 'Form and meaning', 1982, 188/158). Perhaps a deconstruction of the text of metaphysics might show trace or différance, Derrida implies, but this entails a different work, a double reading other than that of an 'interpretation of Platonic or Aristotelian conceptuality' (188/158). Within phenomenology's own terms, Derrida goes on, the submission of sense to the sense of sight – putting an object on view, able to be intuited in the temporal form of the living present of an act[13] – is clear in several directions (189/158). Derrida will focus on the distinction Husserl wants between sense and discourse, sense and meaning, *Sinn* and *Bedeutung*, and show that the system linking language, form and theory is 'worked over by a certain exterior of the relation to the exterior that is the relation to form' (189/158), a 'something' which Derrida will come to name 'trace' at the end of the essay.

The next section, 'Meaning in the text', links the analysis of *Ideas* undertaken in 'Form and meaning' to that of the *Logical Investigations* given in *Speech and Phenomena*. Beginning the close analysis, Derrida remarks that two-thirds of *Ideas I* passes as if sense were silent (Derrida, '*Form and meaning*', 1982, 189/158). Husserl is able to do this because he believes he has shown in *Logical Investigations* that expression is reducible (as we recall this is Derrida's focus in *Speech and Phenomena*). In *Ideas I*, expression is thought as a 'stratum,' that is, as both founded and delimitable. 'Stratum', Derrida notes, is a metaphor used blithely at first by Husserl, but then brought under suspicion at the end of the section (Derrida, '*Form and meaning*', 1982, 190/159).

In focusing on Husserl's use of 'stratum,' Derrida is here addressing the problematic of philosophic metaphoricity he will analyse at great length in 'White mythology' (in *Margins*). Briefly stated, neither philosophy nor rhetoric can dominate each other. A philosophic domination of rhetoric – the establishment of a rigorous concept of 'metaphor' for instance, as the raising of sensibility to conceptual meaning[14] – is ruled out, since the metaphoric nature of philosophemes such as 'con-cept' (*Be-griff*, grasping) would then go unanalysed. Conversely, the rhetorical domination of metaphysics – the tracing of concepts as dead metaphors back to sensibility (the so-called Nietz-schean position) – is ruled out, since the philosophic nature of 'metaphor' as transportation of meaning would in the latter instance go unanalysed. Implicitly relying upon the analyses of other essays in *Margins* – analyses to be taken up again in *Glas* – Derrida then generalizes this structure in a formal rule of haunting or movement of quasi-transcendentality whereby any element in a field that attempts to raise itself to the level of domination of that field will find itself haunted by the gap in the field left by its elevation and will fall back into the field.[15]

To return to our analysis of 'Form and meaning', we see Derrida showing us that the specific metaphor Husserl uses that 'entangles' that of stratum in a 'play of metaphors' is 'interweaving' or 'interlacing' (Derrida, 'Form and meaning', 1982, 191/160), a textual metaphor which recalls the factual interweaving of expression and indication that Husserl had hoped in Logical Investigations 1.1 to untangle by 'essential distinctions'. Derrida recalls at the end of this section the enormous stakes of Speech and Phenomena: if indication were to be irreducible then the very heart of the phenomenological project itself, its principle of all principles, the reliance on intuition, would be threatened by the irruption of indication, sign, delay, relay, space, death, and force at the heart of the self-presence of the acts which abide in the temporal form of the living present (Derrida, 'Form and meaning', 1982, 192/161).

The next section, entitled 'Mirror-writing', is the heart of the essay. In this section, Derrida first simply notes without detailed examination Husserl's exclusion of the sensible aspect of language, and his exclusion of the question of the unity of body and spirit that structures his account of 'animation' (Derrida, 'Form and meaning', 1982, 192–3/161).[16] He then establishes Husserl's goal as the delimitation of the distinctive traits of expression and sense; in so doing he clarifies the terminological distinction Husserl introduced in Ideas I (1982), whereby Sinn now designates the total noematic level of experience – intentional correlates or objects – while Bedeutung designates expressive meaning (193–4/162). Expression is exteriorization for Husserl, Derrida notes, an 'outward transfer' of sense (194–5/163); meaning does nothing but repeat or reproduce a preformed conceptualizable sense. Expression is re-productive; in the terms of Speech and Phenomena, expression is a mere transport of sense to 'a certain outside' (Derrida, Speech and Phenomena, 1973, 34/32), to the space of consciousness of the voice, a movement within an economy of exteriority.[17]

Two metaphors in Husserl's descriptions give body to this non-productivity of expression, Derrida continues, writing and mirroring. We will thematize the hylomorphic production models Derrida allows us to see but does not dwell upon. First, the writing metaphor. In developing this theme, Derrida shows that Husserl can establish the independence of sense from expression using a converse argument centred on a perceptual example. Since the *Logical Investigations* have shown the independence of expression as meaning-intention from perception as meaning-fulfilling intuition, this entails that perceptual sense must also be independent of its expression. Expression thus adds nothing to sense, but it does effect the ascension of sense to what Husserl calls 'conceptual form' (Derrida, '*Form and meaning*', 1982, 195/163). Derrida now makes a point that will assume great importance for his reading later in the essay: all experience must be conceptualizable, because the logical medium of expression has only the originality of not being original, of 'effacing itself as an unproductive transparency facing the passageway of sense' (196/164; translation modified).[18]

Derrida now notes that the transparent nature of expression must have a consistency that allows for impression: prelinguistic (but conceptualizable) sense must imprint itself in conceptual linguistic expression (Derrida, '*Form and meaning*', 1982, 196/164). Thus expression can produce meaning only because 'the expressive noema must offer itself . . . as a blank page or virgin tablet; or at least as a palimpsest given over to its pure receptivity' (196/164). Here we see a hylomorphic production of meaning; expression must be malleable enough to receive the imprint of sense. This is an extremely odd production however, quite literally a chiasmic hylomorphism, which nonetheless goes unremarked by Derrida: meaning, the level of conceptual form, is a material that will be printed upon by sense. This is not the only remarkable chiasm we find here though. Crossing between the analyses of *Speech and Phenomena* (which follows the *Logical Investigations*) and '*Form and meaning*' (which follows *Ideas I*), we see that the expressive medium is conceived as both voice (in the *Logical Investigations*) and as writing (in *Ideas I*). This criss-cross of metaphors proves Derrida's point in *Speech and Phenomena*: for this metaphorical system to operate, both voice and writing must be subtended by a 'third term' governing a general economy (in this case, (arche-) writing).

Returning to the analysis of the writing metaphor, we now see that in its pure receptivity expressive conceptuality is thus the 'redoubling of a preexisting conceptuality' at the level of sense (Derrida, '*Form and meaning'*, 1982, 196/164). As a redoubling, expression is thus both verbal (act) and nominal (stratum), both '*production* and *revelation* . . . united in the impression–expression of discourse' (196/164; Derrida's emphases). Since we are not considering verbal expression, but silent meaning, the radical conclusion is possible: all sense is 'something which by its nature already must be capable of *imprinting itself* in a meaning, leaving or receiving its formal mark in a *Bedeutung*' (197/ 164; Derrida's emphases). Expression is both one of the relata of the relation sense-expression, and that very relation itself, the act of expression as exteriorization. As a revelatory stratum it is transparent, but as a productive act it effects a passage to conceptuality.

Derrida next addresses the 'grave problems' of the inscriptive metaphor of expression as *tabula rasa* (Derrida, '*Form and meaning*', 1982, 197/165). In effect, he will show how the chiasmic hylomorphism of the writing metaphor (that conceptual form is a material for the impression of sense) is embroiled in difficulties that Husserl will himself raise. Basing his argument on the thematics of the later Husserl, especially as he has investigated them in ITOG, Derrida here poses two problems, those of the history and systematic order of the conceptual meaning that is to receive the imprint of sense. Derrida shows in ITOG how writing is necessary for idealization in the passage of sense to meaning (a meaning must be iterable, repeatable 'to infinity', and only writing guarantees such escape from finite subjectivity), even though it brings with it equivocation and sedimentation. Thus writing is both necessary and dangerous for the production and handing down of ideal meaning. In 'Form and meaning,' Derrida concludes from these premises that if the order of conceptual meaning has a history (due to its reliance on writing), then concepts are older than sense. This means that even if one were able to bracket linguistic historicity – but this is the bite of the problem of old words, of metaphysical language Derrida alluded to earlier in setting up this discussion of phenomenology's use of 'form' and its essential ties to presence – then concepts form a text whose systematic order would in fact 'impose its own sense on that sense' (Derrida, '*Form and meaning*', 1982, 197/165), that is, channel sense in the direction of conceptual form. The necessity of writing for the production and maintenance of ideality thus puts the entire phenomenological project of isolating a pre-expressive, preconceptual, ahistorical level of sense given in the living present at risk. But the 'fact' of this channelling of sense by expression cannot be bracketed, Derrida insists, for sense and expression are co-determinant. Husserl's desire to bracket expression's channelling of sense, his desire to protect the production of sense from signitive textuality – to protect the temporal form of consciousness from delay, relay, force – is the non-critical opening of phenomenology, its acceptance of a personal form for the transcendental field (the voice), instead of the impersonal general text of force and signification (writing).[19] These uncritical intentional thematics of Husserl – his metaphysical desire for intuition in the living present – are then hard to reconcile, Derrida concludes, with the faithful descriptions in 'The origin of geometry' of the sedimented history of meaning (Derrida, 'Form and meaning', 1982, 197/165).

At this point Derrida moves on to discuss the second metaphor, that of the mirror. His brief reading shows that Husserl's use of *Bild* (image) metaphors yield a double effect: reflection and imposition, *Abbildung* and *Einbildung*, copy and marking (Derrida, 'Form and meaning', 1982, 198/165). Here again, Derrida allows us to thematize, transversally, the hylomorphism of Husserl's account. The 'improductive production' of the passage of sense to meaning means that the act of expression is the 'imposition of the white mark [*la marque blanche*] of the concept' on sense (198/165; translation modified). This imposition of a mark is a reproduction that 'informs sense in meaning' (198/165; translation modified).[20] As opposed to the odd chiasm of form and matter, of conceptual expression and sense, we noted above in discussing the writing metaphor, here, in the mirror metaphor, we see a straightforward hylomorphic production of meaning in which sense is a material worked upon by its accession to conceptual form. This notion of sense as material for the form of the concept in expressive meaning will be our concern in reading Derrida's next section. In concluding the 'Mirror writing' section, Derrida notes how Husserl is uneasy about the 'metaphoricity' [*Bildlichkeit*] of language, and warns against its seductive power (198/166). Here we can note Derrida's recourse to Fink in ITOG to highlight Husserl's failure to consider the problematic of a language oriented to ontic description being used for transcendental description.[21]

The next section is the 'Limiting-power of form'. As a result of the previous section's bringing together of the dual character of expression, Derrida highlights Husserl's term 'medium': an element and a means (Derrida, *'Form and meaning'*, 1982, 199/166). Derrida notes that the notion of 'medium' serves as a link with the problematic of the history of concepts raised above in the discussion of the writing metaphor, issues that Husserl will deal with in the 'Origin of geometry': 'every science is objectivated in the specifically 'logical' medium, in that of expression . . .' (Derrida quoting Husserl; 199/166). Thus theory needs objectifying expression (it is the element that endows it with omnitemporal validity via iterability) but cannot abide any deformation by the means of reaching that element. Derrida's language implies a recognition of the visual metaphorics behind 'theory': pure meaning discourse allows science 'to preserve and to glance at' [*garder et . . . regarder*] sense (199/167). Sense is fixed in expression at a distance that is at the same time a pure proximity. As the telos of expression, the unproductive productivity of logical–scientific univocal transparency thus serves as 'the model for every possible discourse' (199/167).

This character of expression, Derrida specifies, is designated as 'parallelism', perfect overlap without confusion (Derrida, *'Form and meaning'*, 1982, 200/167). Derrida notes Husserl also uses 'parallelism' to describe the relation of pure psychic activity and transcendental life, a metaphor he investigated in ITOG. Now the overlapping of parallel expression can only occur if expression is a complete reproduction of sense. As always, Derrida notes, Husserl would like to avail himself of the fact/essence distinction to secure a sphere of essentially complete expression from factual incompleteness. Scientific expression as a univocal telos appears as the candidate for complete expression, which would correct the incompleteness of everyday language (200/168).

However, Derrida continues, Husserl shows in section 126 of *Ideas I* that the conceptual form of expression, the *eidos/telos* of expression, entails an essential incompleteness, an essential deformation that occurs in the passage to conceptual form as a result of the raising of sense to the 'generality [*Allgemeinheit*]' of expressive discourse (Derrida, *'Form and meaning'*, 1982, 201/168). Thus the *act* of ex-pression comes into conflict with the *element* of expression. The medium – act and element – of expression is in conflict with itself; the desired coupling of expressive productivity and unproductivity falls apart. The element of expression is to be transparent and reproductive, but the act of expression, the production of meaning, installs a difference between the strata of sense and expression, a difference between the manifold differences of sense experiences and the identity preserved by the generality of conceptual form. Derrida names this 'impoverishing' difference the very 'resource' of scientific discourse, the 'limiting-power of its formality' (201–2/169).

At this point, we need to attend to the first of two major transversals crossing the work of Derrida and Deleuze. Derrida's concern with the metaphysical entanglements of Husserl's notion of conceptual form allows us to highlight the hylomorphic representation of the construction of the organ-ized body politic, as it is revealed by the complicity of the force of form with a social force of identification. In the difference between expression as element and act, in what Derrida calls 'the limiting-power' of form, we read the force of form in hylomorphism. The hylomorphic production of meaning in the expressive act – sense is the material that will be stamped, that will receive the 'white mark' of conceptual form in being raised to expression – undercuts the desire that expression as an element be an unproductive reproduction of sense. Derrida quotes Husserl from *Ideas I*, section 126 on the hylomorphic production of meaning: 'Expression is complete when it stamps all synthetical forms and materials of the substratum in a conceptual–significational way' (Derrida, '*Form and meaning*', 1982, 200/167; translation modified).[22] We should note here that the material element of the hylomorphic production of meaning covers the entire stratum of sense, which itself contains form and matter.[23]

Derrida shows us how Husserl's notion of expression as the achievement of conceptual form is a reduction of difference, a movement in which certain particulars of the sense-giving act are left behind; differences on the sense level are judged as to their formal–conceptual relevance. Husserl writes that 'whole dimensions of variability' of sense are left behind in the elevation of sense to meaning (*Ideas I*, section 126). Regarding their implicit hylomorphism, such conceptualizations are identification machines, selecting for formal identity among material differences.[24] This conceptual reduction of difference is hylomorphic because the material input to the production process – the sense stratum – is homogenized by the reduction of difference to accept the imprint of form. From this hylomorphic perspective, material difference is not itself productive of order in the product, but is only a threat to the order that form alone brings about. We can thus say that in Husserl's hylomorphic production of meaning the material of sense is forcefully stamped by formal conceptuality, or even that conceptual form forcefully stamps out differences of sense, so that a meaningful concept is produced. Thus force, which Husserl wished to exile to empirical indication, forms the heart of transcendental freedom, voluntary and rational conceptual formal expression. Expression is the forcing of sense.

But why do I insist on 'force' in these analyses of form and the hylomorphic production of meaning? Because a certain decision, the political physics of the conscious body politic, is needed to affirm the primacy of logical form in the production of meaning via the reduction of difference in the sense stratum, and this decision is complicitous with forces shaping identitarian social texts that pattern organ-ized bodies politic. These social forces privilege a certain conception of reason as fit for rule, and hence a certain politics of interiority and identity: only the one who rules himself logically and rationally can rule others. (We will examine this fundamental doctrine of Western political philosophy in the Platonic and Aristotelian contexts in Chapters 5 and 6 below.)

Let us trace out the argument here. The form of phenomenological/metaphysical conceptuality, 'the limiting power of form,' is the capture of difference by identity-producing concepts; the hylomorphic production of meaning is the capture of difference by identity, the imposition of formal order on the 'material' sense stratum.[25] What is left behind by the elevating of sense to the conceptual formality of the expressive stratum is precisely the 'non-objective', the 'non-logical'. Now while Husserl mentions only 'the modifications of relative clarity and distinctness, the attentional modifications' as such properties of sense that are left behind, the little phrase 'and so on' (*Ideas I*, section 126), by which he leaves the list of examples open licenses us to bring to bear

38

Derrida's analysis of occasional expressions in Chapter 7 of *Speech and Phenomena*. Derrida highlights the return of indication into expression whenever an irreducible reference to an embodied subject is part of a statement, such as the spatio-temporal determinations 'here, there, above' (Husserl, *Logical Investigations* 1, 1970, Chapter 3, section 26). Such indication is also essential to statements of subjective content: 'All expressions for percepts, beliefs, doubts, wishes, fears, commands belong here' (section 26; quoted at *Speech and Phenomena* 105/94). All reference to embodied subjectivity must be left behind on the level of sense; statements tied to the spatio-temporal body, the corpse, cannot achieve conceptual form.

The exceptions to the spread of indication in occasional expressions are two-fold. The first is relatively innocuous in this context: all theoretical expressions (e.g. mathematical statements) are exempt from this encroachment of indication and hence can achieve conceptual form in expression (although the role of writing in constituting such objectivity can never be reduced).[26] The second exception, however, is the key for our analysis. Husserl wants the statement 'I', when uttered in solitary discourse, to have a self-fulfilling meaning, one differing from person to person. Derrida objects to this notion of a changing meaning; on 'Husserl's own premises', he writes, we should think the opposite (Derrida, *Speech and Phenomena*, 1973, 107/96). The meaning of 'I' must function in my empirical absence (Derrida puts it provocatively: 'I am' is essentially accompanied by 'I am dead'), and so the field of meaning is essentially the field of writing; indication thus 'dictates' expression (108/97).

The consequences of Derrida's analysis of the paradoxes of the 'I' for our analysis of the conscious body politic are striking. The forcing of sense in expression — the forceful imposition of general conceptual form on experience, the stamping out of embodied location and emotion in theoretical meaning, accompanied by the glaring exception of the 'I' in solitary discourse — has a two-fold function. First, in descending from the lived body via the transcendental reduction to the living present animating the lived body, it tames the potentially rebellious material somatic element of the 'animate organism' by excluding it from ruling and relegating it to the level of (what should be) the ruled. Second, in ascending to the embodied level, such desired somatic discipline allows the appearance of immediacy and autonomy in the conscious body politic, allows one the phantasm that the core of the 'I' is a self-present disembodied pure reason, able to ' "rule and govern" immediately' in the animate organism.[27] In the purest sort of metaphysics (see the analysis in Chapter 3 of Aristotle's attribution of life to the prime mover) intention then is life; sense-giving is life-giving via its form-giving, and expression, as we will see, does nothing but preserve the form of sense. This interiority of a conscious, rational self, thinking itself safe from the forced indication and material difference which in fact form its very basis, is gutted by Derrida's thought of forcing as the opening out of consciousness to its inscription in a world of forces. With forcing, as we will see in Chapter 2, we find a making sense which acknowledges force and affirms rather than rules over difference. Forcing thus allows Derrida to think making sense as the non-hylomorphic production of meaning by the hegemonic formation of force vectors in an open, impersonal, directional field.

TRACE AND MATTER

After the exposition of the force of form, Derrida moves to the final section, 'Form "Is" – Its Ellipsis'. In this section he considers the links of form and presence and alludes to a thought of the 'trace' that is 'neither matter nor form'; with this as our clue to a transverse reading, we will delimit Derrida's 'materialism' at this point. Derrida quickly announces that his final section is the payoff to the opening questions (Derrida, 'Form and meaning', 1982, 202/169). He has shown us that the relation between the form of expression and the content of sense is linked to the relation between types of expressions. Two questions ensue: what is the privileged form of statements (the expressive element) that facilitates the passage (the expressive act) of sense to meaning? How does the link of form and the sense of being as presence tie phenomenology to metaphysics? (202/169).

Derrida begins his exposition by showing that the form of judgment, S is P, is the privileged form of expression. This privilege was announced in an analysis of *Ideas I* before the question of expression was even broached: there is a 'doxic kernel' to all acts, even the aesthetically or morally valuational (Derrida, 'Form and meaning', 1982,

203/169). For Husserl, Derrida claims, all valuation is valuation of a being, and the positing of belief in that being is the core on which valuation is overlaid. In an important passage not cited by Derrida, Husserl writes that the doxic posit is the *'archontic'* posit, which rules all other posits in a multi-positional act (Husserl, *Ideas I*, 1980, section 117; Husserl's italics). The doxic kernel thus allows the conversion of the experience of that which is not a present being – emotional or axiological experience – into experience in the form of being-present (Derrida, *'Form and meaning'*, 1982, 203/170). In other words, the analysis of the doxic kernel as the logicity of the pre-expressive stratum – the positing of the being of the noematic correlate of the act – demonstrates that for Husserl one is always credited with the ability to convert the experience of a relation to that which is not present (the absent thing whose presence is desired) into an experience in the form of being-present (the desired *is* what-is-desired, it is present in its being-desired). The theory of the doxic kernel, Derrida continues, means Husserl must try to respect both the originality of practical, affective or moral experience and its character of being founded, of supervening on a fundamental logical core of objectification (204n/ 170n). All experience, in other words, offers itself to logical discourse having the form of predicative judgment.[28] Expression is the forcing of sense, but sense is already forced into the form of object-presentation.

Derrida now asks whether the form of the predicative expression, the privilege of presence, might not have secretly conducted the analysis of the doxic kernel of all experience (Derrida, *'Form and meaning'*, 1982, 205/171). If this metaphysical privilege had essentially directed the analyses, then the entire motif of the separation of sense and expression is questionable, as is the characterization of the passage of sense to meaning as ex-pression. Now Derrida clarifies his aims: he does not wish to contest Husserl's doctrine directly by reducing one level to another. In other words, it is not a matter of naively calling sense a language made up of already formed words – although Derrida has shown the signitive or 'trace' structure of sense and living present in *Speech and Phenomena* – nor of claiming that sense hides ineffable treasures of experience to which words cannot do justice. Rather, Derrida makes it clear that he seeks only to ask questions about another relation of sense and meaning (206/172). This other relation, he goes on, can arise through pondering the unity of sense and word in 'is' and in thinking the relation of 'is' and formality in general. In a classic deconstructive move, Derrida shows that these metaphysical relations rest on privilegings: the privilege of presence in the privilege of predicative judgment over all other forms of language rests upon the teleological promising of all sense to meaning (206/172). In general, Derrida claims, one can surmise that the sense of being has been limited by the form of presence and, conversely, that formalization has been limited by the sense of being (206–7/172). Metaphysics, he concludes, is thus the occlusion of being beyond the form of presence, and form beyond the sense of being as presence. Husserl's project thus shows the identity of the two limits of form and presence: Husserl's formalist demand is limited by his commitment to the form of Being as self-presence in the form of the living present (207/172).[29]

Near the end of 'Form and meaning' Derrida appends a footnote (Derrida, *'Form and meaning'*, 1982, 206/172) that gives a dense and 'infinite' reading project: to see form as the trace of non-presence, as that which is refractory to, yet constitutive of, presence. Thus the epoch of the metaphysics of presence produces marginal texts: any time 'form' appears, 'trace' can be read. We have seen just this supplementation in our examination of Derrida's reading of the living present; the temporal form of all experience is read as trace, as spacing, as *différance*, as force. The final word for Derrida in 'Form and meaning' is that one is not to choose between the form and presence, but to think their circularity, and in thinking thus the closure of metaphysics to deform the circle, to render it an ellipse that is not to be thought in opposition to the circle. Rather the ellipse is produced by the thought of non-dialectical difference: the trace, that which is '[n]either matter nor form, nothing that could be recast by some philosopheme' (207/173). Here we see the Derridean restriction of matter to a 'philosopheme', a crucial move for us in opening our transverse reading of the relation of the thought of trace to that of matter.

To follow up on this restriction of matter to the system of metaphysical conceptuality let us recall Derrida's allusion to the system linking language, form and theory as 'worked over by a certain exterior of the relation to the exterior that is the relation to form'

(Derrida, '*Form and meaning*', 1982, 189/158). How does form relate to the exterior? Although Derrida does not use this terminology, we propose that form is the mastery of 'the exterior', the imposition of order on chaos in hylomorphic production. In the Husserlian context, this means sense is preformed to allow its exteriorization in expression, to allow an object drawn from its conceptualizable nucleus to be held for vision in an intuition with the form of the living present. What then would be a non-formal relation to 'the exterior'? According to Derrida, this pull of the exterior will deform the systematic circle into an elliptical trace; the trace replaces the circle. 'Trace' is the site of the breakdown of consciousness before force in the analyses of 'Form and meaning'; the ellipse of trace brings us to think forcing as the site of consciousness's inscription in the general text. Trace is the deformation of form just as spacing is the pulling apart of the temporal form of all experience, the living present, and forcing is the pulling apart of the form of free consciousness. We should note here, however, that when it comes to deconstructing the opposition of form and matter the notion of trace closes off any notion of material self-ordering as the source of production of the real. In a word, trace, while it cannot be located as either of the poles of the conceptual relation of form and matter, remains bound to that pair as its deformation. For the purposes of this book, then, trace is tied to conceptuality, even as a quasi-concept, a name for the breakdown of the conceptualizing power of form.

To reinforce our claims that for Derrida 'matter' is a concept to be read in metaphysical texts, or at best a marker or trace within metaphysics of a 'radical alterity' that cannot be conceptualized (and hence far from the positive notion of material self-ordering proposed by Deleuze and Guattari in their engagement with complexity theory), let us recall Derrida's answers in *Positions* to the questions posed by Jean-Louis Houdebine about the possible relations of deconstruction with 'dialectical material logic' (Derrida, *Positions*, 1981, 82ff/60ff). Derrida writes:

Above all they [the consequences of his writings] refer to the general economy whose traits I attempted to outline based on a reading of Bataille. It follows that if, and in the extent to which, *matter* in this general economy designates, as you said, radical alterity (I will specify: in relation to philosophical oppositions), then what I write can be considered 'materialist'. (Derrida's italics; *Positions*, 1981, 87/64)

Thus for Derrida 'matter' can function as a marker of 'the absolute exterior of opposition' (89/66), that is, as *another name* for trace, writing, text, and so on, all the names working in the 'deconstructing text' (89/65), but not, we insist, as the site of the production of the real, as it is for Deleuze and Guattari.

CONCLUSION

We have linked indication as the forcing of thought in *Speech and Phenomena*'s analysis of the reduction of indication with form as identifying force in the analysis in 'Form and meaning' of the parallelism of expression and sense. We have also seen the deconstruction of the conscious body politic, the living present as the form of all temporal acts, so that spacing, in rupturing the desired personal form of consciousness and the hylomorphic production of meaning, now is seen as carrying a 'force of repetition' that opens consciousness out onto an impersonal general text. Finally, we have seen the way in which trace, as the deformation of form unthinkable as matter, shows Derrida's inability to engage with matter outside metaphysical conceptuality. In so doing we have shown the transverse line articulating the Derridean analysis of metaphysics in terms of presence and Deleuze and Guattari's analysis of State philosophy in terms of hylomorphism.

We now move to Chapter 2 to examine Derrida's development, through his confrontation with Hegel, of a 'positive' sense of political physics, that of the force of law, a non-hylomorphic production of meaning in a general text of force and signification.

CHAPTER 2

Force and Signification in the General Text

> In a spirit that is higher than another, the lower concrete
> existence [*Dasein*] has sunk to a non-appearing moment;
> what used to be the thing itself [*die Sache selbst*] is now but
> a trace [*Spur*] . . . (Hegel, *Phenomenology of Spirit*, 1977)

Introduction
The Law of Force
Language and Logic
The Determinations of Reflection
The General Text
The Force of Law
Conclusion

INTRODUCTION

In Chapter 1 we saw how Derrida, in his Husserl investigations,
implicitly names force as the limit of thought, the point at which
consciousness breaks down and points to its inscription in a world of
forces. We move now to investigate Derrida's explicit investigation of
force, the way in which Derrida produces a political physics, through
his reading of Hegel, that tries not merely to think force, but to
intervene in a world of forces. We will find, however, that such
intervention consists merely in pointing out the inextricable bind of
force and signification in the general text and hence in the institution
of a body politic. While this Derridean insistence is indeed a welcome
advance compared to those who insist that the use of force in the
foundation of a body politic can be justified by a reason completely
isolated from force, it cannot help us in thinking the detailed material
production of a body politic, an investigation that only the Deleuzean
perspective can enable.

Let us note in beginning our reading that Derrida has tried to make sense of the nexus of force, violence and law in a long series of writings. In this chapter we will consider the writings bounded by the 1963 'Force and signification' and the 1990 'Force of law: the mystical foundation of authority'. In the intervening years essays on these topics such as 'Violence and metaphysics', 'Différance', 'Signature event context', 'Declarations of independence', 'Devant la loi', 'The politics of friendship' and 'The laws of reflection: Nelson Mandela, in Admiration' appeared, as well as interviews like those of *Positions* and the Afterword to the new edition of *Limited Inc*. In this chapter I sketch a political physics that accounts for Derrida's emphasis on force in the context of law and justice. In the first part of the chapter ('The law of force', 'Language and logic', 'The determinations of reflection') I thematize Derrida's treatment of force in his readings of Hegel; in the second part ('The general text' and 'The force of law') I articulate the role of force in Derrida's notion of political physics and making sense in the body politic.

THE LAW OF FORCE

As is often the case with Derrida, his confrontation with Hegel is instructive. Any talk of force and law naturally refers one to the chapter on 'Force and the understanding' in the *Phenomenology of Spirit*. Here we find the failed attempt by natural consciousness to find unconditioned certainty in scientific laws of force. The attempt to find laws of force to explain all phenomena fails; in other words, the attempt to write the book of nature from the outside, nature as observed by consciousness, fails. In seeing how it fails, natural consciousness progresses in its curriculum on the way to absolute knowledge. Derrida knew this in 1963. In 'Force and signification' he writes: 'Hegel demonstrated convincingly that the explication of a phenomenon by force is a tautology' (Derrida, '*Force and signification*', 1978, 45/27). Derrida's next sentence is crucial in understanding his differences with Hegel over force: 'But in saying this, one must refer to language's peculiar inability to emerge from itself in order to articulate its origin, and not to the *thought* of force' (45/27).

As Derrida made clear a few years later in *Positions*, in a passage we will consider in detail below, he is suspicious of the status of Hegelian discourse – suspicious, that is, of its very discursivity, its bookishness, its pretension to being a *pure thought* of force, a purity that relies on the previous work of language as the *Aufhebung des Daseins*, the cancelling and lifting of existence into a pure thought-determination, as the *Phenomenology* puts it (Derrida, *Positions*, 1981, 34/17). The *Phenomenology* is the gathering and ordering of these thought-determinations or shapes of spirit so that the successive failure to provide unconditioned certainty leads one to absolute knowledge, the standpoint in which the pure categories of thought can be gathered and ordered in the *Science of Logic*.

Hegel's system is the dream of a book, a book of nature in which the categories appropriate to thinking nature, force among them, find their proper positions. Derrida's suspicion about Hegel's law of force is not that it fixates an inherent flux, for Derrida knows as well as any Hegel scholar that there is a movement to Hegel's law of force. Derrida is worried, however, that this movement is regulated in a speculative economy of opposition and resolution that is made possible by the work of language, and that turns a profit of meaning from each investment in a lost spiritual shape. This speculative economy is thematically treated in the section of the *Science of Logic* entitled 'The determinations of reflection' and methodologically named *Aufhebung*. And indeed, the movement of 'The determinations of reflection' in the *Science of Logic*, from pure difference to contradiction, does articulate the logic embedded in the 'Force and understanding' chapter from the earlier *Phenomenology of Spirit*. Hegel tells us there that the law of force is 'universal difference', differing even from difference, as seen in the absolute flux of the play of forces and here repeated at the level of thought (Hegel, *Phenomenology of Spirit*, 1977, 119–20/90). At the end of the dialectic of the laws of force, we read that the transition to the Concept, first recognizable in the move to self-consciousness, comes with the recognition that the structure of contradiction is now to be thought: 'We have to think pure change, or *think antithesis within the antithesis itself*, or *contradiction*' (130/99; Hegel's italics).

Reached through the speculative economy of the *Phenomenology*, in which the laws of force play their pedagogic role, Hegel's book of nature is the *Science of Logic*, which arranges the reflexive categories that enable us to think the laws of force. These are then repeated in their externality in the *Philosophy of Nature*. The *Philosophy of Nature* comes second – not chronologically, to be sure, but systematically. As Hegel makes clear, his *Logic* is metaphysics: after physics in the order of knowing, but first philosophy in the order of being.

LANGUAGE AND LOGIC

Derrida reads Hegel's *Logic* as a text. This is not to say as a book in a library, as Derrida has shown us in *Of Grammatology* that he does not equate text and book. Rather we need to see the realm of pure thought that Hegel thinks in the *Science of Logic* as a text that desires the status of 'book', a purely meaningful text. 'Text' here means that the elements of a field gain their meaning or establish their power only in relation to the other elements of the field. Logic – and the *Science of Logic* which articulates it – is a meaningful text; we will see how Derrida thinks fields of forces as texts as well.

Hegel's *Logic* can be seen as a text both thematically and methodologically.[1] The thematic use of contradiction would be contradiction considered as one mark within a field, one category of thought; the methodological use would be contradiction as the master trope for the relation between all the marks, the way the field is ordered. Hegel's term for thematic contradiction is *Widerspruch*, 'counter-speech'; his term for methodological contradiction is *Aufhebung*, determinate negation that cancels while preserving.

Hegel considers the method of philosophy in the Preface to the *Phenomenology of Spirit*, distinguishing determinate negation from abstract or simple negation. Here Hegel claims that the 'proper exposition' of philosophic method is logic, the setting forth of the 'structure of the whole in its pure essentiality' (Hegel, *Phenomenology of Spirit*, 1977, 47/28). The setting forth of this structure is to be distinguished from formalism (48/29). Science consists in following the self-determination of the whole, that is, following the work of negativity: 'this self-identity [of *nous*] is no less negativity . . . having its otherness within itself, and being self-moving, is just what is involved in the *simplicity* of thinking itself' (54/34). The simplicity of internal negativity is the 'pure concept', that the being of each thing is its concept is 'logical necessity', the 'rhythm of the organic whole' (55/34). This rhythm is the *Aufhebung*. Determinate negation, the other name of the *Aufhebung*, is not just any negation, nor certainly an abstract negation, a simple 'no', but is the gathering and ordering of the references to its others, its negations, that each mark carries with it. Determinate negation does not just say category Y is not X or Z, but says instead that Y comes between X and Z, that Y comes from the failure of X and that the failure of Y leads to Z. The *Aufhebung* is thus the putting to work of the negative in what Derrida calls the 'speculative economy' in his important essay on Bataille, 'From restricted to general economy' (in *Writing and Difference*).

From these considerations of the *Phenomenology* we can see Hegel's thematization of the operation of textuality in the *Science of Logic* in the implication of difference and identity as we considered it above. The determinations of reflection thematize the way in which difference is put to work, negativity harnessed in the pattern governed by contradiction, that which difference is already, as such. A thing is what it is only in its difference from other things; thus difference is internal to identity. This is precisely the thought of the trace as developed by Derrida. An element in a field can produce an effect of presence only on the basis of its references, traces, to that which it is not. The thought of the trace does not deny presence, but it insists that we consider presence as produced from absence, identity as dependent upon difference. However, while Derrida thinks identity as dependent upon difference, this is not a reciprocal relation. Indeed, it is precisely in the reciprocal implication of identity into difference that we find the point of Derrida's difference from Hegel (and one of the points of his greatest similarity with Deleuze). Derrida will point out two ways of thinking difference 'as such', difference without identity, which we will take up later in this chapter. The two are the 'radical alterity' of the re-mark, and the irreconcilability of the conflict of forces.

Methodologically, then, logic is treated as a text by Hegel in that the elements of the realm of pure thought, the categories, are meaningful only in their relation to each other. It is precisely the attempt to think any one category in isolation from its others that Hegel names 'abstraction' and that furnishes the failure from which thought learns. Each isolating abstraction fails, and from each failure thought learns. The movement here is named the *Aufhebung*. Now logic can be a text only if the categories, as marks in the field of pure thought, are all meaningful in and through their orderly relation to one another. To achieve such meaningful ordered relation they must be totalizable, must all be on the same level so that they are susceptible of arranging themselves in the pattern Hegel calls determinate negation. The question then becomes, how do the meaningful marks reach the same level, the level of pure thought? Hegel's answer is the purification of nature – which here includes the 'natural' perceptions and feelings of human beings – by spirit. This purification and ordering is only possible as guaranteed in advance.[2] How can thought be exiled into nature in such a way that it can be subsequently purified and ordered? It can be so exiled only if pure thought already functions as a text – if 'exile' or negativity is internal to its structure – so that its exteriorization into nature, and its spiritual lifting into the grammatical categories of natural language – themselves in need of further purification and ordering – would not essentially disrupt a retranslation into pure thought.

Spirit can purify nature and reach the level of pure thought because the patterned movement, the rhythm, of the system writ large – logic–nature–spirit – exile and return – is always already there in pure thought. Now this originary movement of the entire system is most easily seen, because its most abstract, at the beginning of the *Science of Logic*. What is shown there as originary in the famous movement of Being and Nothing is not just a difference, not just a split, but a splitting/healing movement, an originary movement of position– negation–negation of negation. Now such a movement is only possible if healing is possible, and healing is only possible if the originary difference has always been, even in its becoming, a difference within the same sphere, that is, the sphere of thought, of logic. Thus the movement of the system (logic–nature–spirit) is a textuality, a putting of the negative, exile, to work in the guarantee of its meaningful return.

To understand this originary movement it is vital not to focus solely on chronology, to assume that the absolute is solely an historical achievement, although it certainly is in one light. The owl of Minerva tells us that Hegel's success in articulating the absolute in a science of logic is an historical event that displays the maturation of spirit in the age of freedom. However, Hegel's success is possible only as a return to self of thought guaranteed in advance. Now thought returns to itself from its natural exile in language. The very term *Widerspruch*, contradiction, speaking-against — as Derrida points out in an interview in *Positions* on which we will focus — allows us to think the relation of logic to language, the way logic is the ordering of spritual shapes stored in language and brought to pure thought by the *Phenomenology*, which Hegel tells us is the 'presupposition' of the *Science of Logic*.[3] Thus alongside its systematic character Hegel also saw the *Science of Logic* as historical fulfillment, as bringing metaphysics to the level of science: 'the science of logic . . . constitutes metaphysics proper or purely speculative philosophy' (Hegel, *Science of Logic*, 1989, 16/27). To understand how the spiritual shapes *can* be purified we must understand how nature is opposed to thought and brought back to thought in spirit in a way that retains the textuality of originary splitting and healing.

Let us here examine in more detail how the work of spirit is accomplished by language. The spiritual shapes to be purified and ordered are stored in language. How so? For Hegel, language functions precisely as the raising of the material concrete difference that is existence to a universal thought determination. In the Preface to the *Phenomenology*, Hegel writes that a higher spirit can retain previous spirit since the existence informed by those shapes has been reduced to a trace: 'In a spirit that is higher than another, the lower concrete existence [*Dasein*] has sunk to a non-appearing moment; what used to be the thing itself [*die Sache selbst*] is now but a trace [*Spur*]. . . .' (Hegel, *Phenomenology of Spirit*, 1977, 32/16; translation modified). The passage through these stages is precisely the work of the world-spirit, history; the isolated individual who follows this path in the phenomenological forming of the universal individual can do so only because the immediate brute existence of previous stages has been raised to the level of thought:

Yet, at the same time, he [the individual to be formed] does have less trouble, since all this [work of spirit] has already been *implicitly* accomplished; the content is already the actuality reduced to possibility, its immediacy overcome, and the embodied shape reduced to abbreviated, simple determinations of thought. (Hegel, *Phenomenology of Spirit*, 1977, 34/17)

Forming the universal individual in this way entails gathering together previously surpassed and retained spiritual shapes and placing them in the proper order so that a proper interpretation of the relation of finite consciousness and absolute spirit might occur. Such gathering of spirit to itself requires the self-conscious history of a culture, which depends on writing, as Hegel tells us in the *Lectures on the Philosophy of World History* (1975, 83–4/135–6). The thought determinations that are the vestiges of previous shapes of spirit and that are to be gathered in the proper order are precisely linguistic expressions of theoretic intelligence retained in literature and the writing of history. The shapes are purified to the level of pure thought in the *Phenomenology*, then ordered in the *Science of Logic*.

Let us now turn to the precise role of language in the *Science of Logic*. There, language is the storehouse of logical forms (Hegel, *Science of Logic*, 1989, 20/31). A science of logic would then be the gathering of such forms in such a way as to demonstrate their movement as the movement of spirit. In the Preface to the second edition (1831) of the *Science of Logic* Hegel links language, thinking, and logic, thereby taking advantage of their common root in the Greek *logos*. Hegel writes: 'The forms of thought are, in the first instance, displayed and stored in human *language*' (Hegel, *Science of Logic*, 1989, 20/31). Hegel then shows the penetration of language into all the appropriative representations that perform the very process of interiorization we encountered in the *Phenomenology*: 'Into all that becomes something inward for men, or representation in general, into all that that he makes his own, language has penetrated . . .' (20/31). Thought is stored and displayed in language in such a way that it can be retranslated into thought after this exile; Hegel uses an intralinguistic term ('metaphor') to designate the depositing of thought in both nature proper and in the natural 'mental impressions' of experience. Hegel writes in the Introduction to the *Encyclopedia*: 'Mental impressions such as these [feelings, perceptions, desires] may be regarded as the metaphors of thoughts and notions' (Hegel, *Science of Logic*, 1989, 44/6). Spiritual purification would then be de-metaphorization, and the originary metaphor (*meta-pherein*: carrying over) by which thought entered nature would be enabled by an originary splitting, the text-nature of thought itself.

Now a natural language does not contain a science of logic already worked out, but the elements of logic, categories, are contained in varying states of clarity in the linguistic expressions of thought that make up man's very nature, as the *Science of Logic* makes clear: 'and everything that he has transformed into language and expressed in it contains a category – concealed, mixed with other forms or clearly determined as such; so much the logical is natural to him, or better, is his own peculiar *nature*' (Hegel, *Science of Logic*, 1989, 20/31). Once the absolute viewpoint is achieved the *Science of Logic* can procede as the ordering of categories lying dormant and disordered in the grammar of natural languages.

One of those categories is contradiction, *Widerspruch*. As we will see, Derrida claims in discussing the reference of *Widerspruch* to 'dialectical *discourse*' that the *Spruch* points back to the linguistic nature of the *Science of Logic*. By 'linguistic' I do not mean the *Science of Logic* is a book, for Derrida would claim that the concept of 'book' is a desire for meaning divorced from the world, force, materiality, etc. Thus for Derrida 'book' names the desire to efface an inscription in the 'general text'. The linguistic nature of dialectical discourse refers to a textuality of logic in which the categories would be marks in a text rather than signs in a book, and *Aufhebung* would be the means by which Hegel attempts to order the field of meaningful marks. To repeat the earlier-developed distinction between the thematic and methodological uses of contradiction, the thematic use would be contradiction considered as one mark within a field; the methodological use would be contradiction as the master trope for the relation between all the marks, the way the field is ordered. Although Hegel uses a single term for methodological contradiction, *Aufhebung*, deter-minate negation that cancels while preserving, we must of course recognize different movements in each book of the *Science of Logic*. These movements – going over, reflection, development – are all recognizable as inflections of the *Aufhebung*, if we see the *Aufhebung* as the basic movement of the system, a guaranteed-in-advance healing of originary splitting. Thus determinate negations can be seen as specific at each transition, but there must be a minimal structural identity so that each transition is recognizable as a 'determinate negation', as an instance of the concept 'determinate negation'.

Now the *Aufhebung* can order a field of marks only if the marks are opposable, on the same level. The guarantee for such total opposability, total self-reflection, is that healing is co-originary with splitting, that the absolute level of pure thought is that of a field of marks restored from its natural exile via spiritual purification.

THE DETERMINATIONS OF REFLECTION

We have seen the spiritual work of language in producing the *Science of Logic* as a field of marks at the level of pure thought. Let us now examine more closely Derrida's remarks about the *Science of Logic*, starting with one of the interviews in *Positions*, where Derrida claims that:

> I have attempted to distinguish *différance* (whose *a* marks, among other things, its productive and conflictual characteristics) from Hegelian difference, and have done so precisely at the point at which Hegel, in the greater *Logic*, determines difference as contra- diction only in order to resolve it, to interiorize it, to lift it up (according to the syllogistic process of speculative dialectics) into the self-presence of an onto-theological or onto-teleological synthe- sis. (Derrida, *Positions*, 1981, 59–60/44)

After the word 'contradiction', Derrida appends a note in which he says:

> If I have more often spoken of conflicts of forces than of contradic- tion, this is first of all due to a critical wariness as concerns the Hegelian concept of contradiction [*Widerspruch*], which, in addition, as its name indicates, is constructed in such a way as to permit its resolution within dialectical *discourse* . . . (Derrida, *Positions*, 1981, 60n6/101n13)

Derrida continues the original passage:

Différance . . . must sign the point at which one breaks with the system of the *Aufhebung* and with speculative dialectics. Since this conflictuality of *différance* . . . can never be totally resolved, it marks its effects in what I call the text in general, in a text which is not reduced to a book or a library. (Derrida, *Positions*, 1981, 60–61/44)

As we will see in more detail, here is the point where Derrida's political physics departs from Hegel's political logic. Derrida insists on the irreducibility of force beyond discourse, on the plurality of forces whose mutual workings cannot be captured by a logic of contradiction. The forces of the general text exceed the realm of pure thought, leaving always a remainder of force beyond signification.

Before we detail Derrida's thought, though, let us work through Hegel. The realm of pure thought reached at the end of the *Phenomenology* and articulated in the *Science of Logic* is for Hegel a realm in which all opposition can be resolved precisely because of its posited character. We see this precisely in the 'Determinations of reflection', which is, for Derrida, marked out as 'the point at which Hegel . . . determines difference as contradiction'. To find this point let us return to Hegel's *Science of Logic*. The *Science of Logic* articulates the different ways we have of thinking Being.[4] These different ways of thinking are called by Hegel 'categories'. A category is a particular mode of thought; thought can have nature as its object, but in logic the categories are themselves considered in the absoluteness of thought. Logic is thus thought about thought. We can say that thought 'thinks through' each category. That is, thought is modalized in a particular pattern we call a category so that it 'thinks through (via)' a category. Thought can also be said to 'think through' a category in that it considers all the implications of such a thought pattern. These implications are the ways in which thought breaks down when isolated in any one categorial mode. The science of logic is then the ordering of categories that displays the inability of any one of them to sustain thought in isolation and further displays the way in which the specific failure of each category leads to the following category in a movement of learning. The pattern of failure and learning from failure is called by Hegel 'determinate negation' or the *Aufhebung*. In this articulation of failure and learning, the *Science of Logic* moves from considering Being to Essence to Concept.

Hegel thematically considers difference and contradiction in the section entitled 'The determinations of reflection', the second chapter of Section 1 of the Logic of Essence, 'Essence as reflection within itself'. The Logic of Essence begins when thought's unwillingness to give up its attempts to grasp Being in its immediacy leads it to think essence as the truth of Being. Reflection is that mediation in which thought reflects on its attempts to make sense of Being in terms of essence; the reflective determinations are the steps reflection goes through, the ways it determines itself, in learning from the failures of its attempts at making sense of Being in terms of essence. The determinations of reflection follow this order: identity, difference, contradiction (*Identität, Unterschied, Widerspruch*). In other words, thought first tries to think the essence of Being as identity, then as difference, and finally as contradiction. The failures of these attempts lead thought to consider the essence of Being as ground; ground in turn fails, and the movement of failure and learning from failure continues on, eventually leading to the Concept and finally to the Absolute Idea.

The movement of thought in reflection is difficult. As thought thinks through each category it breaks down until it appears to be both a part and the whole of which it is a part. The next stage takes up the result of this reflection but finds itself suffering analogous breakdowns. In the next few paragraphs I will go through each reflective determination in a bit more detail. In the determinations of reflection, thought first thinks essence as identity; the essence of Being is so conceived that things are what they are by being identical to themselves and by being different from everything else. We thus see that the category of identity implies the category of difference, for, thematically considered, it is different from all other categories insofar as it is identical only with itself. Identity must therefore be grasped as essentially implicating difference; the attempt to think essence as simple identity, identity in itself, fails (Hegel, *Science of Logic*, 1989, 2.38–45/411–16).

After the failure of identity, thought is now led to think difference, *Unterschied*, as the essence. *Unterschied* suffers a tripartite breakdown: absolute difference, diversity and opposition (*absolute Unterschied, Ver-*

schiedenheit, Gegensatz). Absolute difference is the first category to be considered, difference *simpliciter* (Hegel, *Science of Logic*, 1989, 2.46–7/ 417–18). But as such it is different even from itself, and hence is identity (that which is different from difference). Thus absolute difference cannot be thought as difference; absolute difference ends up not being thought as itself, as difference, but as what is different from itself, as identity. To think difference as difference some identity must be implicated in difference, so that difference stands still long enough to be thought as difference. This giving of a meaningful identity to difference, this rendering difference meaningful via the implication of an identity is the first stage in which, in Derrida's words, Hegel 'determines difference as contradiction'. The introduction of identity into difference (or the recognition that identity is necessary to think meaningfully difference) is only possible on the level of thought and meaning. As we will see, this reconciliation of difference does not obtain with the power relations established between forces in the Derridean body politic, the general text of force and signification.

At this point of the *Science of Logic* thought has learned that the difference of identity and difference cannot be absolute, but must be thought as relative. Absolute difference here gives way to a relativized difference: diversity, *Verschiedenheit* (Hegel, *Science of Logic*, 1989, 2.47–55/418–24). With the giving up of the thought of absolute difference the full structure of reflection is first realized. Identity requires difference to be identity, so that identity is both a part and the whole – the whole being identity and that difference necessary to identity. Similarly, difference needs to posit identity, because thinking difference as difference entails recognizing an implicated identity. Furthermore, the identity needed by difference is itself self-reflected, so that difference is here seen to be composed of identity and difference, both self-reflected.

Thought has now reached the thought of difference as *Verschiedenheit*, simple diversity in which the self-reflected moments are indifferent to each other, simple likeness and simple unlikeness. Thought soon recognizes the structure of reflection once again, however, for likeness is composed of likeness and unlikeness, while unlikeness similarly needs likeness: both sides are both part and whole. Thought as simply opposed to its other, 'likeness' is seen as positive and 'unlikeness' as negative (and vice versa). Now, positive and negative relate to each other as opposites, so thought has now arrived at the concept of opposition. *Gegensatz*, opposition, is described as 'opposed diversity' (*entgegengesetzte Verschiedenheit*; Hegel, *Science of Logic*, 1989, 2.36/409), and as the 'completion of difference' (*Im Gegensatze ist die bestimmte Reflexion, der Unterschied vollendet*; 2.55/424). Thought in this way realizes that positive and negative are each in themselves positive and negative. At the end of the breakdowns positive and negative are thus both seen to be moments of each other. Both are mutually indifferent and exclusive of its other, that is, both are 'self-subsistent' (2.64/431).

Totality is the key here to the thought of self-subsistence. Reflection must be total: each moment must be both part and whole, with no remainder, forming a self-subsistent whole. But the attempt to think this exclusive self-subsistence proves the downfall of opposition, for as self-reflected (containing its opposite), each moment succeeds only in excluding itself when it attempts to exclude its opposite. That which excludes itself from itself is contradictory. Here is the point to which Derrida alludes, where difference is determined as contradiction, via opposition. Hegel writes at the beginning of the section on contradiction, 'Difference as such is already *implicitly* contradiction' (*Der Unterschied überhaupt ist schon der Widerspruch an sich*; Hegel, *Science of Logic*, 1989, 2.65/431. The 'already in itself' in which difference is destined to realize itself in contradiction marks the reining in, the putting to work, of the negative in the service of speculative meaning. Derrida will attempt to think *différance* as something related to that which goes by the name of *Unterschied* in Hegel, but which cannot be kept in the bounds of the pattern of meaning derived from failure and learning from failure.

Now we must emphasize here that opposition does not fail because of an unthematized remainder; rather it only moves on to contradiction through the success of its totalizing. The first moment of contradiction is a nullity, a ceaseless vanishing of the opposites into each other (Hegel, *Science of Logic*, 1989, 2.67/433). Secondly, however, contradiction sees such self-excluding reflection as positing the moments as self-subsistent (2.67/433). Finally, opposition is not only destroyed in the final movement of contradiction, but 'withdrawn *into its ground'* (2.68/434), which thinks the essence as the 'unity of positive and negative', as contradiction and resolution of contradiction (2.79/ 442).

We must again note the total self-reflection of both sides: there can be no remainder, as both sides are reflected, both part and whole. The important thing for us to consider is that the claim to totality in opposition allows for contradiction. Now, both sides of an opposition that becomes contradictory must be *able* to be opposed. This ability to be opposed entails being on the same level with no remainder. We will now explore why Derrida thinks the Hegelian aspiration to the level of pure thought, that which allows difference to be determined as an opposition resolvable in contradiction, is impossible due to the irreducible difference in forces in a general text of force and significa- tion. This is a key move in defeating all the false claims that Derrida 'imprisons us in language' or is a 'semiological reductionist' or what have you. It is equally key, however, for our overall thesis that the thought of the general text, as the overflow of metaphysics, cannot guide us in the detailed empirical investigation of the production of bodies politic, as can the historical libidinal materialism of Deleuze and Guattari.

THE GENERAL TEXT

When we return to 'Force and signification' we can see the basics of Derrida's reading of Hegel – the reading of the general text as a field of force and signification – in place years before *Positions* and *Glas*. Derrida writes: 'Force is the other of language without which language would not be what it is' (Derrida, *Force and signification*, 1978, 45/ 27). This 'other' is not oppositional, of course. Derrida continues, 'Force cannot be conceived on the basis of an oppositional couple. . . .' (46/28). How, then, is it to be thought – for Derrida does want to think it, although not in a pure thought ('one would seek in vain a concept in phenomenology which would permit the thinking of intensity or force' (46/27; translation modified), but in a Nietzschean mode: 'like pure force, Dionysus is worked by difference' (47/29). Worked by difference – or as he will say in a few years, worked by *différance*, which as we have seen, 'marks its effects in . . . the text in general'. Instead of the pure thought of laws of force in the book of nature, Derrida writes of a differantial, signifying force in the general text, a political physics of a body politic.

Let us now consider the 'Différance' essay (in *Margins*) for more details on the way in which the general text is one of force *and* signification, a site of non-hylomorphic production of meaning as 'making sense'. Derrida begins by insisting that we think *différance* in the 'general structure of [its] economy' (Derrida, *Margins*, 1982, 4/3). He proposes the term 'sheaf [*faisceau*]' to mark that: 'the assemblage to be proposed has the complex structure of a weaving, an interlacing which permits the different threads and different lines of sense [*sens*] – or of force – to go off again in different directions' (4/3). On the basis of this passage, let me advance this formula: *différance* 'is' the interweaving of sense and force in the political physics of the body politic conceived as the general text.

Force reappears in the 'Différance' essay in a thread that is, interestingly enough, not mentioned in Rodolphe Gasché's important and influential treatment of the essay in *The Tain of the Mirror* (1986, 194–205). Derrida names *différance* as the structure of the ever-shifting relations in the field of forces described by Nietzsche. 'Thus, *différance* is the name we might give to the "active", moving discord of different forces that Nietzsche sets up against the entire system of metaphysical grammar, whenever this system governs culture, philosophy and science' (Derrida, *Margins*, 1982, 20/18). Nietzsche sets up *forces*, not the vain thought of force, against metaphysical grammar. In hammering away at metaphysics, the naming of force as *différance* is itself a force, a countervailing force to metaphysical grammar, the thinking of force in opposable, resolvable categories. In describing as differantial what metaphysics would name as equal and opposed there is a performative force, challenging the interpretative structure that is metaphysics. This challenge is not opposition, for the forces are not equatable, the discourses incommensurate to each other. The thought of laws of force might move through opposable and resolvable categories, but *forces* are never equal, as Deleuze insists in his interpretation of Nietzsche. In the 'Différance' essay (Derrida, *Margins*, 1982, 18/17), Derrida quotes Deleuze from *Nietzsche and Philosophy*:

Quantity itself, therefore, is not separable from the difference of quantity. The difference of quantity is the essence of force, the relation of force to force. The dream of two equal forces, even if they are granted an opposition of sense [*sens*], is an approximate and crude dream, a statistical dream, plunged into by the living but dispelled by chemistry. (Deleuze, *Nietzsche and Philosophy*, 1983, 49/43)

A footnote by Deleuze refers here to passages not available in the English translation of *The Will to Power*, but found only in the French edition at II 86 and 87, where Nietzsche writes: 'In the chemical world, the sharpest perception of the difference between forces reigns. . . . With the organic world imprecision and appearance begin' (Deleuze *Nietzsche and Philosophy*, 1983, 49n3/204n5). For Nietzsche, it seems, the 'chemical' world is one of the sites of the production of bodies politic.

How are we to understand the claim by Nietzsche and Deleuze that an opposition of sense is but a dream? The economy of 'sense' in modern Western European languages (e.g. French *sens*, German *Sinn*, Italian *senso*) includes 'directionality' and 'sensibility' as well as 'mean-ing'.[5] Sense is not simply reducible to 'meaning' due to these other elements in its economy, for with directionality and sensibility 'sense' is installed in a field of exteriority and force; 'sense' is a term of political physics. A direction implies a space within which two points can be ordered, and a sensation implies a receptivity to the forceful action of that which is sensed. A political physics of sense would claim that meaning is the most superficial element in the economy of sense, that meaning is the effect of configurations of directional forces in the general text. On this view, meanings as iterable marks arise from the confluence of forceful vectors in the body politic in all its registers.[6] But this means that forces can never be op-posed, because they are never posed from a point outside the field of forces, nor can they be matter for the im-position of transcendent form in hylomorphic meaning production. Since meaning and hence subjectivity arises on the basis of a field of forces, there is no meaningful subject outside the field of forces to do the posing, no Husserlian hylomorphic production of meaning, as we saw in Chapter 1. The dream of opposable sense is the dream of opposable categories isolated from a field of always oblique and never reconcilable forces. In other words, it is the dream of writing a book of nature, the dream of metaphysics. Naming the differantial character of force and the force dimension of the general text, thinking in terms of political physics, dispels that dream for those that hear and understand that naming.

But dispelling the dream is not enough, for precisely what is to be understood is that understanding is not pure, that understanding and signification do not exhaust the general text. We know that bodies are in force in the general text, that bodies are produced by the clash of forces. We have previously cited Deleuze on Nietzsche, from a point in *Nietzsche and Philosophy* only a few pages prior to the quote that Derrida selects: 'every relationship of forces constitutes a body – whether it is chemical, biological, social, or political' (Deleuze *Nietzsche and Philosophy*, 1983, 45/40). Despite this point at which Derrida and Deleuze are so close, Derrida cannot articulate the production of bodies politic from clashes of forces in the general text. He can show that bodies politic are forceful, that force is inextricably part of their institution, but he has no resources, as do Deleuze and Guattari, for elaborating the principles of an empirical research project into the material production of forceful bodies politic. For Derrida, bodies politic, formed in the general text, are simply the point of 'overflow' of sense. A body, as constituted by forces, is always in excess of pure meaning; it is always the overflow of sense in its full economy beyond the single moment of meaning. In *Positions*, Derrida claims that:

> *There is* such a general text everywhere that (that is, everywhere) [metaphysics] and its order (essence, truth, sense, consciousness, ideality, etc.) are *overflowed* [*débordés*; Derrida's italics] that is, everywhere that their authority is put back into the position of a *mark* in a chain . . . (Derrida, *Positions*, 1981, 82/59)

Despite Derrida's inability to grapple with the material production of bodies politic, because of his concentrating on phenomenological/ metaphysical meaning and the breakdown of its claim to self-ruling isolation from force due to its inscription in the general text, we *can* say that the overflowing of sense into the general text, the recognition of its inscription in a field of forces, does allow a certain Derridean purchase on political action. In the general text, the directional forces or the vectors of the play of forces are relatively stabilized as 'meaning', that is, as iterable triggers of the same thought/action (indicating here the interweaving of constative and performative we will explore below). For Derrida, forceful meaning is produced not by a self-ruling consciousness which operates by a hylomorphic imposition of formal conceptual order on sensuous matter, but by a hegemonic formation of forces that grants only relatively, only temporarily, stable identity to marks. The forcefield of the production of meaning is why Derrida will claim in 'Signature event context' that 'an opposition of metaphysical concepts . . . is never the face-to-face of two terms, but a hierarchy and an order of subordination' (Derrida, 'Signature event context', 1982, 392/329). Conceptual opposition, opposition of categories posited in a book, is a dream; forceful meanings are non-hylomorphically produced in the general text, the interweaving of force and signification. As we will see, recognizing such an interweaving of force and signification is an important dissolution of the dream of metaphysics and its attempts to justify hierarchical patterns of social forces by a reason allegedly free of force.

The general text is an interwoven field of forces and significations. The interweaving of the field is named *différance*, while its elements are named 'marks'. The general text is a field of marks. Now just as we have disabused ourselves of the dream of a book of pure signification, so we must beware of the temptation to think we have arrived at a *pure* physics of force, for a mark is force *and* signification. Let me advance another formula to parallel our recognition that meaning is forceful, by claiming that force is a significant element of the general text. Writing, inscribing a mark to render it iterable, is a performative signifying and a meaningful performance – we could call it *making sense*. Making sense is the construction of a hegemonic formation of forces in which meaning or iterability is produced from the clash of force vectors, rather than the hylomorphic scheme of formal conceptual imposition on sensuous matter. Derrida writes in the Afterword to *Limited Inc.*: 'the semantic level [is not] . . . entirely semantic or significant' (1988, 145). Speaking of the stability of interpretative structures, Derrida specifies that he is not speaking of ahistorical 'semantic structures' but of 'stratifications that are already differential and of a great stability with regard to relations of forces and all the hierarchies or hegemonies they suppose or put into practice' (144). In the general text force is interwoven with sense, so that forces must make sense and making sense is forceful.

Now, force is not a ground closed off onto itself. To fit in a general text, a coalition of forces must make sense, they must be iterable in a mark that has a minimal identity over the time and space of the series of its iterated marks. A mark is thus a relatively stable inscription, never self-present, yet repeatable. On the other hand, making sense is forceful. I've noted above the force of Nietzsche's countering of metaphysics. We could also refer, in anticipation of this chapter's next section, to the primacy of the performative Derrida articulates in 'Force of law': any constative is preceded by a performative affirmation: 'yes, I promise, testify, pledge, that this is true'; any constative is also performatively reinforced by a reading code that guarantees its legibility (Derrida, 'Force of law', 1990, 969). In other words, the reading of marks is institutionally enforced. Reading strategies outside the institutionally enforced reading code make no sense, as anyone who reads the bewildered responses to deconstructive readings can tell you.

Having been warned against the dream of a pure physics, we should, however, remember that in the academic/political culture still dominated by the metaphysical reading code, which commands us to ignore differantial force and stress pure meaning, it is disruptive to stress force. But, of course, stressing force is a new way of making sense, one that possesses its own reading code. Reading meaningful force and forceful meaning is a way of reading the general text as the interweaving of force *and* signification.

The general text is a field of marks skewed into hierarchies, as forces never rest in opposition. The hierarchies, which give themselves off as oppositions to a metaphysical reading, are pairs lifted from a differantial reserve. As Derrida writes in 'Plato's pharmacy' (in *Dissemination*):

[the *pharmakon*] is the *différance* of difference. It holds in reserve, in its undecided shadow and vigil, the opposites and the differends that the process of discrimination will come to carve out. Contradictions and pairs of opposites are lifted from the bottom of this diacritical, differing, deferring reserve. Already inhabited by *différance*, this reserve, even though it 'precedes' the opposition between different effects, even though it preexists differences as effects, does not have the simplicity of a *coincidentia oppositorum*. It is from this field that dialectics draws its philosophemes. (Derrida, *Dissemination*, 1981, 158/127)

We must be careful here to note that the field is already 'inhabited by *différance*'. That is, it is already structured by force. Deconstruction is political physics, the diagnosis of the metaphysical lifting of opposites from the reserved field or general text as a skewing of them into new hierarchies, a twisting of them on the basis of previous hierarchies. Any hegemonic formation of meaningful force and forceful meaning is, however, never total, but has held in reserve the possibility of reinscribing its elements in different, disseminative, formations and contexts.

THE FORCE OF LAW

The skewing force is the *coup de force* that establishes an institution, a new way of making sense. It is always a marshalling of force against force, a differantial shift of meaning by a shift of forces, the non-hylomorphic production of a forceful body politic. To emphasize the role of force, we insist on the term 'institution', with its connotation of forceful temporal beginning, rather than 'constitution', with its phenomenological connotation of the transcendental subjective establishment of meaning. The instituting event is a performative–constative undecidable, in other words, one that interweaves performative force and constative signification. In several essays, Derrida shows how any instituting event must grant itself, in advance, the right to act with a force that will only be justified by the institution brought into force by that act. In the 1986 essay 'Declarations of independence', Derrida writes of the 'fabulous retroactivity' of the *coup de force* by which a people constitutes itself by signature in an undecidable constative–performative (Derrida, '*Declaration of indendence*', 1986, 10). The 1986 essay, 'The laws of reflection: Nelson Mandela, in admiration', clarifies this difficult point. Derrida writes here that the violent act of institution must at once produce *and* presuppose the unity of the nation that is to be instituted (Derrida, 'The laws of reflection: Nelson Mandela, in admiration', 1987, 17). In the case of South Africa, this act *remained* a *coup de force* because its violence was excessive and deficient – it remained excessively visible because it enfranchised only the European minority, yet it was deficient in that it was not violent enough, not genocidal enough, in leaving behind too many African witnesses (18). The instituting *coup de force* is violent in the sense that it precedes the institution of a state authority that can legitimately use force.[7]

Now, it should be stated here that Derrida's reading is not, despite a certain family resemblance, mere ideology critique. Critique finds the truth of the critiqued text outside that text in another, scientific, text. Critique would simply describe a higher-order law of force by unmasking positive law as the instrument of forces that would remain foundational. Rather, force and law must be thought together as the force of law, where the conceptual explication of the interweaving of force and signification reaches a limit. Derrida writes in 'Force of law':

> the operation that consists of founding, inaugurating, justifying law (*droit*), making law, would consist of a *coup de force*, of a performative and therefore interpretative violence that in itself is neither just nor unjust and that no justice and no previous law with its founding anterior moment could guarantee or contradict or invalidate. . . . Here the discourse comes up against its limit: in itself, in its performative power itself. It is what I here propose to call the mystical. (Derrida, 'Force of law', 1990, 941–43)

The instituting discourse of a body politic comes up against its limit: signification cannot fully explicate the interweaving of force and signification in instituting in the general text, cannot fully explicate the production of a forceful body politic.

As is so often the case, the German language is fortuitously undecidable in helping articulate this limit. *Gewalt*, as in the title of the

Benjamin piece, *Zur Kritik der Gewalt*, examined in the second half of the 'Force of law' essay, means both violence and legitimate authority. For instance, as we will detail in Chapter 7, *Gewaltätigkeit* is the word Kant uses to describe the violence of the state of nature in *The Metaphysical Elements of Justice*, while *Staatsgewalt* is a common expression for the authority of the state. The social contract tells us that individuals must delegate their natural right to violence to the state, which has a monopoly on the legitimate use of force. The delegation of natural *Gewalt* to the *Staatsgewalt* is the social contract. But, on Derrida's reading, the institution of the *Staatsgewalt*, the *coup de force*, cannot be located in this economy of violence/legitimate force.

This instituting event, even though it is irruptive and resistant to account, is iterable. In the terms of the Benjamin essay, its law-making violence is interwoven with a law-conserving violence. As Derrida says in 'Force of law', 'a foundation is a promise' (Derrida, 'Force of law', 1990, 997). What is set up must be or ought to be repeated. The *coup de force* sets up the law in force here and now. The *coup de force* sets up a hierarchy by skewing differantially what went before. On that basis, it allows for the institution to continue. As Derrida makes clear, this continuation has the structure of auto-affection in which the law-conserving violence iterates the institution and keeps the skewed hegemonic formation of forces in force. Derrida writes: 'Iterability inscribes the promise as guard in the most irruptive instant of foundation. Thus it describes the possibility of repetition at the heart of the originary' (997). And again, a few pages later, 'Iterability requires the origin to repeat itself originarily, to alter itself so as to have the value of origin, that is, to conserve itself' (1007–9).

But iterability is also the basis of dissemination. In 'Signature event context' we read of yet another force, the 'force of rupture', which accompanies any mark and forbids the saturation of any context (Derrida, 'Signature event context', 1982, 377/317; translation modified). In other words, the iteration of the institution is open to a force of rupture because the enforcing of the hegemonic formation of forces is never assured. It is never assured, because any mark is not self-present. Rather, a mark is spaced over the series of its iterations; in this series, the sameness of the mark is constituted from its different occurences. The *coup de force* is a writing, the inscription of a mark in the general text. The *coup de force* makes sense, though its sense is undecidable as to its ultimate justice over time. Derrida writes in the Afterword to *Limited Inc.*:

> I say 'undecidability' ˙rather than 'indeterminacy' because I am interested more in relations of force, in differences of force, in everything that allows, precisely, determinations in given situations to be stabilized through a decision of writing (in the broad sense I give to this world, which also includes political action and experience in general) (Derrida, *Limited Inc.*, 1988, 148).

What, then, does deconstruction do? It diagnoses and intervenes when the skewing *coup de force* at the institution of a body politic forces certain elements to bear the weight of the institution in force by forcing them into economically exploited, politically dominated and culturally marginalized positions. This exploitation, domination and marginalization is revealed in the concrete call for justice made by others forced into those positions. The enforcing of the law, the iteration of the institution, bears down on the point of tension. Reinscription in another context, the so-called 'second phase' of deconstruction, is the unleashing of the force of rupture that makes an institution tremble along the incisions, the lines of force that traverse any institution along the skewing brought into force by the instituting decision, along the lines of production of a forceful body politic. The incision follows the path of the decision. A quote from *Positions* makes this clear: 'An incision, precisely, can only be made according to lines of force and forces of rupture that are localizable in the discourse to be deconstructed' (Derrida, *Positions*, 1981, 109/82). What is to be deconstructed is not simply a signifying discourse, as this quotation might seem to imply, but also the forceful institution that reinforces a certain reading of that discourse and that enforces the performance of the action dictated in the imperatives and performatives of the discourse.

The lines of force that call for incision are key undecidables that are forced, by decision, into positions that allow for the dominant interpretation of the institutionalized discourse. Forced into decided positions, they are prone to release forces of rupture when shown in their undecidability. Deconstruction is called for whenever one of the effects of institutional reading codes is to make hierarchies seem natural and not constructed, that is, to attempt, impossibly, to purify signification of contamination by force and thus attempt to make the general text appear as a book of nature. Since Derrida has written many times that deconstructive intervention is, in the words of 'Force of law', 'a maximum intensification of a transformation in progress' (Derrida, 'Force of law', 1990, 933), we could identify at least three of the incisive lines of force and forces of rupture of our institutions as the denaturalization of the seemingly natural hierarchies of gender, race and class.

But *why* deconstruct, assuming that we have some decision here? In the name of what does deconstruction release its forces of rupture? Derrida answers: in the name of justice. Derrida's political physics looks like a 'might makes right' position. And in one sense indeed it is, in the sense that might makes *droit*, that is, the fact that positive law can be analysed in terms of social power. Derrida reminds us, however, that might does not make justice. Instead, 'Force of law' tell us that 'deconstruction is justice' (Derrida, 'Force of law', 1990, 945). Institutions, or sets of positive laws [*droits*], are deconstructible because they are not justice. Deconstruction is justice, that is, 'deconstruction is already engaged by this infinite demand of justice' (955). Deconstruction also finds its 'force, its movement or its motivation' in the 'always unsatisfied appeal' to justice (957). In the notion of justice that Derrida develops in 'Force of law' there is an aporetic structure in which a universal law commands the recognition of a singular case. The aporetic structure of law is justice. At this point Derrida mentions his debt to Levinas, to whose notion of justice as the face of the other, always singular and hence infinite, Derrida 'would be tempted to compare' his own notion (959).[8]

Although infinitely in excess of positive law, justice is not opposed to law. The law of law, the *loi* of *droit*, might be formulated as: always do justice to those who stand, singularly, before the law. Those before the law are also those whose concrete calling out for justice, interweaving the saying and the said, the primary and secondary affirmations of deconstruction, provoke the 'transformation in progress' to which deconstruction responds with its 'maximum intensification'. We might want to say here that *democracy* is the future, the 'to come' of this transformation, intensifying itself to the point where instituted bodies that muffle or distort the calls of others are overflowed and reinscribed in other contexts. Deconstruction is democratic justice, responding to the calls from all others.

Democracy is not without institution, of course, just as justice is not without law. Justice demands that justice be done in the name of law, and law must be just. Yet, as Aristotle knew well, the universal law cannot always do justice to the singular case before the law. In this case, Aristotle would have us consult the intention of the law-maker in order to do justice (*Nichomachean Ethics*, 5.10.1137b22ff). Derrida would have us do justice to those brought before the law, and that always means doing justice to 'the third' always already there in these cases (Derrida, 'Politics of Friendship', 1988, 641). Doing justice for Derrida does not take recourse to a standard, as in Aristotle,[9] but does articulate the impossible demands placed on judging. Judging is a trial, an undergoing of impossible tasks demanded by the aporetic structure of law. In 'Force of law' Derrida gives us three examples of the same aporia of the universal law to do justice to the singular case: 1) judging must be free and responsible, but not without rule or reference to previously established (positive) law (Derrida, 'Force of law', 1990, 961); 2) judging cannot be arbitrary, yet it cannot be mere calculation either (963–7); and 3) judgment must have all the information, it must not rush to judgment, but justice cannot wait, justice must be served to those here and now before the law (967–79). Judging must undergo these trials of the 'undecidable', but judging cannot be decisionistic. Rather it must be bound to the other and to the third. Decisionism merely chooses one side of the paradox, opting out of the trial too soon, while calculation is merely its mirror-image. Here, in deconstructive justice, the judge is always on trial, yet one can never point to a just decision, for justice is always to come.[10]

CONCLUSION

The *coup de force* is iterable. Iteration occurs as auto-affection, timing and spacing, the turning space of time and the forcing open of consciousness. Time exploded as spacing is the time of justice, the always past of responsibility, the infinite alterity of futural democratic justice. In this economy of exteriority, the supposed inside, signification, is turned out, opened up, to force. In this opening out the construction of an institution of positive law and its deconstruction in the name of justice depends upon the opening of signification to force, the move from the law of force to the force of law, the turning of the book of nature into the general text.

Following this line of thinking, along the lines of the Derridean general text, can show us the irreducible role of force in the institution of a body politic, but it cannot however help us investigate the ways real bodies are produced by material self-ordering processes. For help in such investigations, we must turn to Deleuze and Guattari, whose terms 'singularity' and 'abstract machine', brought about through the transverse communication of philosophy and contemporary science, and a willingness to think the reality of matter, allow us to thematize the production of real bodies. Such brute claims are forbidden the cautious deconstructions of Derrida. As great as the thought of the general text is, as strong as its political effects can be — a strength I hope to demonstrate in the next two chapters — it falls short of the radicality of matter as thought by Deleuze.

CHAPTER 3

Given Time *and the Gift of Life*

If the generative residue in the menstrual fluids is properly
concocted, the movement imparted by the male will make
the form of the embryo in the likeness of itself. (Aristotle,
De Generatione Annimalium, 1965)

Introduction
The Gift of Life
On the Generation of (the Body Politic of) Animals
The Quasi-transcendentality of the Gift of Life
The Demand to Keep Hope Alive

INTRODUCTION

In this chapter we examine Derrida's writings on maternity and the
gift of life to elucidate a thought of the production of bodies politic
beyond formal/hylomorphic re-production; in doing so we will show
how the gift of life forcefully ruptures the circle of species-form. We
first examine an excessive force of maternity beyond a basically
Aristotelian patriarchy, thus breaking the force of form we examined
in Chapter 1; we then develop a politics of life that articulates the
force of rupture we first broached in Chapter 2.

To speak of the gift of life is to speak of the mother. To speak of
the mother is to speak of feminism. To speak of feminism is to speak
of democratic politics, the restructuring of the patriarchal body politic.
Life, maternity and democracy form the general field of this chapter,
which thinks along with, and departing from, the work of Derrida –
specifically, the thoughts of gift, time, and life in *Given Time*.

To speak of Derrida in the context of feminism is a daunting task,
now beyond the scope of a chapter.[1] Analyses of Derrida and feminism
have tended to focus on two major themes: the effects of using woman

as a figure of alterity, and the effects of deconstructing subjectivity even as women struggle to claim their own subjectivities. Little work to my knowledge has been done on the thought of the mother in Derrida, other than some commentary on a few remarks in *Glas*.[2] Rather than pursue the themes of the alterity and subjectivities of woman and women, through either an analysis of the Derridean texts explicitly devoted to sexual difference, or an investigation of Derrida's influence on major feminists, the present chapter takes up and extends Derrida's writings – in this case, not on the questions of performativity and citationality, but on the question of maternity in light of his thought of the gift. In this way I hope to demonstrate the strength of the Derridean approach to the question of the body politic.

It might at first seem a bit strange to think of Derrida and the thought of life. Might one not say that Derrida suffers from the *déformation professionnelle* that has afflicted all philosophers since Socrates paid his debt to Asclepius: an obsession with death? After all, death appears in many guises in his work: 1967's *Of Grammatology* features the (in)famous 'There is nothing outside of the text' (*il n'y a pas de hors-texte*; Derrida, *Of Grammatology*, 1975, 227/158), which is just another way of announcing the death of God along with that of the author, while 1993's *Aporias* focuses on the universal singularity called 'my death'. A typical trajectory, one might say: the young man shooting at big targets, the older man aware of himself in the cross-hairs.

From the focus on death it's a short step to the familiar Derrida the destroyer, Derrida the nihilist. Yet with a moment's reflection, it's relatively easy to document that life has always been one of Derrida's major topics, from his earliest investigations of Husserl's living present onwards, through *Spurs/Eperons*, *Glas*, 'To Speculate – On Freud' (in *The Post Card*), 'Otobiographies' (in *The Ear of the Other*), 'Survivre. Journal de bord' (= 'Living On/Borderlines'), *Memoires – for Paul de Man*, and other texts.

Derrida the affirmer of life; Derrida the speculator on death. Now on any sort of Derridean logic, life and death cannot be opposed – any more than any two other concepts, say, space and time. Technical precision would then have me write 'life–death' at every instance in this chapter, instead of the bare 'life'.[3] Yet life has a specificity to be protected, even if its putative purity is an illusion to be analysed, so I will simply write 'life'. In investigating the life of the Derridean body politic, I show the way the deconstruction of the metaphysical representation of the body politic as hylomorphic re-production of patriarchal form contributes to a rethinking of life.[4]

Now that the gift, present in many of these same texts, has been 'thematized' in *Given Time* — more precisely, as we will see, the withdrawal of the gift from thematization has been brought to the fore, since for a gift to be a gift is for it to go unrecognized — the way is open to think along with Derrida the gift of life. And with this withdrawal of the gift, one should read Derrida's repeated qualification ('the gift, if there is any') in this chapter, even if I sometimes write simply 'gift of life'. For if there were to be a gift, it would be the gift of life.

Two preliminary warnings. First, although I will address the mother in giving life, in all truth, the positive approach is to see sexual difference 'itself' as generative of life. Thus in another setting one could have referred simply to 'parents'. But as such 'positive' thought — if it is at all possible — requires propaedeutic deconstruction, my focus on the mother should be seen as a historical and political strategy against the backdrop of patriarchal thought and practice. In adopting this strategic focus, however, I refuse the identifications of women and woman, woman and mother, and maternity and biology. Rather I wish to retain a maternal specificity as a starting point for articulating my discourse with discourses of sexual difference.[5] Although I cannot undertake a full discussion, I will note along the way such starting points, particularly with the work of Kristeva and Irigaray. Second, although I acknowledge the risk of some dangerous complicities in such a reference to the mother — from Hallmark card sentimentalities about 'Mom', to the 'family values' of fascism, or even, if I may be aggressive enough, the fascism of 'family values' — despite these risks, I intend here no support for any of these discourses, nor by any means, any so-called 'pro-life' position.

THE GIFT OF LIFE

Although the dead might be said to present 'we the living' with gifts of fond memories, and we might give honor or shame to the name of the dead,[6] any gift must include life within its 'trajectory', though not its circle, a circular movement of the gift being impossible. In *Given Time*, Derrida addresses this demand through the thought of 'living on' (*survivre*): 'No, only a "life" can give, but a life in which this economy of death presents itself and lets itself be exceeded. Neither death nor immortal life can ever give anything, only a singular *surviving* can give. This is the *element* of this problematic' (Derrida, *Given Time*, 1992, 132/102).

When we consult Derrida's essay 'Survivre' ('Living on'), to which a note to this passage in *Given Time* refers us, we find instead of a direct discussion of life, the thought of text, that is, meaning and context. Thus while in *Given Time* the gift is thought from life, in 'Living on' life is thought from writing. In 'Living on', Derrida indicates his 'first principle': 'This is my starting point: no meaning can be determined out of context, but no context permits saturation' (Derrida, 'Living on Border lines', 1979, 125/81). The non-saturability of any context is due to 'the structure of remnant or of iteration' (125/81). But typically for Derrida, the 'first principle' is not a simple starting point. Life is not only thought from writing, but writing is also thought from life, for the structure of the remnant is the structure of living on, in which written marks survive their authors and primary audiences: 'The statement survives them a priori, lives on after them. Hence no context is saturable any more' (122/78). Living on past the author and audience, the mark inscribes the death of the author and audience in its life, its survival. With the structure of living on, the element of the gift in writing is adumbrated, for the life of the author and audience is now bound up with an economy of death inscribed in the marks the one gives to the other. Death is the name for that which exceeds the intentional living presents (temporal and donative) of author and audience.

As we return to *Given Time* from 'Living on', the exceeding of living intention in the death-marked surviving mark is explicitly named as a gift. In writing as a giving, marks are given from one to the other, but need not be received or returned ('counter-signed'). In *Given Time*, Derrida writes:

> the structure of trace and the legacy of this text – as of anything that can be in general – surpasses the phantasm of return and marks the death of the signatory or the non-return of the legacy, the non-benefit, therefore a certain condition of the gift – in the writing itself. (Derrida, *Given Time*, 1992, 130/100)

Trace exceeds return, the given mark survives.

Writing is then a gift in which death exceeds life and life exceeds death. The survival of marks inscribes the death of the giving/taking author and audience; death-marked marks live on beyond the temporal and donative present. In writing as a gift, the economy of death presents itself and lets itself be exceeded. Let us now ask the converse: if writing is a gift, is the gift a writing? More precisely, let us ask, how is the gift of life a writing?

The gift of life is a writing at first in sharing the structure of non-return. But instead of the possibility of non-return being irreducibly inscribed, we find necessity, for the gift of life can never be repaid in kind. The taking of life can be repaid by giving death, by the revenge of another or by order of the state, but all the symbolic equivalents that might be paid to parents do not match the initial gift of life; despite all the gifts given on Mother's or Father's Day, a child can never give life to the parent. In the gift of life we thus find an irreducible excess of gift over exchange.

Derrida notes this excess in referring to a certain non-exchange of thanks between mother and son concerning a kidney transplant: 'This [unconditionality of the gift] is what the literature on organ donation brings out. One of these studies records that the son who donates a kidney to his mother does not want any gratitude from her because she had borne him in the first place' (Derrida, *Given Time*, 1992, 31n/17–18n). The mother has already given life to the son, and the son's gift, even if it results in the loss of his own life, cannot give life to the mother, although it can give a supplement – it can give more life in the sense of more time.

In an indescribable coincidence, I ran across the following headline while writing the first version of this chapter, which describes the converse situation, a parent's gift again to the child: 'Father gives his son life for second time'. The subhead reads: 'Hanh Ngoc Nguyen, 51, donated a kidney. But first, he needed a visa to get here from Saigon'. The story describes the victory over red tape of the father, who 'feels very proud to do this', and who was an 'interpreter for the Marines during the Vietnam War'.[7] Here indeed we have a family scene worthy of the one limned in 'Otobiographies', the dead father and the living mother of Nietzsche. Here we find father and son, set against the backdrop of the giving over of the living maternal tongue to Uncle Sam's death machine. But even without being able to exploit the resources of this scene more fully, we can at least note that here again the gift is not life, but more life, more time.

Thus there is here in the gift of life an absolute excess of life over symbol, of the initial gift over the economic return. Even in the most tragic, or merely melodramatic, scenarios the child or parent can only trade less life for him or herself in return for more life for the parent or child; life can never simply be given again. This is not to say there are no real or symbolic returns, simply that there are never returns in kind. Parents or children, in knowing themselves to be givers of life, the first or 'second' time, can certainly constitute themselves as generous subjects in a circle of symbolic self-congratulation. This can occur with the first or 'second' gift, as in the case of the kidney-donating father who feels proud, or with those who, in denying themselves such direct self-constitution – as in the case of the kidney-donating son who declines recognition – open the door for a supplementary surcharge of congratulation from self or others as 'noble', as more truly generous, precisely in declining thanks or recognition. The possibility of such a surcharge haunts the nobility of the Nietzschean advice to beat all the onlookers to an act of generosity, or more prosaically, haunts the otherwise glorious Italian *prego*, said in response to *grazie*: please, I beg you, do not thank me. Real returns are also possible in that parents or children can calculate in the restricted sense of 'economy' on the return in terms of the child's labour or parent's gratitude over the initial outlay in suffering and care. Fundamentally, though, these returns can never be in kind – no kidney gives life, only more life. The gift of life never returns. Thus, even with the structure of symbolic recognition and debt, the gift of life, precisely in this excess of gift over symbolic exchange, is, if not quite the paradoxically self-effacing 'gift itself', perhaps the closest to the gift of all of our idioms. If there were to be a gift, it would be the gift of life.

ON THE GENERATION OF
(THE BODY POLITIC OF) ANIMALS

Given this excess of life over gift in the gift of life, let us continue with the thought of the gift of life as writing. 'Writing' can indeed be generalized to cover life: Derrida writes in *Given Time* that the structure of traces governs 'anything that can be in general' (Derrida, *Given Time*, 1992, 130/100). Now we have seen the way in which living on structures writing, so we must say that writing structures life and life, writing. The restricted opposition of life and (dead) writing gives way to an infrastructure: writing-life. In writing-life, the inscription of a mark is giving birth and vice versa; while marks live on, we can also say that life is a text of traces, that each living being is an inscribed mark.[8] Just as the death of the author is inscribed in the mark, which survives him or her, so the child shows life–death back to the parent. The child can always survive the parent, and vice-versa, so that the parent's or the child's death is inscribed in the child's or the parent's life. Living on is thus the risk of giving or receiving life, as Derrida writes in 'Aphorism Countertime': 'One of us will see the other die, one of us will live on, even if only for an instant. One of us, only one of us, will carry the death of the other – and the mourning' (Derrida, *Psyché*, 1987, 524/Attridge, *Acts of Literature*, 1992, 422).

With the thought of life–death sketched here, the life of living on past the death of the other, let us take the opportunity to enter the Aristotelian orbit, so consistently evoked by Derrida in *Given Time*. Writing-life, a tracing: how does it come into line and circle, to modify the questions of 'Ousia and Grammè' (Derrida, *Margins*, 1982, 67/ 57)? Given the structures of non-return and the risk of living on in writing-life, can we think the gift of life as an 'exteriority' in excess of the circle of exchange, a space–time of the gift of life that would not be representable as a circle and yet would provoke the circle?[9] Is the gift of life the 'first mover of the circle' to which Derrida alludes in *Given Time* (Derrida, *Given Time*, 1992, 47/31)? We know that for Aristotle in *Metaphysics* Lambda the prime mover moves others as does the object of eros (*kinei hôs erômenon*; Aristotle, *Metaphysica*, 1957, 1072b3). We also know that the erotically provocative being of the prime mover is 'constant life' (1072b28). For Aristotle, divine life is the first mover of the circle, provoking the erotic circles of stellar locomotion and species-generation, which mimetically supplement, in their motion and generation, the unreachable constancy of divine life.[10]

The 'closed circle', that curious pleonasm, is indeed the very medium of Aristotle's thought of generation, the encircling of life. For Aristotle, generation is a change, and all change is ecstatic, moving 'from this to that' (*ek tinos eis ti*; Aristotle *Physica*, 1950, 5.1.225a1). But in generation the ecstasis is recaptured in the passage of form from father to child, the circle of the species. Generation for Aristotle is hylomorphic production – the re-production of the same form via material relay – *par excellence*. *On the Generation of Animals* portrays generation as immanent change within the protective borders of the circle of the species, oriented to the ideal case in which the superior male principle, working in the spermatic motions of the father that victoriously overcome the motions inherent in the maternal material on which it works, provokes the appearance of the same form in a father-resembling male child: 'If the generative residue in the menstrual fluids is properly concocted, the movement imparted by the male will make the form of the embryo in the likeness of itself' (Aristotle, *De Generatione Annimlia*, 1965, 767b15–17). We see here a hylomorphic political physics of generation, the attempted formal domination of a refractory material at the heart of re-production. The maternal material is to be mastered, so that the detour of the mother's matter does not break, but only provides the circumference of, the circle of the species.[11] The material mother is only a sign, a relay, even a mirror for the formal self-reflection of the father in the son.[12]

Within the circle of hylomorphic re-production, change is tamed, kept within the bounds of form. When Aristotle says: 'from humans come humans' (*inter alia*, Aristotle, *Physica*, 1950, 2.1.193b8; *Metaphysica*, 1957, 7.7.1032a25; 12.3.1070a29), the orienting ideal case, the closing of the circle in father-resembling male children, must always be kept in mind. With this orientation, the immanence of circular species-generation is reflected in the motif of change being attributed to a thing of the same name (Aristotle, *Metaphysica*, 1957, 12.3.1070a5) or the same form (7.7.1032a24). So there is no leaving the shelter of form in proper generation, and immanence is preserved in the paternal–filial passage. This teleological semenology of animal generation is literally a patri-archy, since the father, the one responsible for form and finality, is also the efficient cause, the source of the change, the *arché kineseôs*. The formal identity of father and child recuperates the exteriority of generation via numerical material/maternal difference. Thus form dominates repetition in the political physics of the Aristotelian body politic, the circular and hylomorphic reproduction of the species.

Derrida's work provides the resources for a counter-reading to patri-archal teleological semenology, a way to think writing-life outside the circle of the species, the gift of life as a forceful rupture of formal immanence, a non-hylomorphic production of bodies politic. In this reading, we start from the Aristotelian determination of motion as life (Aristotle, *Physica*, 1950, 8.1.250b16), which is then oriented to an unreachable goal, the prime mover, the pure presence of pure act. The prime mover is that to which the mimesis of the mimetic supplementation of generation is oriented. But change is incomplete (Aristotle, *Metaphysica*, 1957, 9.7.1048b28), and the accomplishment of motion is its end. To reach the end of kinetic life would be death, as Aristotle notes in analysing the metaphoric resources of *telos* (Aristotle, *Metaphysica*, 1957, 5.16.1021b28–30), so pure divine presence would be death to moving life. Since pure divine life is death, the life of writing-life – let us call it species-being life, a terminological choice I will discuss shortly – must be impure life; the mimetic supplement of generation, while indeed mimetic, is in the end only a supplement of divine life. In species-being life, presence is deferred (attaining presence is death, the end of life/motion) and differed (generation proceeds via numerically different individuals (Aristotle, *Metaphysica*, 1957, 7.8.1034a7)). Generation, the mode of life of the universal, the species, is a temporal deferring and a numerical or spatial differing. Generation is *différance*; the gift of life is the gift of differantial species-being.

I use 'differantial species-being' here to describe writing-life in the context of generation, despite the not-inconsiderable difficulties in making Derridean sense of Marx's 1844 definition of species-being (*Gattungswesen*) as 'free conscious activity'. I'm attracted to the term 'species-being' because it indicates, in Michel Henry's words (and there are difficulties with Henry's work as well), an 'opening to the universal'.[13] In the Derridean account of universals via *différance*, the formal identity of the universal is constituted by the indefinite repeatability of its numerically different instances.[14] Thus while Aristotle's thematic account of generation, the paternal immanence of teleological semenology, privileges formal identity, *différance* highlights the strange, contaminating interweaving of real members and ideal species. In differantial species-being – and this is the point I will pursue in the conclusion – the final closure of ideal identity, the totalizing saturation of the defining context of the universal, is deferred because it must wait for different contexts, while species-being lives in the difference spaced among its real, different marks. Thus the final moment of form never arrives and the way is open to a non-hylmorphic thought of species-being.

To think writing-life or differantial species-being counter to patriarchal teleological semenology, as the positive notion of the Derridean vital body politic, let us concentrate on the material mother left behind. In Aristotle's orienting case of the circular re-production of paternal form, the mother is relegated to matter; mother/matter is – bastardizing the words of Derrida in *Glas* ('reste – la mère'; Derrida, *Glas*, 1974, 162/115) – what remains behind the march of the species. To emphasize alterity in our counter-reading, let us write '(m)other',[15] and let us say that the non-hylomorphic production of an other, the gift of life, proceeds by the (m)other, rather than the hylomorphic re-production of the species which proceeds via the maternal relay back to the form of the father.[16]

With the gift of life thought as differantial species-being, the circle of the species is broken, and 'there is' an exteriority that is not recuperated. Here the opening to the universal, the identity and difference of species-being, is the differantial logic of living on. In our patrilineal and patronymic patriarchy, the name of the father is passed on, beyond his death, while it is only the mother herself that lives on.[17] Focusing here then on the mother who survives only in matter, without name, left behind or outside the circle of the species, we can follow the words Derrida writes in *Glas*: '*je suis la mère*', 'I am/I follow the mother' (Derrida, *Glas*, 1974, 164/116). The trace of the other constitutes the identity of the child: 'I am the mother', but this identification is not complete, for the child (or, indeed, the mother) lives on: 'I follow the mother'. In the gift of life as differantial species-being there is an alterity that can only be followed, a tracing that is not a line and an exteriority that cannot be captured in a circle, a gift in excess of any return.[18] The gift of life forcefully ruptures hylo-morphic re-production and frees a thought of maternal production of life; the gift of life breaks the force of form we investigated in Chapter 1, and gives us the 'positive' thought of the Derridean body politic, the vital body politic.

However, the 'positivity' of the Derridean vital body politic is characteristically attentuated. In the materiality of the mother we see once again the deconstructive logic of matter as marker of radical alterity in the text of metaphysics, as we analysed it in Chapter 1 above, rather than the straightforward materialism of Deleuze. Thus while we can think along with Derrida differantial production in negative terms as non-hylomorphic, we cannot approach the positive Deleuzean thought of material self-ordering.

THE QUASI-TRANSCENDENTALITY OF THE GIFT OF LIFE

In *Given Time*, the gift of life, as a gift, is the gift of time: 'the gift only gives to the extent that it *gives time*' (Derrida, *Given Time*, 1992, 59/41; Derrida's italics). The gift gives time, but 'time' is not univocal for Derrida; there are at least three temporal registers: (a) the 'vulgar' time line of nows; (b) 'temporalization' or temporal synthesis of nows by retention and protention in which the line becomes circle; (c) *différance* as the differing and deferring that opens time–space (59/40). These registers are set in motion by the gift: the gift demands the becoming-temporization, that is, the *becoming-différance*, of temporalization. Temporalization – which in its synthesis of neutral time, the 'vulgar' now-procession, would pretend to be originary – is shown by Derrida to be constructed by the effacement of *différance*. In a stunning line, Derrida writes that the *becoming-différance* of temporalization, the spacing of time, is 'the animation of a neutral and homogenous time' (59/40). Animation – becoming alive. The gift of giving time gives life, even to time itself; the gift of giving life gives time, the time of life.

Thus we see here the equation of giving time and giving life. The temptation to think such a gift as a transcendental category must now be addressed. Derrida discusses what I claim should best be called the quasi-transcendental status of the gift of time-life in two compact paragraphs, first as a transcendental signified, an ordering principle for a field of empirical diversity, and then, in a more complicated move, as a transcendental condition, as the site of appearance for appearing things.

The question of a transcendental signified that would unify the multiplicity of categories of giving (Derrida, *Given Time*, 1992, 72–5/ 51–3) arises as a consequence of the thought that these empirical categories might be clarified first of all 'in the style of analytic philosophy or of ordinary language analysis' (71–72/50–51). As is his wont in particular circumstances, Derrida thinks the empirical deter- minations of the transcendental signified as 'metaphorico-metonymic substitutes' (74/53). The power of the tradition of transcendental thought Derrida analyses here comes from its ability to 'inscribe the transcendental given in the present in general' (74/53). In other words, this tradition gives us the thought of a transcendental unifying given as the effect of a mastering force, as that which is first given by the gift of an origin which could be named in a variety of ways: 'Nature, Being, God, the Father – or the Mother' (74–5/53). Derrida here warns us away from attributing a simple transcendental ordering status to the gift of time-life or its giver, the capital Mother.

The difficulties in thinking the transcendental–empirical relation that are brought to the fore in thinking it in terms of metaphor are reinforced by Derrida's observations on idiom: 'the essential link that passes from the thinking of the gift to language, or in any case to the trace, will never be able to avoid idioms . . . is it not impossible to isolate a concept of the essence of the gift that transcends idiomatic difference?' (Derrida, *Given Time*, 1992, 76/54). Derrida now asks the question of the transcendental status of the gift of time-life not in terms of a transcendental signified that orders a multiplicity of metaphoric determinations, but in terms of condition–conditioned. He poses the distinction between a gift that gives something determinate, and a gift that gives 'the *condition* of a present given in general' (76/ 54). Here Derrida has complicated the question of the transcendental from his first analysis. A transcendental signified slides rather easily into place as the given of masterly force, an organizing principle or capital whose presence would guarantee the unity of the empirical field, but the giving of a condition of presence is not 'itself' present, nor does it give 'anything' present – the scare quotes marking the problem of a terminology drawn from an empirical language that would nonetheless be adequately respectful of the distance between empiricity and transcendentality.

Derrida specifies the complication of thinking the gift of time-life as a transcendental condition in terms we will have to analyse:

'[T]o give time' is not to give a given present but the condition of presence of any present in general; 'donner le jour' [literally to give the day, but used in the sense of the English expression 'to give birth' – JP] gives nothing (not even the life that it is supposed to give 'metaphorically', let us say for convenience) but the *condition* of any given in general. (Derrida, *Given Time*, 1992, 76/54)

Here Derrida shows that the life given in the gift of life cannot be thought simply as an object of biological science – hence the break with any simplistic 'pro-life' political stance. Rather, to be given life or time is to be given the condition for determining life or time, to be given the condition for giving to oneself or others determinate stretches of time or life – and also to be given the condition for giving the condition, and so on. Derrida writes: 'to give time, the day, or life is to give nothing, nothing determinate, even if it is to give the giving of any possible giving, even if it gives the condition of giving' (Derrida, *Given Time*, 1992, 76/54).

With these complications, it is no longer so clear which gift is conditioned and which is the conditioning, nor indeed what is to be the value of the gift: 'One perceives there no longer the sharp line that separates the transcendental from the conditioned, the conditioning from the conditioned, but rather the fold of undecidability that allows all the values to be inverted: the gift of life amounts to the gift of death . . .' (Derrida, *Given Time*, 1992, 76/54).[19] How does this 'fold of undecidability' contaminating the transcendental–empirical relation arise? Derrida's text here is compact, elliptical, accelerated. It seems to me that an exegesis in terms of the structure of 'quasi-transcendentality' worked out by Derrida in his earlier work would be helpful at this point.

Let us first rule out the temptation to think that the gift of time-life, as a condition, is the long-sought key to a transcendental philosophy, the ultimate working out of the transcendental horizon for the question of the sense of being, to borrow Heidegger's phrase. We must not think the gift as transcendental, but as inscribing the peculiar ascent/fall movement of quasi-transcendentality. The transcendental is not an atemporal position from which to order or condition an empirical field, but a movement in which a member of the field aspires to a position of ordering or conditioning, but in so elevating itself, leaves behind a mark of its absence from the field.

The key to understanding the notion of quasi-transcendentality as ascent/fall is to return to the notion of metaphoricity Derrida alluded to earlier in his discussion of the transcendental signified, and to link it to the notion of the transcendental condition. The transcendental as condition is the site of appearance for things which appear. As such a condition, it withdraws from appearance, ceding room for the things which appear – it is no-thing, to speak Heideggerian again for a moment. Now any naming of this site of appearance can only be a name drawn from a thing which appears – again in Heideggerian language, an 'ontic metaphor'. This means that a name drawn from a figure of the empirical field is given to that which is elevated to the position of conditioning the field, of accounting for the possibility of the field by providing its site of appearance. But the empirical character of the elevated term can be read as the mark of an absence in the empirical field, the inability of the conditioning figure to account for its elevation to the role of conditioning power. This inability to account for the necessarily empirical name of the transcendental condition can be called a fall back into empiricity of the elevated term. Thus the stability of the transcendental condition is rethought as the unstable movement of ascent/fall, the movement of quasi-transcendentality, or to use another Derridean phrase, the contamination of the transcendental–empirical distinction.[20]

The structure of quasi-transcendental movement, worked out by Derrida at *Glas* (1974) 340–41/244 and commented upon by Gasché, Bennington, Lawlor, Thompson and others,[21] can be further specified with regard to the gift of time-life. To repeat, the movement of quasi-transcendentality occurs as part of a field assumes the ordering or conditioning position for that field, but in so doing cannot account for its own power of ascending to the position of ordering or conditioning principle; this failure to account for the elevation of that which orders or conditions is a fall back into empiricity that leaves behind a double. In the case under examination here, we leave behind the 'gift of gift', a gift too many and a gift too few. A gift too many in the ordering or conditioning position: the givenness of the ordering or conditioning gift, its elevation from empiricity, remains unthought, as the ordering or conditioning principle brings along with it in its elevation the mark of the empirical ordered or conditioned field from which it arose. What remains unthought is that we have given ourselves, or taken upon ourselves, 'gift' as that which will order or condition the field, just as, in the analyses of 'White mythology' (in *Margins*), the philosophic nature of 'metaphor' cannot be accounted for when 'metaphor' ascends to the position of transcendental principle for the field of philosophemes. Conversely, with the elevation of the gift of life-time to an ordering or conditioning position we find a gift too few in the ordered or conditioned field, for the givenness of the empirical concepts of gift, time and life, remain unthought. The ascension leaves a blank in the field, so that our being given 'gift', 'time', 'life' in their idiomatic specificities by linguistic tradition is overlooked, just as in 'White mythology' the metaphoric nature of philosophemes such as 'concept' or 'ground' cannot be accounted for.

These complications of quasi-transcendentality lead me to write '(m)other' to capture the quasi-transcendental ascent and fall in thinking the gift of life as condition of any other gift. Otherwise we risk the fall from a complicated condition to simple ordering principle, the fall to the capital Mother. The capital Mother, the giver of life as an ordering principle, is what *Glas* warns us against in calling attention to the maternal remainder. Or in spelled-out form, if we may lift the analysis from the context of the reading of Genêt and let the marks live on:

> The mother would present for analysis the term of regression, a signified of the last instance, only if you knew what the mother names or means (to say) . . . Now you would be able to know it only if you had exhausted all the remain(s) . . . To the extent you will not have thoroughly spelled out each of these . . . there will remain something of the mother . . . you will not have exhausted. (Derrida, *Glas*, 1974, 162–5/115–17)

The fall from (m)other as quasi-transcendental condition to the capital Mother, the giver of the gift of life thought as transcendental ordering principle would result in that which lies behind just another transcendental signified, and as we have noted, Derrida lists it among the usual suspects he rounds up in *Given Time*: 'Nature, Being, God, the Father – or the Mother' (Derrida, *Given Time*, 1992, 74–5/53). The gift of life, thought from the (m)other against patri-archal teleological semenology, must be seen as the quasi-transcendental gift of differantial species-being, the positive thought of the Derridean vital body politic.

THE DEMAND TO KEEP HOPE ALIVE

A discourse on the gift cannot remain purely theoretical, Derrida writes, but is only a part of a 'normative operation' (Derrida, *Given Time*, 1992, 85/62). The norms of the gift are not simple: we must opt for the gift, affirm its excess, but we must also acknowledge the necessity of economic calculation (86/62–3). In such a political physics, as we will see, the gift of time-life demands both an affirmation of the excessive demands for justice in the singular case and an acknowledgment of the regulative demand of universality in judgment.

In the move to the civic body politic, we must break with the family as the field of the gift of life, even if the politicization of the domestic economies of labour and violence is an undoubted advance.[22] Following Levinas, it is for Derrida always the third, disrupting the couple and the home, who is the figure of the call for justice.[23] But the break with the family in the political must not be seen as an essentialism consigning the female to the home and reserving the political for the male, the Antigone syndrome analysed in *Glas*. Rather, civic body-political demands are placed on all, male and female, by the way we have revealed to us the ruptured immanence of the Derridean vital body politic, our species-being, by our being born of the (m)other, the remains of the patriarchal circle. The force of maternity lets us think the non-hylomorphic production of vital bodies politic rather than the hylomorphic formal re-production of patriarchy. Again, another system might have enabled us to speak simply of parents and children, but today we must emphasize the material/maternal. Thus I am not here arguing for the ethical significance of the feminine as the possibility of mothering – not because I think this impossible or unworthy – but rather for a notion of political responsibility to the other figured in the debt incurred in accepting the gift of life by all of us born of the (m)other.

Despite the emphasis on alterity in the preceding account of the gift of life from the (m)other, and the alterity of the third that ensures the move to the political, it remains to be said, however, for vital political reasons – from the perspective of both liberalism and the left, and within them, from the perspective of a deconstructive politics under attack from protectionist liberals and leftists – that 'we' all deserve democracy and justice, that the thought of differantial species-being in the Derridean vital body politic is indeed an opening to the universal, albeit differantially constituted.[24] The gift of life is given to all of us, and our responsibility in the civic body politic is not to the singular (m)other, but to (and for) all of us born of (m)other(s). Universality must not be neglected, for the liberal notion of universal rights remains a necessary safeguard in its negative guise, and a promise, in its positive guise, of access to conditions of life, the economy of life. This right of the living to share in the economy of life need not, however, license state intervention in the lives of women, forcing them to become mothers. Such an intervention under the guise of a specious 'right to life', in forcing motherhood on women, precisely removes any hint of gift-character from the gift of life.[25]

We broached the subject of the economy of life earlier when we demonstrated that the ability to give more life, that is, more time, falls short of the ability to give life again. Here we see the double significance of Derrida's claim in *Given Time* that time is the 'most important stake of political economy' (Derrida, *Given Time*, 1992, 44/28). The economy of life is a political economy of time, interweaving the vital and the eco-civic bodies politic: the owning class has both more leisure time than the working class, more time to 'really live', rather than just 'live for the weekend', but it also has a lower infant mortality rate and longer life expectancy, hence more life in the sense of 'time on earth'. Forced bodies give surplus time to leisured bodies, as we will see in Chapter 6.

With the introduction of the political economy of time to the discussion of the gift of life, let us turn to 'Force of law'. Here Derrida thinks, via the thought of the gift, the civic body politic as oriented to a justice or democracy 'to come' in terms of the gift. Justice demands, Derrida writes, 'gift without exchange' (Derrida, *Given Time*, 1992, 965), while we are bound to the 'giving idea of justice' (971). To extend these phrases in the direction of the gift of life, let us turn to Kant, to whom Derrida turns in 'Force of law' and *Given Time*. The just democracy to come can be seen as a differantial rewriting of the kingdom of ends, the transcendental condition for moral discourse and the orienting horizon for political reform.[26] Now the 'typic' of the kingdom of ends is provided by natural science's need to presuppose a lawful universe, so in the kingdom of ends each member is both universal legislator and subject to universal legislation.[27] The kingdom of ends thus brings together universality and singularity: it is the regulative idea of a universal legislation respective of the singular end-structure of each legislative moral subject.

Just as the guiding yet generated structure of iteration or *différance* is, in its own thought of universality and singularity, a rewriting of the passage to the limit of the Idea in the Kantian sense,[28] so is the just 'democracy to come' a rewriting of the kingdom of ends as a differantial civic body politic. In thinking justice Derrida thinks universality and singularity, but as *aporia*, as in the three *aporiai* of 'Force of law' we encountered in Chapter 2: judgment, undecidability and urgency (Derrida, 'Force of law', 1990, 961–79). A differantial structure underlies these aporias, so that the just democracy to come, in being just, must be open to the call of the other — it must be engaged, must say yes — but in such a way as to be democratic, that is, institutionally open to rewriting — the yes must be doubled, the tradition counter-signed. Hence the kingdom of ends is 'differanced' in the thought of the just democracy to come: no longer able to function as a horizon that might be realized or that would allow for a period of waiting, the just democracy to come must be opened to the future, as it strives in the urgent judgments of today to take up the institutionally given promise of perpetual openness to rewriting.

Our task now is to show how the just democracy to come is demanded by the quasi-transcendental gift of life as differantial species-being, that is, the crossing of the vital and civic bodies politic. While membership in the kingdom of ends is granted by virtue of the transcendental status of the rational moral subject, membership in the democracy to come is by the quasi-transcendental gift of life, the giving of the mark-structure of differantial species-being. As we have seen, differantial species-being is not an immanent circular transfer of ideal form between individuals, but is constituted by the repetition of real material inscriptions, real births. The gift of life is thus not a transcendental condition, but the quasi-transcendental interweaving of ideal species and real members. Consequently, the final form of the species is always deferred, while the members of the species differ from one another, taking the risk of living on past the other. The moment of saturation of the form thus never arrives due to this logic of survival, so the final meaning of 'humanity' or whatever other criterion one might have for membership in the kingdom of ends or its equivalents never arrives. The civic body politic, for Derrida, must always remain open-ended, its final meaning always deferred.

Thus differantial species-being demands a certain, although always inadequate response, a double affirmation — a holding the future open while counter-signing the past that demands such openness — that forbids our complacency in identifying 'is' with 'ought', or law with justice, or the members of the species with any determinate examples. Such a double affirmation of openness ruptures any totality, any totalizing saturation of the context that would determine a final content that would fill in the idea of justice or democracy or humanity and justify the forced exclusion of 'others'. This structural deferral of totality drives the extension of rights demanded by the thought of the just democracy to come beyond the historical examples/exemplars who orient Kant's discourse,[29] and who, today, beneath the formal equalities of democracies in the New World Order, maintain their exemplary status. We must, in other words, in being open to the rewritings demanded by the others newly arrived in the courts and the academy, drive beyond gender, race, class marginalizations, beyond the exemplary 'white guys with ties' whose talking heads blare out at us so regularly on the television news programmes. We must denaturalize the exemplars and deconstruct the hylomophic representation of the production of hierarchical and authoritarian bodies politic along the line of gender, race and class.

This deconstructive drive beyond previous constructions of justice, democracy or humanity is in response to the quasi-transcendental gift of life as differantial species-being, writing-life as a text of traced marks, life that takes the risk of living on. The Derridean civic body politic follows the openness given in the vital body politic. Our acceptance of this gift, which in the fact of recognition destroys one aspect of the gift, nevertheless inscribes an excess of the gift over any return that indebts us not only to the singular mother of our family, and not even solely to the preceding generation, but also to the others to come;[30] as vitally excessive, even though recognized, the gift of life comes close enough to a gift that it demands our work in service to democracy and justice, engaged and re-affirmed. And so, in a way, in holding open the future we allow the past its due, and this provides a guide to always mad, incalculable political decision. An incalculable yet urgently demanded decision can only have a guide but not a rule, and Derrida specifies such a guide in 'Force of law': 'Nothing seems to me less outdated than the classic emancipatory ideal' (Derrida, 'Force of law', 1990, 971). So in accepting the gift of life, in affirming its demands, in holding open the future and giving the past its due, counter-signing the tradition in the name of the just democracy to come that ruptures any totality, in following the vital body politic in constructing the civic, we keep hope alive.

CHAPTER 4

Economies of AIDS

But in my work on the AIDS retrovirus in the laboratory, I do not confront the individual victims of a dreadful disease. I deal with knowledge, with the science of retroviral disease. There are no patients in a research laboratory, no pain, no suffering, no disease, no death. Instead there are cells, viruses, and molecules; and the questions are scientific – not moral, not political, not even humanistic. (Robert Gallo, 1991, *Virus Hunting*)

Introduction
Economies of Truth in the Scientific Body Politic
Economies of the Border in the Somatic Body Politic
Economies of Identity in the Sexual Body Politic
Economies of Meaning in the Academic Body Politic
Conclusion

INTRODUCTION

In this chapter we conclude the Derridean portion of this book. We depart from the analysis of Derridean texts to attempt a Derridean-inspired reading of the representations of bodies politic constructed in AIDS discourse; in doing so we use the distinction between restricted and general economy crucial to Derrida's notion of the general text. We examine the economies of truth, border, identity and meaning in the scientific, somatic, sexual and academic bodies politic, respectively; we strive to identify the lines of force in standard constructions of AIDS through a shift from a restricted to a general economy, from a logic of opposition to a general text of force and signification.

AIDS was once the most frightening thing in the world, even for those who felt themselves relatively safe for the time being. Now, for those of us in the 'First World', it has been normalized for the 'general population': it is just another disease.[1] Other apocalyptic threats loom larger: asteroids seem to have been the summer movie season's favorite during the first drafting of this chapter (1998). In countless publications, we are told that science knows roughly what AIDS is, whom it strikes, how it works. The mop up work of developing and testing vaccines or maintenance regimes is just research money and public health education (for those who believe in 'science') and grants, careers and pharmaceutical company profits (for those with a more 'cynical' outlook).[2] On either score, in the early part of the new millennium, after two decades of scientific investigation, there's nothing about AIDS any more significant to philosophers than the issues raised by any other disease.

Or so it would seem. This chapter seeks a way out of the complacency that has settled over AIDS discourse in the 'general population' – and over most philosophers, to judge by the striking absence of AIDS discourse in most journals and conferences – by a use of the Derridean thematics developed earlier: the general text and the body politic. I try to shake up this complacency not to restore fear so much as to restore the thought-provoking force of considering the AIDS epidemic in all its facets. In other words, thinking about AIDS in ways other than the normalized provokes thought precisely about that normalization. I try to restore this thought-provoking force of AIDS by rehearsing the effects of a shift in discursive framework – a shift in 'economies of AIDS' – on the series of topics that most seems to relegate AIDS to normality.

This shift in economies is the move from a restricted to a general economy. By these terms I mean respectively a scheme in which mutually exclusive opposition is put to work so that risk is rewarded with a guaranteed profit (the 'restricted' economy), and a scheme in which these formerly opposed terms are reinscribed as a distribution in a wider economy in which genuine loss is possible, an economy of the general text of force and signification.[3] Why this move? What is the relative superiority of a general economy in investigating AIDS over a restricted economy?

The shift in framework from restricted to general economy seeks a way out of the complacency brought about by the congruence between the oppositional discourse of the restricted economy with the medical, economic, political and symbolic forces that have normalized AIDS discourse. In other words, I will show how the logic of opposition, whose derailment we traced in Chapter 2, underlies the language used by those that articulate the official discourse and the cultural imaginary – the realm of accepted channels of desire and fantasy – on AIDS. Rehearsing the shift to a non-oppositional logic of difference, a general economy, should then reveal the assumptions and limits of the official discourse and rob it of its complacency-inducing effects by showing the boundary-crossing force of 'generalized' AIDS discourse – its liminal effects.

The shift from restricted to general economy is thus the shift from following a logic of opposition to tracing the production of forceful bodies politic in a general text of force and signification. Restoring the thought-provoking force of AIDS discourse by showing how it reveals the production of forceful bodies politic would restore AIDS to its status as the most economical point of departure for analyses of the various economies – logical, ontological, epistemological, productive, political, medical, bodily, sexual – that used to be called 'the system'. At once concise and illimitable, generalized AIDS discourse occasions a listening to the clear and muffled call of forced bodies produced in the multiple, concrete and overlapping ways we call racism, misogyny, capitalism, homophobia, etc.

Putting it this way, though, is the language of restricted economy: my approach pays off, it produces more insight per unit of time invested in discussion. In other words, I seem to be paradoxically claiming that switching to talking about AIDS in terms of a general economy pays off with more lessons than can be learned from discussing it in terms of a restricted economy. So to take account of this crossing of economic effects, I focus precisely on this return on investment in learning from AIDS in my discussion of the last category. What does it mean to learn from AIDS? Is this philosophically defensible at all, the attempt to make AIDS an object? As we will see, 'thinking about AIDS' is itself a philosophically questionable activity. Thus AIDS, when viewed from a certain angle, when thought about in a certain way, is such as to take away the complacency with which it can be comfortably viewed, discussed, and thought about – even as it demands such thought. AIDS, the wearing away of the border of inside and outside, won't allow an outside from which it can be viewed so easily.

ECONOMIES OF TRUTH IN THE SCIENTIFIC BODY POLITIC

As we were all taught at one point, and as various forces would still have us believe, knowledge relates to force as truth to corruption. The philosopher or scientist battles not only cryptic nature, but also seductive or dominating power. Between the figures of Socrates and Crito in prison, Galileo and the Inquisitors in the dungeon, the brave individual must stick to a vision of the truth in the face of the temptations or threats of forceful power. The philosopher king, after all, was the greatest of the scandals of the *Republic*, greater even than the destruction of the patriarchal family. Dragged back down into the cave only by the fear of being governed by worse people, putting power to work after the fact in the service of an already achieved truth, the philosophers assigned to puppet master duty are nonetheless tormented by nostalgia for the clear air up above, as their eyes, which once feasted on the light of the Sun/Good, atrophy in the flickering light of the cave's fire. Thousands of years later, testifying to the solidity of this cultural structure, Kant also knew force would destroy philosophy's necessary purity; disdaining the rei(g)ns of force, putting truth over immediate justice, he thus forbade the philosophy faculty of the university any but a critical role.[4]

We see here the restricted economy of truth in the scientific body politic: it turns a profit only in isolation from its opposite, force, which, if it must, it will grudgingly put to work implementing policies directed by a truth gained in splendid isolation from power. The restricted economy of truth presupposes a restricted economy of human being that separates inside from outside: the mind sees truth, force works on the body. (We have seen in Chapter 1 how Derrida deconstructs the phenomenological version of the metaphysical representation of body politic as self-ruling 'animate organism', the rule of the living present in the conscious body politic.)

The everyday picture of AIDS truth is a restricted economy. Here we are told of the healthy competition – or even if we're cynical enough, the patent, profit and Nobel Prize-corrupted competition, which should have been disinterested – between the heroic American and French investigators, Robert Gallo and Luc Montagnier. By a prodigious intellectual feat of uncovering a piece of nature gone awry, wresting the truth from a recalcitrant world, in 1984 they break the mystery of the retrovirus, they isolate the truth about AIDS: it's caused by what will become known as HIV, the human immunodeficiency virus.[5]

The mutually exclusive opposition of force and truth, as another story would have it, comes under fire from the masters of suspicion, Marx and Freud. They taught us to look to labour and desire as the very condition of mainstream scientific constructions of truth. That Marx and Freud – at least on some, institutionalized readings, which one could no doubt render problematic – would have us look to another truth, a truly scientific truth, shouldn't detract from their critical import: they've taught us to look at the worldly context governing the production of first-order scientific statements claiming truth. It's the third master of suspicion, Nietzsche, who turned a genealogical eye not to false, insufficiently scientific truths, but to truth itself. Truth: a lie told for the increase of power by a force always already in a power relation with other forces. Nietzsche's self-acknowledged heir, Foucault, completes the deconstruction of the opposition of force/power and truth by coining the phrase 'power/knowledge'. The general economy of truth: force/power does not corrupt, then, after the fact, an innocent search for truth. Force/power supplements knowledge; power/knowledge is the very medium of truth: knowledge is only produced on the condition of the power necessary to control situations, while power depends upon knowledge for its deployment and reproduction. In Derridean terms, power/knowledge, or the general economy of truth in the scientific body politic, means we must acknowledge our living in a general text of force and signification by deconstructing the restricted economy that would oppose force to truth and by thereby recognizing the production of forceful meaning, as we have seen in Chapters 1–3.

Before sketching the outlines of a general economy of truth about AIDS, let me first make it clear that I am not aspiring to historiographic standards of factual determination about the establishment of the hegemony of the HIV-only paradigm in American AIDS research and policy during the period 1981–95. Leaving aside the controversies over the epistemology and methodology of historiography, about which I am no expert, this chapter is philosophical, not historiographical; in brief, I do not speculate about facts, but propose ways to explain facts, specifically, the hegemony of a paradigm which posits HIV as the sole cause of AIDS.

Just as I do not speculate about facts, I do not advocate a thesis about political influence in AIDS science. Such a thesis assumes science and politics are independent spheres whose *de facto* mixture is to be condemned. The logical model for such a thesis is precisely a restricted economy, that is, an exclusive disjunction or forced choice: either pure science or dirty politics, or their products, scientifically purified politics or politically contaminated science. Any sarcasm in this chapter is directed to caricaturing restricted economy views of truth, bodies, identities and academic writing – including my own – in AIDS discourse.

Certainly, a general economy that articulates science and politics should not be seen as insulting to the integrity of scientists, although it may disappoint some who feel threatened by such attention. But one might hope these are a dwindling few; about the general issue of the appropriateness of using political economy to analyse scientific research I defer to none other than Paul Gross and Norman Levitt, whose *Higher Superstition* lies behind the notorious Sokal hoax:

> We are all, in a commonsensical way, cultural constructivists in our view of science. . . . It would be idle to pretend that the projects taken on by science, the questions that it asks at any given period, do not reflect the interests, beliefs, and even the prejudices of the ambient culture. Clearly, certain kinds of research get the strongest encouragement – funding, recognition, celebrity, and so forth – in response to the recognized needs of society. (1994, 43)

For strategic reasons, I accept Gross and Levitt's implicit offer to trade 'weak cultural constructivism' in exchange for dropping questions of realism in physics and molecular biology, including virology.[6] Thus I will not argue, for instance, that HIV does not behave the way Gallo claims it does, nor that it is a mere 'construct'. Instead, I argue that the potentials to discover evidence that would fit a broader immunological model that would incorporate virologically derived HIV evidence were foreclosed by the establishment of the hegemony of the HIV-only model.

I propose three principles for investigating the hegemony of the HIV-only model in the scientific body politic: (a) consider the problem with reconciling a first-level multi-factorial model with the theory-discriminating meta-level preference for parsimony; (b) consider the political economy of funding agencies and paradigm establishment; (c) consider the political economy of the scientific research/pharmaceutical industry connection. I advocate these as principles for further research, together making up a 'general economy of truth', not in order to speculate about the facts of the case, but to propose a model to explain those facts.

Finally, though, one more question before we begin: is it even plausible to question the utility of the HIV-only model? Are there biological rather than philosophical reasons to question it? Here I can only refer to the very strong case Robert Root-Bernstein brings against the monocausal virology or HIV-only model, and for a multifactorial immunology model, in his *Rethinking AIDS*. Although I cannot rehearse Root-Bernstein's arguments here, he presents a strong case that the HIV-only model fails Koch's postulates, in other words, that HIV does not provide the necessary and sufficient conditions for AIDS, and hence cannot be the sole cause of AIDS. I take it that Root-Bernstein's alternative scenarios for AIDS at least gives us the room to investigate the history of the establishment of the HIV-only model.

(a) *Models of causation.* Pursuing the general economy of truth about AIDS first takes us to the question of scientific models of causation. Ockham's razor commands us to parsimony in explanation. Hume may have shaken the belief in causality of philosophers, but the everyday operation of the production of scientific truth was spared the tortuous path through Kant's Copernican turn, by accepting constant correlation as good enough as long as it produced predictable, verifiable, and repeatable results identifying necessary and sufficient conditions. So

HIV as 'the cause' of AIDS fit right in to a long-standing scientific predilection for simplicity.[7] So it seems one could explain the widespread acceptance of the HIV-only model in the scientific network on the basis of intra-scientific reasons, as a classic example of finding the cause of a disease.

But what was the state of early AIDS research, in those primitive days before 'GRID' become a historical footnote?[8] What became of the leads investigated? Were they dead-ends gladly abandoned when the truth became known? Or were they marginalized when the NIH adopted the HIV-only model? What is the counter-history of AIDS research? It turns out that in the wide-open field of 1981–4, all sorts of hypotheses were entertained. Multi-factorial models, based on immunology rather than virology, were proposed.[9] Thus, even in an 'intra-scientific' discussion, the question of monocausal vs multifactorial disease models would have to be settled, before one could laud the establishment of the HIV-only model as scientific progress.

(b) *Political economy of agency funding*: beyond the question of scientific models lies a further issue, the possibility of analysing a political economy of medical funding that would explain the HIV-only model's hegemony. To simply point to the hegemony of the HIV-only model, as in the endlessly repeated phrase, 'almost all leading scientists agree that HIV is the cause of AIDS', begs the question of the establishment of that hegemony, as does pointing to a proponderance of evidence without examining the constraints on evidence discovery. Given Gross and Levitt's formulation of 'weak cultural constructivism', we can say that 'evidence' is developed not only in response to social desire, but also on the basis of previous social investment. By 1984, virology was a well-established, hard-science field as opposed to the fragmented and less-respected field of immunology;[10] as such, virology enjoyed considerable evidence-gathering advantages over immunology in early AIDS research. Thus, pointing to the greater evidence gathered by a science that already enjoys an established hegemony (pre-AIDS virology) explains but does not necessarily justify the re-establishment of that hegemony in a new area (AIDS).

Proposing a single cause, elegant virological laboratory experiments could be designed to control for all factors but the one impacting HIV.[11] The adoption of the HIV-only model, HIV as the necessary and sufficient condition for AIDS, by the NIH – the major source of funding for biomedical research in the US – meant that grant writers had better write HIV-only model grants. After a few years, the HIV-only model literature piles up and literature reviews in the introductions of grant proposals are filled with HIV-only studies. A few more years, and students new to AIDS work are referred to the classic studies in the field, all of which work with the HIV-only model.

(c) *Political economy of drug treatment*: isolation of a single cause could lead to a 'magic bullet'.[12] The patent on such a weapon would yield enormous profits on a global arms market in the war against AIDS. The adoption of the HIV-only model and the hegemony over research funding it established thus allowed the articulation of government research with drug company research. The tangled story of Burroughs–Wellcome and the drug/poison AZT,[13] its testing and government approval, would have to be told here, as well as the struggles over test structures, and the ethics of the double-blind placebo study. In other words, AIDS 'politicizes' medical research and practice – the scare quotes marking the political struggle to recognize the always already political nature of medical practice and research, its articulation in a general text of force and signification productive of forceful meaning in a process of 'making sense'.[14]

The first lesson of AIDS is to recognize the general economy of the production of truth claims in the general text of force and signification that is the scientific body politic.

ECONOMIES OF THE BORDER IN THE SOMATIC BODY POLITIC

The HIV-only model rests on a restricted economy of the somatic body politic, in which a border is breached and an interiority exposed to an exterior invader. Processes may result from the interaction of these entities, virus and body, but these processes are supervenient upon the entities involved. The HIV-only model might also have some 'co-factors' along for the ride, to account for the observed differences in survival times after seroconversion was registered, but these are never granted the dignity of the category 'cause'.

The restricted economy of truth about AIDS in the scientific body politic – the victory of Gallo and Montagnier over cryptic nature in isolating the entity upon which a pathology might be constructed – was thus historically correlated with a restricted economy of the borders of the somatic body politic. In this picture, the virus comes from outside, breaching the walls that should separate the unitary body from its opposite, the outside world.[15] The body is seen as an interiority encased by a protective barrier, a frontier. According to the oppositional cultural imaginary, the ideally seamless mucuous membrane walls are in fact fragile, prone to tiny invisible tears, opening the inside to an outside that should stay outside. The response to this factual degeneration from ideal separation is to police the borders of the somatic body politic. The messages we all know by now: separate inside and outside. Avoid mixing the famous bodily fluids. The truth about AIDS is a liminology, a discourse on borders: keep your fluids to yourself! Don't bring foreign blood inside! Clean your needles, watch your blood supply: regulate the purity of outside substances, if you must – through perversity or medical order – incorporate them. Keep your penis and its fluids to yourself! The condom keeps the outside, even when it is inside, outside. Keep your clitoris and vaginal secretions to yourself! The dental dam keeps the inside, even when it is outside, inside. Latex is life; fluid exchange, death.

The general economy of the somatic body politic in the AIDS context, by contrast to the oppositional liminology of virology, focuses on immunology. Immunology is the study of a process, a discourse that attempts to explain the regulation of a site of interchange. Immunological models are fuzzy and soft compared to the elegant precision of virological experiments. Disturbing new logics are called for. There is, frustratingly enough, no one 'cause'.[16] Information theory and cybernetics, as Donna Haraway demonstrates in her important essay 'The biopolitics of postmodern bodies', are the paradigms of immunology. The immunological system's task is one of reading, of espionage and counter-espionage. The endgame of auto-immune disease – especially when it targets the immune system itself (Root-Bernstein's position in his *Rethinking AIDS*) – is that of the impossible task of undoing the mistakes committed by internal police who confuse internal police for foreign agents masquerading as internal police dedicated to tracking down foreign agents masquerading as internal police. . . . Suspicion taken to the limit; hermeneutics *in extremis*. Compared with the paranoia of immunology, the virological war model, where the task is the defence of the garrison from the enemy storming the walls, is relatively reassuring.

For immunology, the question is never one of inside and outside, but of the economic distribution between intake, assimilation or rejection and excretion. The unitary, self-present body is exploded into a systemic interchange, a point of exchange of forces; in other words, immunology studies forceful bodies politic. The outside is always already inside, in relation to the inside; the regulation of this interchange is the job of the immune system. A general economy of the somatic body politic is not simply a process-ontology, in which entities like virus and body are snapshots of an underlying process that would be in principle knowable by an intellect able to synthesize into a grand present the series of present nows that make up the process. Rather, 'body' is the presentifying effect of a reifying language; it marks the stilling of a process to be sure, but also, if we read the scare quotes, the re-marking of language in general, the non-present ground of presence as an effect.[17] This is not a 'dematerializing' of what should remain the stable basis of our politics: the body as source of surplus value, as field of desire, as locus of disciplinary biopower, was always thought as a site of force relations, whose present appearance through invocation in language was itself a force relation in a general text whose ground could never present itself in the way its effects present themselves.

The general economy of the somatic body politic brings with it a mutual contamination of science and politics, so that the body as site of interchange with a manifold environment feeds back to demand a reconceptualized general economy of research, an acknowledgement of the general text of force and signification. The multifactorialists felt a second form of resistance from the scientific establishment, who not only had to face a messy scientific model, but also a contamination, on the basis of that very model, of biological science with social science and critical political analyses. The supposedly pure 'medical' factors of toxins, allergens, immunosuppressives and disease loads that make up a multifactorial immunological model of the AIDS disease process would have to be articulated with psycho-socio-econo-political analyses of homophobia, racism, misogyny and the capitalist production of poverty and commodification of medical information and service.[18] Discomfort with this 'politicization' of supposedly pure science only served to further isolate multifactorial model proponents – already weakened by the adoption of the HIV-only model and the higher prestige of the elegant simplicity of virology – from the big science establishment.

With the marginalization of multifactorial models and the funding hegemony of the HIV-only model secured, virologists could leave 'politics' to the 'activists', who themselves embraced HIV for their own reasons, as we will see. As Gallo puts it in *Virus Hunting*:

> But in my work on the AIDS retrovirus in the laboratory, I do not confront the individual victims of a dreadful disease. I deal with knowledge, with the science of retroviral disease. There are no patients in a research laboratory, no pain, no suffering, no disease, no death. Instead there are cells, viruses, and molecules; and the questions are scientific – not moral, not political, not even human-istic. (1991, 10)

Before we proceed, I want to note four points: (1) Gallo's is an entirely appropriate, and in fact the only valid, stance that a practising virologist, while in the lab, can adopt; (2) Gallo is a great scientist, whose reputation is secured for breaking open the entire field of retroviruses, even if his own-horn-tooting is gauche and his remarks that slight the social factors of epidemics are silly (see note 18 above); (3) virological results are an important part of responding to the AIDS crisis; (4) the results of virological research need to be incorporated in a general immunological approach that articulates the socio-political connections virology by definition cannot and should not be concerned with.

The second lesson of AIDS is that the general economy of the somatic body politic must be a multifactorial immunological model of a process of interchange between 'body', 'environment', 'medicine' and 'politics', as they interact in the general text of force and signification.

ECONOMIES OF IDENTITY IN THE SEXUAL
BODY POLITIC

The April 1984 press conference by Margaret Heckler of the US Department of Health and Human Services to announce Gallo's upcoming breakthrough to what would become known as HIV brought a sigh of relief and a groan of despair, at once dissipating and heightening the unspoken fear of the early 1980s, that this mysterious 'gay plague' – mysterious enough without the bizarre and inexplicable Haitian connection – might start infecting the 'general population'. So AIDS teaches us that the economies of identity in the sexual body politic must be put to the test.

With a restricted economy of sexual identity we deal with an essentialist sex/gender politics, and a crossing of medical and political discourses. A full-fledged theoretical discussion of sex/gendering processes, to say nothing of sexual identity or orientation, is of course impossible in the context of this book. We can say, however, that in the cultural imaginary sexual identity is a restricted economy in which straight and gay are opposed and mutually exclusive. In the 1980s an essentialist model of homosexuality had powerful incentives that gained it support from some elements within the gay community. One was psychological, the reassuring discovery of an identity within the centrifugal whirl of late capitalism. Another was civic-political, coming out being the gesture around which a community, the gay body politic, could be formed. When this announcement was seen as the acknowledgement of a biologically determined identity, both guilty parents and gay-baiting politicians could be mollified that a 'choice' was not being made. Even those for whom coming out was discursive and performative, not simply ontologically revelatory, could insist on a sexual identity for community-building purposes, even if only for a short time, until the straight community grew up and homophobia could decrease.

When the restricted economy of gay vs straight identity in the sexual body politic was crossed with a general economy of the somatic body politic, disaster loomed. Immune system overload theories inevitably brought up the question of 'lifestyle', which was and is dangerously prone to reinscription in moralizing contexts. Discussions of the immuno-suppressive effects of amyl nitrate, cocaine and alcohol as toxins; antibiotics, steroidals and others as immuno-suppressives; foreign proteins from semen and blood as allergens; run of the mill sexually transmitted dieseases like syphilis, gonorrhea and herpes simplex, and other multiple and repeated infections – Epstein–Barr, hepatitis, etc. – as disease loads, with the synergistic effects of all the permutations of these factors, could easily be lifted from a 'medical' context – assuming for a moment the merely relative specificity of such a context, particularly difficult in the case of AIDS, as we saw above – and adduced as evidence for the 'unnaturalness' of a 'gay lifestyle'.[19] To some when considering the political cost of overload theories, the dissemination of dis-semen-ation seemed too great a risk.[20]

And perhaps these intuitions were accurate, the civic-political calculation a good one. Current proponents of non-HIV-only models, from the simple toxicity model of Peter Duesberg[21] to the sophisticated auto-immune endgame theory of Root-Bernstein, are in fact plagued by retrograde and essentialist sociologies. The early multifactorialists, many of them themselves gay men like Joseph Sonnabend[22] and his popularizer Michael Callen,[23] even though themselves relatively free of such problematic discourse, nonetheless found themselves at odds with sectors of the gay community that saw in the non-discriminatory reputation of viruses a political wedge that could force funding from a homophobic establishment that may have been happy to see gays and drug addicts die, but that couldn't take the heat from a sufficiently frightened 'general population'. Isolated from big science and from the most politically visible parts of the gay community then, accused of self-hatred from unacknowledged internalized homophobia, and able to appear only in their own marginalized journals or in the overwrought conspiracy-theory framework of the New York Native, the early multi-factorialists found themselves doubly marginalized. And, to repeat, it's by no means clear that the calculation backing the HIV-only model within the gay community wasn't the most effective in the short run.

A general economy of bodily practices is then called for by AIDS. An anti-essentialist discourse, a general economy of bodies and prac-tices, rather than a restricted economy of sexual identities, is always tricky to establish. Let us continue with our strategy of exploring the cultural imaginary and examine therein the tortured category of the 'bisexual'. Brought in to supplement the restricted economy of sexual identity, the 'bisexual' category, when pushed, can nevertheless explode the sexual body politic into a general economy of bodies and practices enmeshed in a general text of force and signification.

To support the restricted economy in the cultural imaginary, the bisexual is always conceived to be a sexually identified person whose sexual practices sometimes exceed that identification. To explain this gap between identity and practice, to channel the excess, is the task of an explanatory scheme that sees not pleasure and desire but politics, escape from others or from the truth about oneself, or even revenge, as the 'motive' of bisexual behaviour. A self-congratulatory and reassuring patriarchy can be easily seen here. Bisexual women, on this model, are essentially straight, but out of solidarity with the struggle against patriarchy or in disgust with past abuse by men, turn to the naturally gentle sex for the comfort and tenderness unavailable in straight beds. Bisexual men, on the other hand, are essentially gay, and sleep with women only to avoid confronting their internalized homo-phobia or because they are unable to negotiate coming out. By the 1980s the Don Giovanni 'repressed homosexual' explanation of multi-ple seduction became the horror story of the HIV-positive gay man gaining revenge on the straights by 'knowingly infecting' the women with whom he 'had sex' – defined, of course, as penile–vaginal contact.

What this model reveals is the desperate attempt to salvage a reassuringly patriarchal sexual identity out of a welter of bodies, practices and possibilities, to save an oppositional logic of the sexual body politic. The cultural image that 'bisexual' women are really straight but simply disappointed in the small sample of acutally existing men they happened to have met assures straight men that they might just be the ones who could show them the supplemental nature of settling for other women by showing them what real heterosex is all about. Similarly, that bisexual men are essentially gay is an obvious attempt at sheltering 'straight' men from acknowledging the possible pleasures their bodies might achieve in combination with other mascu-line-coded bodies. Stripped of these protective fantasies, the 'bisexual' – the mark of the excess of practice over identity – becomes the figure from which a general economy of 'bodies and pleasures' (Foucault, *History of Sexuality I*, 1978, 208/157) might emerge in a disseminative sexual body politic.

The political implication of this general economy of bodily practices on the self-support and anti-homophobic strength of a gay body politic gathered around the notion of a shared sexual identity is difficult to address here. Nonetheless, some elements of the gay community adopted this general economy, *sotto voce*, in connection with a restricted virological economy of the AIDS body, in order to combat the ghettoization of AIDS, its restriction to the gay 'risk group'. Doing so was a paradoxical gesture, however, for even though the general economy of bodies and practices and the restricted economy of the virus brought about a politically efficacious heightening of anxiety, a general economy would seem to threaten the notion of gay-body-politic-under-siege-by-AIDS that proved an effective mobilizer. No conspiracy theory is advocated here, but simply an articulation of cultural logic: If 'viruses don't discriminate', as the slogan goes, and if different acts are widely distributed among people whose practices seem to violate their socially assigned identities, then perhaps there is no 'general population' only now coming to be at risk. If 'bisexuals' are everywhere and seemingly healthy – because of the time lag between seroconversion and symptom – then everyone is at risk![24]

The third lesson of AIDS is that an anti-essentialist general economy of bodily practices, exploding the oppositional logic of identity in the sexual body politic and consequent confining of AIDS to a 'gay' 'risk group', was necessary but problematic, for it also exploded the identity politics on the basis of which a gay body politic could be formed which could be effective in combating homophobia in AIDS issues.

ECONOMIES OF MEANING IN THE ACADEMIC BODY POLITIC

This chapter and all academic writings on AIDS need to be seen in its economy of meaning. What is gained and lost in glib announcements to academic audiences of 'lessons' about AIDS, as if it were a sort of social litmus test? A restricted economy of AIDS meaning would see academic profiteers pouncing on the AIDS phenomenon as a pretext either for CV-fattening publications or as a chance to give suffering a meaning. At stake is the very practice of AIDS discourse in the academic body politic.

The first option seems too intentionalistic to have much critical edge. Given the structures of academic publishing, such interpretations are irreducible, but what would be the criterion for deciding the 'reason' behind this or any other publication? Author's intention? But who's to decide that? The author's testimony? Someone else's? Now one could always claim a certain Kantianism and try to explain that the risk to one's status – difficulties with hiring and promotion – from tackling a 'controversial' topic outweighed any possible benefits which might come from oneself in the form of self-congratulation on adopting academic 'risk behaviour' or from the marginalized group of academics reading and writing about AIDS in the form of approval from a group of like-minded comrades, and perhaps a conference invitation or two. On balance, then, one might discount the probability that inclination rather than duty determined the will in this case.

But precisely that opposition of self-interest and altruism leads to another restricted economy of meaning, one that, unfortunately, is closer to the heart of the academic body politic. Nietzsche taught us to beware the nihilistic impulses behind the attempt to render suffering meaningful, to turn a profit of intelligibility from pain. Thus it is precisely the very notion of learning from AIDS, learning from fiddling about with the economies of truth, borders and identity in the scientific, somatic and sexual bodies politic that is the gravest injustice, for it turns the suffering and death of others into a heuristic device. Is this not the anti-tragic gesture *par excellence*?

But, as with the implacable logic of the Holocaust, the seemingly noble gesture of a dignified silence is indistinguishable from a callous ignoring of tragedy. Is there a discourse of AIDS that would not be anti-tragic but a bearing witness to tragedy? In the terms of this chapter, can the Derridean-inspired move I advocate of moving from discussing AIDS in terms of a restricted economy to a discussion in terms of a general economy, be itself not a restricted economy turning an intellectual profit in the academic body politic but a general economy acknowledging an irretrievable loss in the general text? Is Derridean politics a simple move into a general text of force and signification as if it were a simple change of world-view? But of course, with these questions we now have to rethink the very relation of restricted and general economy. They cannot be opposed, because opposition is the structure of restricted economy. They themselves must be in a general economy, an economy of economies that allows both profit and loss. I hope I have adequately demonstrated the profit from the move I advocate of switching from restricted to general economy. The question now is: what is lost? And, concomitantly, what is gained from acknowledging a loss from which no gain can be made?

Perhaps such an economy can be sketched in the Levinasian perspective which has always haunted Derridean discourse.[25] Levinas is one of the contemporary thinkers who have most taught us to beware the desire to profit simply through learning from suffering. For Levinas, such profitable learning occurs through the construction of an immanent totality, a horizon of meaning within which an object can be determined: 'The meaning of individuals (invisible outside of this totality) is derived from the totality. The unicity of each present is incessantly sacrificed to a future appealed to to bring forth its objective meaning' (Levinas, *Totality and Infinity*, 1969, 6/22). Such horizons of meaning abound in the case of AIDS discourse: we are told how AIDS teaches us God's wrath, or the dignity of the human spirit, or the folly of disregarding our bodily limits. In each case, the people living with and dying from AIDS are seen from the outside; a clear border is drawn in the academic body politic between observer and object, a border across which travels a lesson to be learned and applied to the observer's stock of knowledge about the world.

For Levinas, the refusal of totality occurs in the opening to infinity announced in the face of the other. In the face of the other, phenomenology fails, no object can be seen; seeing the face is objectifying it, so that the seen face is no face at all. Rather than sight, the face is 'revealed' when it is responded to in discourse: 'here I am, what do you need?' The response to the face does not seek knowledge about an object in the world; rather the response performs the subjectification of the respondent, the acknowledgement of offering oneself as hostage to the other. The act of response is a 'saying' that underlies the content of the response, the 'said'.

For such an infinite response, each death does not yield up a truth at the end of the day by being placed in a wider scheme – the academic body politic disintegrates – but draws its significance at the very moment of its occurence in the response it evokes, the response that opens an ethical dimension. This ethical 'beyond' of totalities 'restores to each instant its full signification in that very instant . . .' (Levinas, *Totality and Infinity*, 1969, 8/23). In the response evoked by AIDS, the saying animating the said of all AIDS discourse – the very gesture of writing about AIDS – can we not glimpse such a restoration of significance beyond subjective-intentional meaning, beyond all lessons learned? And wouldn't this not be an anti-tragic gesture, but precisely a tragic bearing witness? That is, not a simple learning of lessons, but an un-learning? Can AIDS discourse ever become tragedy stripped of recognition and catharsis?

If that is the case, then the final shift in economies of AIDS I advocate would be one that highlights the most unsettling thing that comes from thinking about AIDS discourse: that the most important thing to learn about AIDS discourse is that its normalization, and the resistance to this normalization by recourse to the lessons learned in the shift to a general economy, both need to learn that it is the very structure of learning about AIDS that hides that unlearning, that loss, which motivates the struggle against AIDS. We must learn not to learn about AIDS, we must profit by acknowledging the loss that interrupts every profit; this second learning or profit can only take the form of a non-learning, non-profiting response, the recognition that the move to a general text of force and signification wherein forceful bodies politic are produced is the move not to a field of thought, but to a site of struggle.

CONCLUSION

We have now brought Part I to a close. I hope that in these four chapters that I have been fair and sympathetic to Derrida in sketching the possibilities and limits of the deconstructive approach to the question of the body politic. We have seen Derrida's deconstruction of metaphysics move us from the phenomenological representation of the conscious body politic to the general text, the move from the rule of the living present to 'making sense' via the inscription of marks of force and signification. We then attempted our own deconstructions of the Aristotelian patriarchal body politic and the body politics of restricted economy AIDS discourse, attempting also to show the positive thoughts of the Derridean vital body politic as differantial species-being and the general economic effects on the scientific, somatic, sexual and academic bodies politic of AIDS discourse. Along the way we have seen how the question of hylomorphism allows a certain articulation of Derrida's discourse with Deleuze's materialism, as well as the limits of that engagement given the starting point of deconstruction in 'metaphysical' claims to presence. We now move to Part II, in which I develop readings of the implicit hylomorphism in the body politic as thought by Plato, Aristotle, Heidegger and Kant.

PART 2

Deleuze: Historical–Libidinal Materialism and Organ-ized Bodies

CHAPTER 5

Master and Slave in the Platonic Body Politic

> [S]lavery, state, man and world all illustrate a single
> hierarchic pattern . . . the slave lacks *logos*; so does the
> multitude in the state, the body in man, and material
> necessity in the universe. Let to itself each of these would
> be disorderly and vicious . . . Order is imposed upon them
> by a benevolent superior: master, guardian, mind, demi-
> urge. Each of these rules (*archein*) in his own domain. The
> common title to authority is the possession of *logos*.
> (Gregory Vlastos, 'Slavery in Plato's Thought', 1981.[1])

Transition to Part 2
The Platonic Body Politic
Platonic 'Hylomorphism'
Body and Soul in Man
Production in the Household
Rule and Custom in the City
Reason and Necessity in the Cosmos
Conclusion

TRANSITION TO PART 2

In Part 2, we show the way Deleuze's engagement with complexity
theory, especially the notions of hylomorphism and material self-
organization, illuminate the political physics of the body politic in
Plato, Aristotle, Heidegger and Kant. In particular, I focus on the
distinction between 'artisanal' and 'architectonic' production and on
the notion of the organic (or organismic) body politic in those readings.
Here I present the second transversal: instead of looking for traces of
a Deleuzean critique of hylomorphism within Derrida's work, here I
develop independent readings of classic philosophers which, in the

style of Derrida's close reading, thematize hylomorphism in its own right.

But what dictates the choice of these philosophers as my test cases? When it comes to illustrating the power of using the Deleuzean/ Simondonian concept of hylomorphism to read the history of philosophy, we cannot follow the procedure of Part I, that is, we cannot hope to locate detailed readings of the hylomorphism of other philosophers in Deleuze the way we are able to follow the close readings Derrida devotes to articulating the metaphysical engagements of particular philosophers. This is due to the fact that Deleuze's synthetic and wide-ranging original work, from which we draw the concepts of hylomorphism and material self-ordering, do not develop detailed readings of historically important philosophical texts. Thus, due to the difference in method of Derrida and Deleuze we are free to choose the philosophers we will examine in our transverse approach of crossing Derridean 'method' and Deleuzean concepts; we begin by examining Plato as the one who sets forth with particular clarity many of the basic concepts of Western political philosophy, so that revealing his hylomorphism will enable us to see similar patterns in Aristotle, Heidegger and Kant.

THE PLATONIC BODY POLITIC

The body politic is one of the most basic structures of Plato's thought.[2] In the Introduction, we defined the forceful body politic as a body composed of force relations; the Platonic 'soul' is a body politic, then, for in a well-ordered soul the rational part of the soul *rules* the non-rational parts. We will thus use the term 'corporeal' for 'body' in the extended sense of any ordered system of force relations (to match Deleuze and Guattari's *corps sans organes* or BwO) and the term 'somatic' for body in the restricted sense (as opposite of 'soul').

The particular contours of the Platonic body politic result in the isomorphism of soul, man,[3] household, city and world, an isomorphism that allows terms historically most clearly associated with political entities to describe the internal relations of soul and man (reason should rule the appetites; the soul should rule the somatic body) and terms historically most clearly associated with soul and man to describe

the internal relations of political entities (cities can be healthy or sick).[4]
For Plato, the body politic in all its registers – body, soul, man,
household, city, and cosmos – is isomorphic because all the registers
are (or should be) technically produced organic unities. The Platonic
body politic is technical, since each body is (or should be) produced
by outside sources possessed of logos and techne.[5] The Platonic body
politic is also organic, since in each body the parts are (or should be)
subordinate to the function of the whole.[6]

With regard to our other qualification of the body politic – its
'forceful' nature – I take it as a relatively easy exercise to demonstrate
the forceful nature of the Platonic body politic in the realms of
household and city, especially when the problem is posed in terms of
the relations of master and slave in the household or the group of
citizens and the group of slaves in the city rather than in terms of the
relations among citizens. As is well known, the forceful and organic
nature of the Platonic body politic is the basis of the charge of
totalitarianism first made famous by Popper in the struggle against
fascism in the early 1940s and continued during the anti-Communism
of the Cold War. At roughly the same time as Popper's *Open Society*,
Gregory Vlastos saw to the heart of the Platonic body politic in a
brilliant article the key passage of which serves as the epigraph of this
chapter. In that article Vlastos demonstrates the forceful nature of the
Platonic body politic by pointing out how Plato equates artisans'
submission in the just city with slavery (Plato, *Republic*, 590c), even
though he doesn't wish to obliterate the distinction between the artisan
citizen and the slave. Vlastos thus contends that Plato idealizes slavery
as amiable submission to one's betters and makes democracy the result
of unnatural force (Vlastos, *Platonic Studies*, 1981, 159). Vlastos thus
unmasks the forceful nature of Plato's organic body politic by revealing
the way Plato likens the guardian rule of artisans to the citizen
domination of slaves. While this view is not without its detractors, I
find it convincing. A full demonstration is not possible here, but we
can note an important passage of the *Republic* to support this view. The
divine and intelligent, Plato writes, should govern in the city as in the
soul and man. It would be best if this could be indwelling in each
citizen (as the result of proper psychic and anthropological education),
but in default of that, it should be 'imposed from without' (Plato,

Republic, 590d). Here we see the iron fist of compulsion within the velvet glove of persuasive education. The forceful nature of the relation of soul and body in man is also quite clear from the prescription that the soul is to rule the body as does a master (Plato, *Timaeus*, 34d), as is the forceful nature of the intra-psychic regime, as shown by the bloody discipline imposed on the bad horse by the charioteer at *Phaedrus* (254e). The relations of force and persuasion in the cosmological register are more complex and interesting than in the registers of city, soul and man, however, and will be the focus of the last section of this chapter.

In our talk of basic structures we should not overlook several significant differences among the registers of the Platonic body politic. In man and cosmos, the task is to mould an organic whole of body and soul (the difference between man and cosmos is that the body of the cosmos is multiplicitous).[7] But such order is only possible on the basis of a well-ordered soul, in which reason rules spirit and appetite and is thus capable of logos and techne, that is, planning that subordinates parts to their function in a whole. In household and city, the task of the psychically and anthropologically well-ordered master/ruler is to mould an organic whole from a human multitude by proposing an order of ends in which the work of the slaves or citizens can be functionally organized for what the master/ruler judges to be the good of the whole.

However, although the registers of the Platonic body politic differ in these ways, the production of each relies on the technical rendering determinate of indeterminacy (the most basic of all ontological processes for Plato, as we can see at *Philebus*, 35e). That a single process produces all the bodies politic is revealed by the fact that for Plato, mastership, statesmanship and kingship are the same eco-political science (Plato, *Statesman*, 259b; see also Aristotle, *Politics*, 1253b18; 1252a8). And it is because Timaeus is both learned in politics (Plato, *Timaeus*, 20a) and astronomy (27a) that he can describe the cosmogenesis directed by the Demiurge in the dialogue that bears his name.[8]

In investigating the Platonic body politic we find a complex interchange between the order of discovery, the order of being, the demonstrative order, and the pedagogic order. The order of discovery proceeds from instance to form (ascent, eidetic purification) while the order of being moves from form to instance (participation). The demonstrative order, the arguments Plato allows Socrates to offer to his interlocutors in the *Republic*, follows the ease of eidetic purification, beginning with the city – justice writ large – and then moving to soul and man, where it intersects the pedagogic order. The pedagogic order shows what is necessary to reproduce the philosophic knowledge on which rest the demonstrations Plato allows Socrates' character to present. On either side of the central images of the *Republic* we see the pedagogic order of the production of ordered souls governing corporeal and somatic bodies, first through musical and gymnastic education for the entire guardian class (Plato, *Republic*, 376e–412b), then through the specialized training for the philosopher kings in arithmetic, plane and solid geometry, astronomy (that is, knowledge of the cosmos) and harmonics as prelude to an ascent via dialectic to the study of the Good (that is, knowledge of Being; 522c–34b). The complete course of training of the philosopher kings thus provides them with a comprehensive onto-cosmo-psycho-anthropo-eco-political wisdom so that they can in turn use their insight into the principles governing all of Being to produce the Platonic body politic: moulding the character of the souls and somatic bodies of the next generation of citizens as fits their natures to produce the ordered whole of the good city, resting on the ordered whole of the household, and fit to the order of the cosmos and all of Being.

PLATONIC 'HYLOMORPHISM'

Our Deleuzean critical analysis of the Platonic body politic focuses on hylomorphism: the external, psychic, technical *archē* of corporeal organic order as the imposition of form on chaotic matter.[9] Since he assumes that there can only be one source of order for a corpus, Plato always wants to identify the *archē* when analysing the genesis of an organic body, assuming further that the oldest element is the source of order, deserving of rule (Plato, *Timaeus*, 34c; *Laws*, 892a).[10] If we remember that *archon* is the name for the highest Athenian political office, then we can recognize *archē* as a term of political physics par excellence. Now we must recall that the source of organic order is external even for the soul; hence the Platonic emphasis on education.

The source of order of the body politic is not only external but also technical: the *archon* must have the kingly techne to produce order and hence to rule in the city (Plato, *Laws*, 968a; *Statesman*, 305d) or cosmos (Plato, *Sophist*, 265e; *Timaeus*, 28c; 53b).

After Aristotle, we are used to distinguishing the technical from the organic (*Physica*, 1950, 2.1.192b9–23). But the technical and the organic are but two sides of the Platonic body politic, seen from the side of the (technical) producer or the (organic) product. Following up on this duplicity of technical organics, in this chapter we will analyse the Platonic body politic with the help of the term 'hylomorphism', even though the typical Platonic discussion of technical organic production does not use the terms 'matter' (*hylē*) and 'form' (*morphē*). Given the Platonic focus on architectonic vision, the usual Platonic target in discussions of production is the relation of form to finished product (the copy, the instance of the form), rather than the hylomorphism strictly speaking of Aristotle, in which the analysis begins with the finished product and moves back to form and matter as its constituents (matter as input to the production process). However, the key for us in discussing the Platonic body politic is its technical nature, the external source of order in psychic and somatic systems, not the direction of analysis. Furthermore, since the Platonic notion of the technical production of an organic body politic is in its deepest sense the imposition of determinacy (as measure or number) on indeterminacy,[11] and since for Aristotle 'matter' is the name for the principle of indeterminacy, an extended and looser sense of 'hylomorphism' can cover both the Platonic and Aristotelian instances, especially since we have no received term for the privilege of measure, number, or determinacy over indeterminacy ('metrism'? 'arithmetism'? 'perasitism'?).

The organic nature of the Platonic body politic is the target of the charge of 'totalitarianism' levelled by Popper against Plato in *Open Society*, which is historically linked to the mid-twentieth-century struggle against fascism and Stalinism. Although this topic is of course worthy of the most intense study today, due to the upsurge in interest in biology and the philosophy of biology, and is of course also amenable to a Deleuzean analysis,[12] the organism-status of the Platonic body politic is so well-founded that we are better served by a focus on the technical aspect of the hylomorphic construction of the Platonic body politic, with only brief attention in passing to the organism as ideal state of the body politic.

Since the grasp of the form is the hallmark of techne, our analysis of 'hylomorphism' will focus on the technical interpretation of production. The Platonic notion of techne has three major characteristics, all of which are associated with the vision and command of the architect: (1) the look to a paradigm; (2) the use of numbers, measure or limit to render determinate indeterminacy;[13] (3) the construction of a system of ends. This notion of technical production is evident in the *Republic* in the context of the city and in the first part of the *Timaeus* in the context of the cosmos, and is characterized in Platonic terms as the work of reason. The major features of Plato's view of techne are illustrated in the following passage from the *Gorgias*. Among craftsmen [*dēmiourgoi*], Plato tells us, each one works with the goal of giving a form [*eidos*] to the work, and so 'disposes each element he contributes in a fixed order and compels [*prosanagkazei*] one to fit and harmonize with the other until he has combined the whole into something well ordered and regulated' (Plato, *Gorgias*, 503e). In the key verb 'compel' we see the root *anagkē*, 'necessity'; we will investigate the relations of reason and necessity in detail in the last section of this chapter.

Over against this strict sense of techne, Plato's texts also include a notion of a productive process superficially closer to that of the artisan than to that of the architect: a close working with materials. But this productive process is both denied the status of techne and subordinated to a science of ends as the mere production of means. For Plato, the hallmark of techne is the ability to teach, to give a supplementary logos explaining production, as we see at *Apology* (22d) and *Gorgias* (501a) in the cases of craftsmen and doctors respectively. Conversely, at *Apology* (22b) and *Gorgias* (465a), we read that poets and rhetors have no supplementary logos; hence they have no techne. It is important to stress here that Plato does not judge poets or rhetors by their effectiveness at production, but by the lack of rational grounding of that production. It is undeniable that poets and rhetors effectively produce [pleasure], but they produce through enthusiasm (Plato, *Ion*, 533–5) or non-logos grounded habit, what Plato calls 'experience [*empeiria*]' (Plato, *Gorgias*, 462c).

David Roochnik shows how such productivity, relying on embodied skill and an ability to recognize the appropriate moment for intervention (the *kairos*), is thematized by Hippocratic medicine, Protagoras, Isocrates and Aristotle (under different terms, to be sure) as 'stochastic techne'.[14] This form of techne fails to meet the Platonic standard of the logos-driven application of measure or number, however, and so is not recognized as techne by Plato, but is denigrated as mere knack or what we can call 'artisanal sensitivity'.[15] We have seen, in the terms of Deleuze and Guattari, that artisanal sensitivity is what allows for the tracking of the machinic phylum through linking traits of expression and singularities via productive operations. Artisanal sensitivity is thus a 'nomad science' of working with continuous variations rather than a 'royal science' of establishing laws between constants (ATP, 446–64/ 361–74). Nomad science is not hylomorphic in that it works with the implicit forms of matter, coaxing a material system to one or more of its thresholds of self-ordering, rather than imposing a form on chaotic matter.

In the second part of the *Timaeus* in the context of the cosmos and in the *Laws* in the context of the city we find a notion of 'persuading necessity' which seems closer to our notion of artisanal sensitivity than the strict sense of Platonic techne, as well as a notion of material self-ordering. As we will see, however, even in these seeming exceptions, the strict Platonic sense of techne shines through, as the architect's vision of the form, either as the use of number to render determinate indeterminacy (*Timaeus*) or as the establishment of a system of ends (*Laws*), garners the predominant share of the credit for the production of the organic body politic in question, even though material self-ordering and artisanal sensitivity are mentioned.

As we have defined it, then, Platonic hylomophism is the notion that organic corporeal order is imposed by an external technical source in soul, man, household, city and cosmos; this is the root of the isomorphism we call the Platonic body politic. In Deleuzean terms, hylomorphism is a transcendental illusion: the architect arrogating to himself, to his vision of form and his directions for its imposition in formless chaotic matter, all credit for the production which actually occurs through artisanal work with the implicit forms of matter. As we have seen, Deleuze and Guattari's analysis relies on Simondon's work showing that hylomorphic conceptions of production are based in the social conditions of slave society: all production is credited to the direction provided by the eidetic vision and ordering command of the architect/master/ruler. The work of the artisan is unworthy of notice; he only follows orders, merely allows the realization of form in matter. He himself is in need of direction from above, and the matter with which he works is only a hindrance to the reproduction of form. Plato thus either sees artisanal labour as in need of philosophic direction (childrearing nurses attending to the implicit forms of human psyche and somatic body, for instance, as we will see in our analysis of *Laws*, 7), or as mere production of bodily means, to be controlled by a science of ends (Plato, *Gorgias*, 517e; *Statesman*, 287d).

From our perspective, then, Plato gives too much credit to architectonic techne in production: all overarching, finalized order is due to technical logos rather than artisanal sensitivity, even in those passages in which an artisanal 'persuasion of necessity' is thematized. Regarding the inputs to production, Plato ignores or denigrates material self-ordering, which happens without psychic control; regarding the production process itself, Plato ignores or denigrates artisanal sensitivity, which happens without logos. Thus he has the wrong conception of production, focusing on techne in the strict sense, the perception and command of the architect, rather than on 'stochastic techne' as the aesthetic sensitivity of artisans – even when he seems to be talking about artisans. According to the Simondonian and Deleuzoguattarian analyses of production, the appearance of an ordered object – which the architect thinks is the result of his vision directing the artisanal imposition of form on chaotic matter – is really due to artisanal sensitivity to operations linking the way actual traits express virtual singularities of material self-ordering so that a material system can be coaxed to one of its thresholds of self-ordering.

Platonic hylomorphism is uncritical in the strong Deleuzean/Kantian sense: it posits that order must have an ordered source. But such positing accounts for the production process in terms garnered from the state of the products. In other words, to account for ordered products Plato posits a prior order as the source of the ordered product, because he denies that order could arise from the chance/ necessity of the collision of atoms. But this Platonic attack on atomism assumes that a material system is mechanist in the sense of being nothing but a collection of parts. From the perspective of complexity theory, however, it's the total systematic interrelations plus implicit self-ordering processes that produce order, as virtual self-ordering potentials are actualized via either natural processes or artisanal sensitivity. As we saw in the Introduction, the secret of the success of Deleuze and Guattari in working out the implications of contemporary science is thus their ability to construct a non-mechanistic materialism via their distinction between the virtual self-ordering processes and the actual properties of physical systems.

The production of the Platonic body politic is thoroughly hylo-morphic, either in the ideal case of the *Republic* and the first half of the *Timaeus*, where the royal science has a clean slate to work with, or in the cases that appear to grapple with material or historical content, such as the second part of the *Timaeus* and the *Laws*. Even these seemingly artisanal cases still betray a fundamental hylomorphism, as matter is never a positive contribution to order and artisanal labour needs philosophic rescue. In our examination of Platonic hylomorphism we will thus attend to overlooked material self-ordering and to overlooked or denigrated artisanal labour: body and soul in man (*Ion; Republic*); childrearing in the household (*Laws*), custom in the city (*Republic; Statesman; Laws*), and necessity in the cosmos (*Timaeus*).

Let us now consider each of the registers of the Platonic body politic.

BODY AND SOUL IN MAN

The key to uncritical Platonic hylomorphism is the denigration of the somatic knowledge and aesthetic sensitivity of artisans in favour of psychic logos and architectonic vision and command. The connection of body (aesthetics, chaotic motion) and soul (logos, self-caused regular motion) in man is thus crucial to understand. As we have maintained, the psychic body politic is the key notion here, as soul is to rule the body as master (Plato, *Timaeus*, 34c).

For Plato, the body is the point of contact of soul and world. Although he provides a detailed physiology in the second part of the Timaeus, it's enough for us to notice that material 'influx and efflux' cause the psychic motions known as sensation, pleasure, pain and emotion (fear, anger and the like, Plato, *Timaeus*, 42ab). As provoking such a cauldron of unruly motions, the body can only be only a hindrance to intellection, although its passions can be tamed and hence the hindrance minimized. Now let's be clear that Plato would never accept a characterization of intellection as a flight from the body. Plato knows perfectly well, even though he sounds like he regrets the fact at times (e.g. Plato, *Phaedo*, 66d), that while living the philosopher will always be embodied: the key is to have a certain kind of body, a philosophic one whose passions and pleasures come from knowing (Plato, *Republic*, 485d).

We can attempt an explanation of the Platonic attitude to the body's drag on knowledge through reference to the Greek male aristocratic disdain of the biological realm as one of unfreedom and necessity. The daily bodily needs of the citizen are to be met by the labour of others so that the citizen is free for politics, war and perhaps philosophy. When the system of meeting bodily needs is in place and working well, it fades into the background, hidden behind the important things.[16] Similarly, we can surmise that, for Plato, when the body is fit, trained into harmony, well-fed and rested, then bodily actions and states become transparent, fading into a background so one can concentrate on the object of intellection. But that doesn't mean the philosopher has literally left his body, only that it has faded into the background, just as the labour of women and slaves fades into the background of the city.[17] Thus the body in man, like women and slaves in the household, and workers in the city, can never be sources of knowledge: all they can do is get in the way. The two forms of distraction, desires stemming from the body and the eco-political entanglements they entail, are linked at *Phaedo* (66d) in the notion of leisure:

All wars are undertaken for the acquisition of wealth, and the reason why we have to acquire wealth is the body, because we are slaves in its service. That is why, on all these accounts, we have so little time [*ascholian*] for philosophy. Worst of all, if we do obtain any leisure [*scholē*] from the body's claims and turn to some line of inquiry, the body intrudes once more . . .

(On this point, see the link of bodily desire, wealth and war at *Republic*, 373de; we will consider leisure in a Heideggerian/Aristotelian context in Chapter 6.)

Another important clue to the chaotic somatic body in Plato is his view of medicine. At *Gorgias* (504a) we read that doctors 'give order [*kosmousi*] and discipline to the body'. Here is an explicit example of a technical origin to the order of a somatic body plagued by a tendency to disorder. (Plato, *Statesman*, 273b-e, gives a mythic account of 'the bodily [*to sēmatoeides*]' as the source of cosmic disorder which is fixed by divine cosmo-medical technical intervention: 'he takes control of the helm once more. Its former sickness he heals'.) These medical interventions are but specific cases of the general psychic control of the somatic in the cosmos. But there are social–political implications to mundane medical intervention to combat somatic chaos. The doctor should only step in to fix 'wounds and an attack of seasonable diseases'; it is shameful to use medicine to supplement the failure of regulated custom, that is, education (Plato, *Republic*, 405c). Although Plato uses medicine as an example of a techne that can be imposed on someone against their will for their own good (Plato, *Statesman*, 293b), such use of medicine to remedy the deleterious somatic effects of a poor lifestyle is shameful for a man who should have been in possession of a self-directing somatic body politic, just as one would be shamed in the city at having 'a justice imposed upon one by others, as by masters and judges, because of one's lack of inner resources' (Plato, *Republic*, 405b). In these cases, one is a slave to the body that should be one's slave; one has a perverted body politic, for 'it is a good soul which by its own excellence ensures that the body shall be as fit as possible' (403d). In these matters Plato is strict enough to insist that excessive recourse to medicine to remedy any somatic defect, lifestyle-related or not, destroys either the practice of a craft and the contribution to the city that makes a craftsman's life worth living to him (406d–7a) or the leisure necessary for eco-polemico-politico-philosophical action:

Excessive concern for the body beyond physical training is pretty well the greatest obstacle of all; it puts difficulties in the way of managing a household, of military service, or of holding a sedentary public office. The worst of it is that it makes difficulties with regard to learning of any kind, or thought, or self-training . . . (Plato, *Republic*, 407bc)

To avoid such shameful dependence by regulating the somatic body and thus achieving the philosophic corporeal body is the task of education. There are two main images of education in the *Republic*: education as moulding or shaping of soul, and education as harmonizing of chaotic motion. Both posit an external psychic source of order in the soul and then in the soul/body corpus. Both are examples of the imposition of determinacy on indeterminacy.

The first notion, education as moulding or shaping of soul, fits the restricted sense of hylomorphism as imposition of form on matter. At *Republic* (377b) we read that music is to be employed before gymnastics in order to seize the moment of youth in children, for 'it is then that it [sc. the soul] is best molded and takes the impression that one wishes to stamp upon it'. Similarly, at 396d–e we learn that the good man 'shrinks in distaste from molding and fitting himself to the types of baser things'. The prime example of the production of humans in the restricted hylomorphic sense of the imposition of form on matter is, of course, the noble lie myth. Here the people are to be told that they have been fashioned out of the material of earth, with the earth as their mother and nurse (414e; see also 470d). We cannot forget, however, that the matter/form schema of the noble lie is presented as a lie by Socrates to Glaucon, even though it is presented as a plausible schema for the inhabitants of the city.

The more profound notion of education, the one with which Socrates carries on his discussion with Glaucon, is the harmonizing of chaotic motion, which falls under the generic Platonic sense of production as the rendering determinate of indeterminancy. But Plato never goes into real detail on how this psychic harmonizing is to occur, and this is the clue to the hylomorphic conception of the production of man in the Platonic body politic. For example, in the discussion of music in *Republic* 3, Socrates claims not to know anything about the exact ways in which musical modes and rhythms affect the soul. He simply describes what he wants, and lets Glaucon (399a) or Damon the expert (400b) identify which ones would work. This is precisely the architectonic viewpoint: he sets the ends and the artisan chooses the means. The idea of musical education, as we know, is to harmonize the soul before it is capable of logos so that it is prepared in such a way that it can receive logos. In other words, we find here the profoundly Platonic emotional/aesthetic basis of moral judgment: 'He will rightly object to what is ugly and hate it while still young before he can grasp the reason, and when reason comes he who has been reared thus will welcome it and easily recognize it because of its kinship with himself' (402a). Here the harmonized soul is the goal of musical education; the philosopher sets forth the criterion of a harmonized soul, but it is left to the artisanal labour of craftsmen set to work under philosophic direction to choose the exact components of the musical regime that will produce the harmonious soul. 'But we must look for those craftsmen who by the happy gift of nature are capable of following the trail of true beauty and grace . . .' (401c).

When it comes to the harmonized body, Socrates' discussion of gymnastics is similarly architectonic, that is, hylomorphic. Socrates lays down the telos, the harmonized body, yet remains vague and abstract about the means of realizing this end, despite the mention of Corinthian girls and Attic pastries (Plato, *Republic*, 404d) as deleterious. Socrates begins the discussion by disclaiming the need to attend to the details of gymnastics by pointing out that the previous psychic training by means of music will be sufficient to produce a good body: 'For I, for my part, do not believe that a sound body by its excellence makes the soul good, but on the contrary that a good soul by its virtue renders the body the best that is possible' (403d). After winning assent on this point from Glaucon, Socrates continues:

> Thus if we should sufficiently train the mind [*dianoian*] and turn over to it the minutiae of the care of the body, and content ourselves merely indicating the norms or patterns [*tupous*], not to make a long story of it, we should be acting rightly? (Plato, *Republic*, 403d)

Here again the technical architect is content to lay down the patterns and leave to the artisans what he assumes will be the imposition of this pattern in a plastic matter.

Platonic somatic, psychic and anthropological education is ultimately a matter of the technical establishment of the organic body politic. Justice is internal self-rule which establishes harmony, order and unity, as we note in the following passage which uses the key body-political terms of household (*oikos*: what is one's own), *archē*, cosmos and unity to describe psychic order: '[Justice] means that a man . . . should dispose well of what in the true sense of the word is properly his own and having first attained to self-mastery [*archanta auton autou*] and beautiful order within himself, and having harmonized these three principles . . . and having linked and bound all three together and made of himself a unit, one man instead of many . . .' (443de).

The conclusion of *Republic* 4 reinforces the body politic one last time in an explicit analogy of health and justice via the production of domination according to nature, with disease and injustice resulting from misrule.

> But to produce health in the body is to establish the elements of the body in the natural relation of dominating and being dominated [*kata phusin kathistanai kratein te kai krateisthai*], while to cause disease is to bring it about that one rules or is ruled by the other contrary to nature [*to de noson para phusin archein te kai archesthai allo hup allou*]. . . . And is it not likewise the production of justice in the soul to establish its principles in the natural relation of controlling and being controlled [*kata phusin kathistanai kratein te kai krateisthai*] by one another, while injustice is to cause the one to rule or be ruled [*archein te kai archesthai*] by the other contrary to nature? (Plato, *Republic*, 444d)

Several things are important to notice about the translation. To translate *kratein* as 'domination' in body but 'control' in soul softens the Greek, which is identical in both cases. We should also note the difference between health and justice as domination (*kratein* is a household term, which Bloom insightfully translates as 'mastery') vs disease and injustice as rule (*archein*): an implicit slap at democracy, or even at any politics not conceived as mastery?

After this treatment of the body politic in the *Republic*'s system of education, we can now ask about the resources of the body overlooked in the *Republic*'s account of education. The body of the philosopher is a key organism in the Platonic body politic. What is the positive contribution of the body that Plato overlooks, analogous to the similarly overlooked positive contribution of material self-ordering tapped into by artisans in production?

We must not think that the *Republic's* recognition of natural differences amounts to a recognition of implicit somatic form, for the body is still only hindrance, not a positive contribution to the organic body politic of the city. The very reason for the noble lie at 415a–c is that, even in the harmonious city, the unruly somatic body renders breeding unpredictable. The meritocratic solution is to test for aptitude at learning across class and gender lines (Plato, *Republic*, 455b). But this testing for a philosophic constitution is precisely testing to what extent one can be trained to give up the pleasures of the body as hindrances to knowledge (485d; see also Plato, *Phaedo*, 66d–7a). There's never any Platonic hint of the body as positive contribution to knowledge. This latter notion would be part of the basis for a radical anti-Platonism, which would link such a rehabilitation of somatic epistemic positivity to two themes of Deleuze and Guattari, the rehabilitation of indeterminacy (the virtual as positive pool of resources: the BwO) and the attack on *a priori* philosophy (the emphasis on pragmatics and experimentation), in addition to Deleuze's previous formulation of anti-Platonism as the rehabilitation of the simulacrum.[18]

The philosophic resources for thinking the body's epistemic positivity lie in the contemporary 'embodied mind' school, one of the most important areas of contemporary philosophy.[19] We cannot go into details here, but a fruitful line of research would be to posit that Plato takes ideal prototypes of basic-level categories[20] as real, and then performs various conceptual operations upon them to produce the highest kinds (*Sophist*) and the Good/One (*Republic*), thereby making abstraction and transcendence the hallmark of philosophy. Further, I would suggest that these operations attain their prestige because they require a calm, leisured somatic and corporeal body politic which provides free time for reflection, thus distinguishing philosophers from workers within the civic body politic. By then claiming that the contents of philosophical abstract cognition are more real than the contents of somatic/aesthetic artisanal sensitivity, Plato ontologically justifies philosophical rule. But the alleged ontological superiority of higher-level concepts as the components of philosophical discourse doesn't account for its systematic or orderly nature. For that, Plato needs to posit the philosophers as possessors of logos, that is, as able to create plans based on part–whole relations and to direct the action of others to far-off ends. This ability, we might say, is the cosmo-justification of philosophical rule, the ability to organ-ize a body politic, while the ability to effectuate those plans, to produce the organic body politic, reveals the forceful nature of the body politic.

PRODUCTION IN THE HOUSEHOLD

Production of the material support for the life of all and for the good life of the citizens occurs for Plato on the model of household relations between master and slave, even if *demiourgos* literally meant one who worked for the people, the *demos*, as an independent craftsman, and even if artisans are technically speaking citizens of the city of the *Republic*. However in that ideal city they are 'citizens' without a voice in the decision-making of the city, a task reserved for the guardians. In the *Republic*, artisans speak only in pathological democracy; in the *Laws*, they are not citizens (Plato, *Laws*, 846d). Thus no matter the economic or political status of real artisans, Plato reflected on production in terms of the relation of master to slave characteristic of the household, which is why teaching, the hallmark of techne, is conceived as command, the characteristic relation of master to slave.[21] At *Ion* (537aff) we find that Socrates wants to convince Ion that he doesn't speak from knowledge about all subjects, even those in Homer. For instance, Socrates says, Homer says lots about the arts, e.g. driving a chariot. Socrates then asks Ion to recite a passage in the *Iliad* from the funeral games of Patroclus in which Nestor instructs Antilochus about the upcoming chariot race. In Socrates' demand we see that teaching by logos is the test of techne. Socrates then wants to know whether a doctor or a charioteer will be better suited to judge whether Nestor's instructions are good hallmarks of his possessing the charioteering techne.

This line of questioning betrays a skewed, hylomorphic, conception of techne, overlooking artisanal labour and privileging the commands of the master. Mere words as instructions can only be implemented by a trained body, so it's the prior bodily training that is the test of chariot driving teaching. In order to judge Nestor's skill at teaching we would have to examine the regime of training that Nestor set up for Antilochus, gradually increasing – through artisanal sensitivity to the boy's performance at each level – the complexity and intensity of exercises so that the boy's somatic sensitivity could be refined. On the other hand, it is chariot driving itself that is the mark of the techne of chariot driving, so we would have to observe Nestor's driving, not his instructions, to judge his skill at chariot driving. Thus there's a double problem with Socrates' demand: techne is judged by production, not teaching, while teaching is not accomplished by commands, but by setting up a regime of somatic training.

Once again, then, in this example we see the hylomorphic emphasis on exterior command in the production of a body politic. Technical teaching is important, but it does not consist of instructions to be obeyed, but in setting up a regime of exercises in which trainees develop somatic skill. Thus the relation of teacher/student is not that of master/slave: a regime of exercises is not an order given on the spot, but an artisanal coaxing that actualizes a certain combination of the virtual potentials of the student's body. The most radical point of our analysis is that somatic skill is more complex than instructions, more precise, more refined. The challenge of contemporary anti-Platonism is to turn around logo-prejudice: it is words that are clumsy, abstract, and so on, not the somatic skills long associated with a brute and stupid 'body'.[22]

But doesn't Socrates explicitly say that, of all the people he surveyed in Athens, only the artisans had a techne, only they knew anything at all? Of course, but again, we must presume that Socrates thinks the artisans of Athens have techne because they have supplementary logos, that they are able to explain their production, not because of somatic skill that enables that production. At *Apology* 22d Socrates tells the jury that although 'craftsmen [*cheirotechnas*]' have specific knowledge, they err when claiming knowledge outside their expertise: 'on the strength of their technical proficiency they claimed a perfect understanding of every other subject, however important. . . .' Presumably they have a supplementary logos for their productive techne but err when they attempt a logos that purports to demonstrate a political techne. Once again, however, we must ask if it is by the possession of logos that artisans produce? An affirmative answer is, I submit, only the hylomorphic assumption at work. For Deleuze and Guattari, as we have seen, production is due to the artisanal/aesthetic following of the machinic phylum, the coaxing forth of material self-organization. Thus even though the artisans Socrates interviews have a psychic logos, that's not how they produce; they produce by aesthetic sensitivity. In other words, Socrates is impressed by their psychic logos, their 'knowing that', but it's their somatic skill, their artisanal sensitivity, their 'know how', that allows them to produce.

To consider artisanal labour at the intersection of household and city, let us examine *Laws* 7, the most detailed account of childrearing Plato gives us. Here the difference between *Republic* and *Laws* is very interesting. In the *Republic*, the philosopher-king has a hylomorphic view of the body as input to an educational production he commands from afar, from 'outside the workshop': he simply commands that a reward/punishment system be set up that will produce the correct aesthetic/emotional/moral response, but doesn't have the hands-on knowledge of childrearing as artisanal labour. The Athenian in *Laws* 7 does, on the other hand, recognize such artisanal child-rearing labour. However, since this labour must be philosophically directed, the home is to be regulated, not by law, but by rational instruction, by rational reform of custom. So the philosopher is still in charge. When artisanal labour is recognized, it must be regulated from above, used as means to an end, rendered as an organ submitted to the overall functioning of an organism.

At the beginning of *Laws* 7, the Athenian warns against overlooking the cumulative impact of trivial domestic transgressions on the character of the citizens:

the privacy of home life screens from the general observation many little incidents, too readily occasioned by a child's pains, pleasures, and passions, which are not in keeping with a legislator's recommendations, and tend to bring a medley of incongruities into the characters of citizens. (Plato, *Laws*, 788a)

Thus, despite the seeming indignity of paying attention to such matters, the legislator must attend to them and instruct the citizens, even though he refrains from legislating about them:

> Now this is an evil for the public as a whole, for while the frequency and triviality of such faults make it both improper and undignified to penalize them by law, they are a real danger to such law as we impose, since the habit of transgression is learned from repetition of these petty misdeeds. Hence although we are at a loss to legislate on such points, silence about them is also impossible. (Plato, *Laws*, 788c)

The discussion of domestic order as the basis of civic order begins by proposing that the perfection of body and soul is the *telos* of the legislator's instructions to the household (Plato, *Laws*, 788c). The discussion then focuses on the body, a departure from the procedure of the *Republic* in which somatic education followed psychic. The Athenian proposes that attention must be paid to the effect of maternal exercise on the embryo (789b), to the shock of Clinias. The prospect of legislating maternal exercise, says the Athenian, would entail that the infant be seen as so much wax to be moulded (789d). In keeping with the Platonic predilection for the harmonizing model of education, such a restricted (matter/form) hylomorphism is proposed only to be shown as unworthy of philosophic interest despite its utility as an image for the masses, as was the case with the noble lie of the *Republic*. Despite the laughability of legislating such matters to the slavewomen who serve as nurses (Plato, *Laws*, 790a; but we will see later that slave nurses are the linchpin of the entire educational system), they must be discussed, so that 'masters and freemen', i.e. heads of households, will recognize the need for proper household regulation as the foundation of public virtue. In so doing, the citizens will take these instructions as 'laws' for themselves and as patterns to be looked at in their 'administration' of house and city (790b). So while the restricted matter–form sense of hylomorphism is rejected as an analytic tool, the wider sense of hylomorphism as architectonic vision establishing order is retained.

When it comes to the training of infants' souls, a similar discussion must be held, the Athenian continues (Plato, *Laws*, 790c). The infants' souls are to be harmonized by a primitive form of music, the lullaby (790e). Plato here relies on unthematized custom for the most efficacious selection of these songs and on the caregiver's sensitivity and skill in delivering them at the proper time, with proper intensity and proper rhythm. He sets the context for their use, but cannot discuss the details of the lullaby or its somatic/psychic effects. When he does attempt to indicate how the lullaby works, he has recourse to a political term ('domination'), a further indication of the fundamentally forceful nature of the Platonic body politic, which informs every relation of part/whole, even reaching to the very level of the lullaby: 'fright is due to some morbid condition of soul. Hence, when such disorders are treated by rocking movements the external motion thus exhibited dominates [*kratei*] the internal, which is the source of the fright or frenzy' (790e). A further proof of Plato's reliance on the artisanal labour of caregivers in these early, critical days of psychic training occurs at 792a where the harmonizing of the body of the infant with regard to the placidity of its temper must also rely on the 'guesswork [*tekmairontai*]' of nurses, who are able to discern the proper course of action in placating a screaming child.

That despite this recognition of the sensitivity of nurses Plato maintains an essential hylomorphic view of childrearing is clear in the discussion of the preference for one hand over another at 794e. Instead of recognizing such a preference as an implicit form of the body with which artisanal childrearers deal, Plato derides the preference of one hand over the other as due to 'the folly of nurses and mothers'. Proper philosophic direction of childrearing, if properly implemented by obedient artisanal childrearers, would eliminate such preference. Here we see once again a restricted sense of hylomorphism, as this is a clear example of an architectonic view of the material of production – the body of the child – as plastic and receptive of the form proposed by the direction of the architect and implemented by the labour of the artisan.

RULE AND CUSTOM IN THE CITY

In moving to discuss the technical production of the civic body politic, we must at first note two models of statesmanship in Plato: one presupposes a *tabula rasa* regarding pre-existing custom and relies on the knowledge of the ruler beyond agreement or law (*Statesman*; *Republic*); the other presupposes the existence of custom and relies on the rule of law, supplemented by an advisory council (*Laws*). While the distinction between the two models seems to conform to the distinction between the architectonic and the artisanal point of view – that is, imposing a form on chaotic matter (or more precisely, harmonizing a chaotic motion) vs working with available materials – both however conform to the hylomorphic and architectonic suspicion of artisanal labour and material self-ordering. Even though these latter factors are at least acknowledged in the *Laws*, they still stand in need of philosophic direction and redemption from on high.

The *Statesman* defines 'ruling [*tēn basilikēn*]' as knowing how 'to control the powers of acting . . . according to its power to perceive the right occasions for undertaking and setting in motion the great enterprises of the city' (Plato, *Statesman*, 305d). The person possessing such knowledge need not secure agreement from the citizens, nor work with a fixed set of laws, no more than need a doctor or ship captain secure agreement from those with whom he deals or work with a fixed set of rules (293a; 296b–7a).[23] In the *Republic*, Socrates practices this techne with regard to the character of the citizens of the ideal city, a techne he implicitly denied was possible in cosmopolitan Athens in examining the sophists' implicit claims of being like horse trainers (*Apology*, 20c).

The key in the *Republic* for the practice of the kingly science is the *tabula rasa* of a construction in logos, looking only to principles and paradigms. As we know, Socrates hedges on the possibility of realizing the ideal city; one clue as to its difficulty is the exiling of all over age of 10 (Plato, *Republic*, 541a).[24] The ideal city of the *Republic* is a construction in logos, built according to a heavenly model (592b; see also 484cd). Socrates finds the principle of the first city in need (369b) and then proposes to 'make' a city in logos according to this principle (*tōi logōi ex archēs poiōmen polin*, 369c). The principle of the city develops, however, until the principle of a just city is announced as something we can paraphrase as 'doing the one task for which one is naturally suited' (433a). This principle is then said to be 'a sort of principle and mould of justice [*tina eis archēn te kai tupon tina*]' (443b). This insistence on models and paradigms to which the architect of the city looks amply demonstrates the technical side of the production of the Platonic body politic in the ideal case of the *Republic*.

Let us here move to consider the status of the *Laws* with regard to hylomorphic production. The city proposed in the *Laws* is the second best, the best earthly approximation of the ideal sketched in the *Republic* (739e). The grappling with historical reality in the *Laws* led Glenn Morrow, one of its leading twentieth-century commentators, to intimate that the *Laws* is more artisanal than the *Republic*. Morrow writes that in the *Laws* the legislator must possess 'a more intimate understanding of the materials that the statesman has to use'.[25] Morrow thus relates the action of the legislator of the *Laws* to the Demiurge's dealing with necessity, which is glossed as dealing with the 'material of empirical science' (Morrow, 'The Demiurge in politics', 1954, 8). But this latter phrase should be construed in the objective genitive as well, to reveal Morrow's perhaps unwitting testimony to Plato's hylomorphic stance in the *Laws*, for we must insist that the material posited by empirical science is not the material with which artisan works; 'empirical science' is still 'royal science' in Deleuze and Guattari's terms, that is, the establishment of laws between constants rather than the 'nomad science' of the artisan working with continuous variations of matter (ATP, 446–64/361–74). Morrow further demonstrates the hylomorphic nature of the Demiurge when he says that:

> [t]he *Laws* shows that Plato did not shrink from the task of putting his political ideal into a determinate form . . . To accept the disadvantages [of the material at hand] is the mark of the demiurge in Plato. (10–11; 12)

But the conception of matter as recalcitrant to an ideal to be realized, as containing 'disadvantages', is hylomorphism *par excellence*, the architect's perspective. The artisan's work is to track the machinic phylum and bring out the positivity of matter as implicit form. For the artisan, matter is never the site of the 'task' of formation; it is never 'recalcitrant', but always a positive contribution to order.

What is the material for the city with which the legislator must work? This can only be custom, and let us note that Plato is almost always condescending toward non-philosophically directed custom. One of the most noteworthy instances of Plato's negative image of non-technically reformed custom is that of the production of social insects:

> I suppose that the happiest people, and those who reach the best destination, are the ones who have cultivated the goodness of an ordinary citizen – what is called self-control and integrity – which is acquired by habit and practice, without the help of philosophy and reason . . . they will probably pass into some kind of social and disciplined creature like bees, wasps, and ants . . . (Plato, *Phaedo* 82a)

Similar passages are strewn throughout the dialogues; the trouble produced in cities without philosophical direction is of course the basis for the reforms proposed in the *Republic* and the *Laws*.

In the early dialogues, Plato investigates Socratic *elenchos* as a method for the purification of custom. But Socrates' refutation of claims that virtue can be taught provides neither an overarching vision of the good city, nor the ability to achieve cultural homogeneity in the complex social and historical dynamics of cosmopolitan Athens, hence the technically legitimated philosopher kings of the *Republic* and their *tabula rasa*. As we have seen, household childrearing, which is beneath the level of legislation, is a key element in the production of the healthy organic body politic. Given the *tabula rasa* of the *Republic* the hylo-morphic legislator can design an unchangeable regime of children's play which, when correctly instituted, will correct degenerate custom:

> When the children play the right games from the start, they absorb obedience to the law through their training in the arts, quite the opposite of what happens in those who play lawless games. This lawfulness follows them in everything, fosters their growth, and can

correct anything that has gone wrong before in the city. (Plato, *Republic*, 425b)

With this base of a properly harmonized soul, unremarkable customs of social and bodily comportment – all of which enforce the hierarchies and reveal the statuses essential to the organic function of the body politic – are preserved from deleterious innovation:

> They then discover those conventions which seem unimportant, all of which those who came before them have destroyed . . . when it is proper for the young to be silent in the company of elders, how they should sit at table, when to give up their seat, care for their parents, hair styles, what clothes and shoes to wear, deportment, and the other things of that kind. (Plato, *Republic*, 425ab)

The disciplining of the body politic in the registers of man, household and city operates below the level of political legislation, reinforcing the need for the *tabula rasa* which enables philosophic control of psychic and somatic education: 'I think it is foolish to legislate about such things. Verbal or written decrees will never make them come about or last . . . They are likely to follow as necessary consequences from the direction one's education takes' (Plato, *Republic*, 425bc).

The situation in the *Laws* is only superficially different from that of the *Republic* regarding custom. It is true that in the *Laws* there is no *tabula rasa*, that the legislator must work with custom.[26] As we have seen, the household artisanal childrearing that forms the character of the future citizens needs the hands-on knowledge of nurses of the implicit somatic forms found in their charges. This embodied sensitivity of the artisanal nurses is passed on in customary child-rearing practices in which the nurses are trained, just as the somatic knowledge of other hand workers is passed on in apprenticeship. Despite its acknowledgment of custom and artisanal labour, the architectonic view remains in force in the *Laws*: custom is to be directed; labour is to be supervised. Custom, the 'unwritten laws' should 'neither be designated laws nor left unformulated' (Plato, *Laws*, 793b). Custom must be philosophically directed so that the second best, the closest approximation to the ideal, can be realized. In this crucial passage Plato's hylomorphic conception of custom is clear, as he shifts from custom as a protective covering to custom as degenerate building material. When 'rightly instituted and duly followed in practice', custom will 'serve to wrap up securely the laws already written' (793b). Thus the proper role of custom is nothing positive and productive but only preservative of the vision of the legislator, a prophylaxis. However, when customs deviate from their correct purpose of guiding the formation of the organic body politic, when they 'perversely go aside from the right way', they desert their roles as support for the architectonic legislator's vision. To bring home the role of customs as material Plato uses the classic image of the building: 'like builder's props [*hoion tektonōn en oikodomē-masin*] that collapse under the middle of a house, they bring down everything else tumbling down along with them, one thing buried under another, first the props themselves and then the fair superstructure, once the ancient supports have fallen down' (793c). No clearer image of custom as matter in need of philosophic rescue is possible than this one of a crumbling house. Here the restricted hylomorphism of matter and form, which Plato usually eschews as too crude for sustained philosophical analysis, is put to use to illustrate the dependence of custom on philosophical direction.

REASON AND NECESSITY IN THE COSMOS

For Plato, cosmogenesis is the technical harmonizing of the material and psychic motion of the universe. In all the dialogues that at least mention cosmogenesis or issues related to cosmology (*Phaedrus* (245c), *Republic* (530a); *Sophist* (265c), *Statesman* (269c), *Philebus* (26e; 28d), *Timaeus*, *Laws* (896a)) Plato is consistent in maintaining a transcendent and non-material source of cosmic order. However, since 'source' (*archē*) is ambiguous between origin and principle, the exact nature of that source changes in different dialogues. In *Republic*, *Timaeus*, and *Statesman* the origin of cosmic order is unambiguously named a divine craftsman or Demiurge, who is not a soul,[27] but in *Phaedrus* and *Laws* the principle of cosmic order is self-moving soul. Some commentators will attempt to read the Demiurge as merely an image of the principle of order, so that the stories of the origin of cosmic order are considered mythic rather than realistic; others disagree and uphold a literal reading of the origin of cosmic order as divine technical production. Strictly speaking, the topic of our investigation, the hylomorphic conception of cosmos, does not require us to make a stand on the issue of the literal or mythic status of the Demiurge or on the compatibility of these two sets of dialogues, as both Demiurge and soul are exterior to the systems they control (cosmos as soul/body complex and cosmos as material system respectively). Furthermore, the soul in the *Laws* is specifically said to produce a technical and non-natural order (Plato, *Laws*, 892b) and to rule over the bodily (896c); thus we see a technical political physics in these passages which brings the *Laws* doctrine close to that of the Demiurgic dialogues. However, regardless of the nuances of specialist scholarship in Platonic cosmology concerning these points, given the spread of scholarly opinion we can pursue a literal reading of cosmogenesis and concentrate on the technical nature of the Demiurge, his use of number.

Plato's cosmology is always set against the materialist atomists, who posit a type of material self-ordering as responsible for cosmic order. Plato's argument against the materialists rests on his splitting of logos and necessity, which the atomists equate;[28] Plato consequently equates necessity with irrational chance (Plato, *Laws*, 889b; *Philebus* 28d). After this reduction to irrationality, necessity is rendered a subsidiary cause to be persuaded by reason (Plato, *Timaeus*, 46d). In addition to the reduction of necessity to irrationality, Plato incorporates the materialist principle of like–like attraction, but restricts its effects; for Plato, like–like attraction is productive not of cosmic order but only of the irrational pre-condition of that which is to be taken over by the Demiurge (Plato, *Timaeus*, 53a–b), the input to his productive process. Since there is evident order in the universe and since matter by Plato's definition is capable only of blind chance or, at best, via the attraction of like to like, is capable of only traces of elemental nature, then only an external source can produce order in a material system. (The cosmological argument against the atomists is tied in with the alleged bad political effects of atheism (Plato, *Laws*, 890a). In this regard we might refer to Aristotle at *Politics*, 1287a28: 'He who recommends that reason (*nous*) should rule may be regarded as recommending that God and the laws should rule'.)

Parallel to the question of the source of cosmic order, of course, is that of the source of physical disorder. One school, exemplified by Harold Cherniss,[29] sees soul as the source of all motion; therefore disorder must come from irrational soul; here matter is seen as utterly passive. The argument is set forth at *Phaedrus* (245) and *Laws* (891), where we read that all motion must have a self-mover as source. Since bodies cannot move themselves, and since the soul is a self-mover, then it is the source of all motion, disorderly as well as orderly. The other school, exemplified by Mohr[30] and Vlastos,[31] argues against extending the *Laws* argument to *Timaeus* and *Statesman* and sees material motion as the source of disorder; here matter is seen as active and tending to the chaotic, though with an inherent capacity for some tentative and fragile order. On this reading, natural motion at best consists only of the attraction of like for like, which can produce only minimal order. Confirming the wide-ranging nature of the Platonic body politic, this chaotic physical motion is called 'bodily' in the *Statesman* myth.[32] On either reading, here again we see that Plato only considers the resistance of passive matter or the recalcitrance or indeed even rebelliousness of chaotic matter to the designs of the Demiurge, never the positive contributions of matter to order. Again, given the spread of scholarly opinion, we license ourselves to pursue a reading of matter as active rather than passive. On the most generous reading of active matter, material systems might have an internal order for Plato, but they are not externally directive: they cannot order a larger system toward the good, cannot produce an organic body politic. (Similarly, in economic terms, slaves will feed themselves every day, but in so doing reduce the household to ruin; in civic terms, democracy is a sort of regime, but one that produces only increasing disorder in the city.)

Let us now consider the trace of material self-ordering in the cosmos, the best known instance of which to be found in Plato's work is in the *Timaeus*. We will spend some time on this dialogue due to both its clarity in presenting our issues and to its ongoing historical importance. First of all, the cosmic register allows for a clear appreciation of the key elements of the Platonic body politic: the organic order of the cosmos is explicitly portrayed as the work of a divine technician. Secondly, the *Timaeus* is often regarded as the most commented upon work in the history of Western philosophy; it is the one Platonic dialogue to have exerted a constant influence on the Latin West during its period of Greeklessness.[33] One of the classic twentieth-century commentators, Cornford, brings forth the reason for our focus on the *Timaeus* in a perfect example of hylomorphic thought:

> Here, then, we may conclude that Plato's Demiurge, like the human craftsman in whose image he is conceived, operates upon materials which he does not create, and whose inherent nature sets a limit to his desire for perfection in his work. (Cornford, *Plato's Cosmology*, 1937, 37)

Cornford's comment is classically hylomorphic because it allows no positive contribution of matter to order; for him, matter can only limit the implementation of the vision of the 'craftsman'. The Demiurge, on this reading, is thus modelled on the architect rather than the artisan as conceived by Deleuze and Guattari; we will pursue this point throughout our reading.

The cosmological portion of the *Timaeus* is framed by several political narratives, one of which recapitulates the technical production of the organic body politic of the city in the *Republic*. We cannot treat the frame narratives, but instead move directly to Timaeus' first discourse, which displays a classic hylomorphism as the technical source of order.

> For God desired that, so far as possible, all things should be good and nothing evil; wherefore, when He took over all that was visible, seeing that it was not in a state of rest but in a state of discordant and disorderly motion, He brought it into order out of disorder. (Plato, *Timaeus*, 30a)

The first account of the demiurgic production of the cosmos, the transcendent imposition of order on chaos, occurs by the look to an eternal model. The universe must have a cause, and that cause is its 'maker and father' (28c). The choice confronting the paternal Demiurge at this point is that of models: eternal or created. Working backwards from the impiety of suggesting that the cosmos is not beautiful nor the Demiurge good, Timaeus can conclude the Demiurge looked to the eternal model to produce the beautiful cosmos as a copy (29a–b).

After the long account of pure imposition-style production, production through looking to an eternal model, Timaeus finds himself constrained to make a new beginning; here he offers the discourse from 'necessity', in which he explains how *nous* is constrained to 'persuade' the elements to accomplish its ends. In this account the motions of the elements become 'auxilliary causes' (Plato, *Timaeus*, 46c), which are used 'as servants [*huperetousi*]' of the Demiurge (46d). Thus the entire second discourse, the analysis of cosmogenesis from the perspective of the rational persuasion of necessity, will be a political physics, the struggle to tame the natural force of necessity, that which gives matter its 'violent potencies [*dynameis ischuras*; 33a4]'. The auxiliary causes move chaotically – they don't have 'reason [*logos*] or thought [*nous*]' (46d4–5); the necessary is chancy, so that the second account entails taking account of the 'errant cause' (48a8–9). The errant cause is to have its chaotic motion patterned, so that it acts for the best. Thus the second discourse is Plato's staging of Timaeus's attempt to bring the natural force of necessity to reason in the patterning of material motion via number, the very essence of techne.

At this point, let us be clear that cosmogenesis by the rational 'persuasion' of necessity is no escape from hylomorphism for Plato; the persuasion of necessity by reason is still the imposition of order by an external source. Vlastos notes that 'persuasion' (*peithō*) could be 'influence' or 'suggestion' as well as rational conviction. '*Peithō* means simply changing another's mind. It puts no strings on the way this is done'. Vlastos also notes the connotation of 'bribe' for *peithō* (Vlastos, *Platonic Studies*, 1981, 148n5). Vlastos' linguistic evidence is welcome, but not necessary; there is evidence enough with in the *Timaeus* to support my reading of persuasion as imposition. In the *Timaeus* persuasion works in a political physics, imposing a rule of reason on that which is without reason: 'reason was controlling (*archontos*) necessity by persuasion' (Plato, *Timaeus*, 47e). This rule by persuasion is not an internal rule freely adopted after argument, for persuasion is without logos (51e); that which rules in the cosmos, *nous*, is 'unmovable by persuasion' (51e); and that which is ruled, we recall, is without logos (46d). In this context then, 'persuasion' is indistinguishable from 'command', for what other name should be used for the bringing of elements without logos into order by a process that is itself without logos? Thus the 'persuasion' of material necessity in the *Timaeus* cannot be likened to the 'coaxing' of material self-ordering potentials we named in the Introduction as the work of the artisan; 'persuasion' in the *Timaeus* is thoroughly architectonic.[34]

After stating the object of the second discourse, Timaeus has by now reached the point where he introduces four accounts concerning the 'third kind' necessary for his new beginning – third, that is, after the pair of Being and Becoming used to begin the first discourse. We cannot enter into the details of all the arguments of these passages, which form one of the densest and most commented-upon sections of all the dialogues; we can only offer a reading oriented to our concerns with political physics and the technical production of the organic body politic of the cosmos. The first account (Plato, *Timaeus*, 48e–49b) introduces a third form, one which although 'baffling and obscure' is variously named the receptacle, the underlying appearance, the nurse. We will follow the different attributes given this third form. The third form, ultimately named *chôra*, will be the site of the struggle with the natural force of necessity, the site of the numeric patterning of material motion, the site wherein the political physics of the cosmic register of the Platonic body politic is enacted.

The second account occurs at 49b–50a, where Timaeus addresses the adequacy of language to articulate material motion outside the framework of the transcendent imposition of order on chaos; in other words, Timaeus here examines to what extent his conception of language is able to articulate the motion of matter 'itself' 'prior' to hylomorphic production. In Timaeus' account the elements (fire, air, water and earth) are indeterminate, and so should be only called 'such', while only that in which the elements appear should be called 'this'. There is an enormous literature on this point, which we cannot deal with in this context.[35]

The third account (Plato, *Timaeus*, 50a–51b) treats the third kind as characterless, like matter for shapes. Here we find the receptacle compared to gold that is constantly reforming shapes. Timaeus continues that the receptacle is 'laid down by nature as a moulding-stuff [ekmageion]' (50c), that which accepts determination while retaining the ability to receive other determinations. This is a key point. In her important article, 'Matter and flux in Plato's *Timaeus*' (1987), Gill reads the *ekmageion* attribution as a metaphor or image for the impassivity of the receptacle as a reflecting surface; thus the receptacle is not matter as this passage intimates on a literal reading (Plato, *Timaeus*, 48). Aristotle, however, takes precisely this literal reading and sees the receptacle as matter (Aristotle, *Physica*, 1950, 209b12–17). This will prove to be crucial for our concentration on technical production by numeric patterning, for Aristotle also uses *ekmageion* to describe the indeterminate dyad in its role as matter for the hylomorphic production of numbers (Aristotle, *Metaphysica*, 1957, 988a1).[36] Whether or not the receptacle is literally matter or only figuratively so in order to highlight its (non)-qualities as a good mirror, we see here hylomorphism: the inputs to production have no characters, no 'implicit forms', no positive contribution to produced order. Of further interest to us is the fact that in the passage we are considering, Timaeus specifies the materiality of *ekmageion* as that upon which figures can be inscribed: 'the figures that enter and depart are copies of those that are always existent [*onta aei*], being stamped [*tupothenta*] from them in a fashion marvelous and hard to describe' (Plato, *Timaeus*, 50c). In the word 'stamping' we read a forecast of the politics of physics we will describe shortly when Timaeus details the numeric patterning of natural motion into triangles. Production by stamping is the core meaning of 'persuading necessity', the imposition of order on passive and chaotic matter; 'stamping' is not persuasion in the sense of winning assent by argument.

The final account, a 'more exact reasoning', names the third kind as *chōra*, a word best left untranslated[37] (Plato, *Timeus*, 51b–3b). After an affirmative answer to the question of the existence of forms beyond sensible beings, Timaeus describes the three kinds: one is self-identical form, ungenerated and indestructible; the other is a sensible object; and the third kind is *chōra*, which 'admits not of destruction, and provides room for all things that have birth, itself being apprehensible by a kind of bastard reasoning . . . for when we regard this we dimly dream . . .' (52b)[38]

Timaeus next provides a summary of the four accounts (Plato, *Timaeus*, 52d1–3b), in which 'the nurse of becoming' receives the

impressed copies of forms, a reception that affects her quite dramati-
cally. The receptacle 'sways unevenly in every part, and is herself
shaken by these forms and shakes them in turn as she is moved' (52e).
This motion is said to be like that of a winnowing basket; in this
manner the motion of the recipient separates the dissimilar and
associates the similar, so that the four elements occupied different
places (*chōran*) before cosmogenesis (53a). Material self-ordering is
hinted at in these passages of the *Timaeus* in which the natural motion
of the receptacle, prior to the work of the Demiurge, produces 'traces
[*ichnē*]' of elemental self-identity (53b). This recognition of the minimal
precosmic order of matter is Plato's incorporation of the materialist
principle of like attracting like. But for Plato, such material self-
ordering, while not complete chaos, is 'devoid of reason and measure
[*alogôs kai ametrôs*]' (53b), and thus provides only the preconditions of
the Demiurge's ordering. Thus the traces of order in the precosmos
due to material self-ordering means that the techne of the Demiurge is
responsible only for 'rational order', not for all regularity.[39] But this
recognition of material self-ordering only serves to reinforce the
fundamental Platonic doctrine that only the techne of the Demiurge,
the royal science of mastery/kingship, can put things to work for
purposes, can fit parts into a functional unity, can form an organism as
the judgment of God, Deleuze and Guattari put it (ATP, 197/159).

How does the Demiurge produce order? Through a numerical
patterning of the elements. The Demiurge uses numbers, the tools of
reason, to dominate a chaotically moving matter and so produce a
cosmos.[40] Timaeus tells us that 'the god' began controlling material
motion, overpowering the natural force of necessity, by 'marking them
out into shapes [*dieschēmatisato*], by means of forms [*eidesi*] and numbers' (Plato, *Timaeus*, 53b). With this revealing of the arithmetical
principles of the elements Timaeus proceeds to posit the principles of
the elements as triangles (53d). The four elements, fire, air, water and
earth, are straightforwardly generated, but a fifth figure remains, which
the god must '(mis)use up [*katechrēsato*]' in 'decorating [*diazōgraphōn*]'
the all (55c).

Thus the technical work of cosmogenesis, the numerical patterning
of matter, produces an excess that must be used up by more
inscription. Now this writing away of the fifth figure would seem to

generate in turn more figures than could be controlled and would thus require more catachresis of the excess. Why is this important? By Aristotle's testimony, Platonic number is itself generated by inscription of the one on the indeterminate dyad (Aristotle, *Metaphysica*, 1957, 988a1). So when hylomorphically produced number is used to determine matter, to pattern the movements in and of the receptacle prior to the production of the cosmos, the doubling of hylomorphic production meets a limit: the attempt founders due to this prior production, a production *of* numbers that maddens production *by* numbers. Number rebels against reason by producing an order and excess beyond rational use, an excess figured as the 'fifth figure' that must be used up in non-utile 'decoration'. This mathematical excess is the trace of, not chaotic matter, but the force of material self-ordering, the natural force of necessity Timaeus sees dimly through the 'bastard reasoning' that focuses on the receptacle.

CONCLUSION

We have investigated six registers of the Platonic body politic (soul, body, man, household, city, cosmos), searching for the implicit hylomorphism of Plato's insistence upon an external technical source for corporeal organic order. In each register we traced Plato's privilege of architectonic vision over artisanal sensitivity, looking for traces of the notions of material self-organization and artisanal labour. Even when grudgingly acknowledged, however, artisanal sensitivity is derided by Plato as mere habit and in ultimate need of philosophical supervision, while material self-organization, even under the most generous interpretations of the *Timaeus*, only amounts to an alogical and non-orderly precondition for the numeric patterning of the Demiurge. Neither matter nor artisan deserves credit for the ordered product then; such credit belongs solely to architectonic vision and philosophical command.

Let us now turn to Aristotle, and to Heidegger's reading of Aristotle, to see a similar hylomorphism; rather than duplicate the detail of our reading of Plato and investigate all the facets of all the registers of the Aristotelian body politic, we will concentrate on the invisibility and/or denigration of artisanship in Heidegger's reading of *Metaphysica* 1.1–2.

CHAPTER 6

Philosophy and Leisure:
The Social Force of Necessity

Happiness extends, then, just so far as contemplation does
. . . But, being a man, one will also need external prosper-
ity; for our nature is not self-sufficient for the purpose of
contemplation; for our body must be healthy and must have
food and other attention. (Aristotle, *Nicomachean Ethics*)

Introduction
Heidegger's Effacement of the Body Politic
The Eco-Ontological Chiasm of Substance
Conclusion

INTRODUCTION

We have investigated in Chapter 5 the natural force of necessity, that
unpredictability of material motion which provides a trace of a concept
of material self-ordering in Plato's *Timaeus*. I suggested that Plato was
unable to thematize material self-ordering because of a tendency to either
overlook artisanal/aesthetic sensitivity (that which enables production by
coaxing forth the potentials for self-ordering of a physical system) or
denigrate it as mere habit in favour of a numeric and eidetic architec-
tonic/hylomorphic production (which imposes order on chaos from a
transcendent authority position). In this chapter I investigate this overlooking or denigration of artisanship as part of the *déformation professionelle*
of philosophers, the conviction that we're smarter and braver than the
great unwashed: all those bakers, bus drivers, housewives, scientists and
literary types about whom we all know deep down that they secretly
wish they could have been philosophers if only they had been able to rise
above their mundane preoccupations to reach the level of pure thought.

The invisibility or denigration of artisanal sensitivity, while first appearing in canonical Western philosophy with Plato, is a deep-rooted philosophical prejudice. My avenue to demonstrating the deep-seated nature of the invisibility or denigration of artisanal sensitivity is Heidegger's reading in his course on Plato's *Sophist* of Aristotle's first chapters in the *Metaphysics*. By showing that even the father of 'continental philosophy' repeats the hylomorphic privilege of the architect over the artisan I hope to show the radical break that Deleuze and Guattari's thematization of artisanal sensitivity to material self-ordering entails for the history of Western philosophy.

In this chapter, I use a brief interval in Heidegger's thought, his insight in 1928, announced in the *Metaphysical Foundations of Logic*, that ontology had an 'ontic presupposition' in the factical existence of Dasein and nature, to criticize his 1924–5 reading of Aristotle in the *Plato's Sophist* volume. I show two 'supplements' to the body politic – teaching for *technē* and leisure for *epistēmē* – that disrupt what Heidegger's reading of the beginning of the *Metaphysics* would have as a homogenous ladder of temporal comportments: *aisthēsis* (sensibility), *empeiria* (experience), *technē* (technique), *epistēmē* (science) and *sophia* (wisdom). Perhaps if Heidegger had pursued the ramifications of the thought of the ontic presupposition, he might have completed what he only started with his notion of being-in-the-world: the opening out of phenomenology from its focus on consciousness as 'origin of the world'[1] to a world of forceful bodies politic in which consciousness is an inscribed effect in a general text of force and signification. Instead, it was left to Derrida to pursue this route, as we have seen in Chapters 1 and 2. For now, let us pursue the social force of necessity in examining Heidegger's notion of the difficulty of philosophy.

Now we all know philosophy is difficult. Conceptually, physically, emotionally, politically, financially difficult. Heidegger found it easy to talk about this difficulty, and it appears as a major theme of 'the hermeneutics of factical life', the project of the early 1920s. The predecessor to the fundamental ontology pursued in *Being and Time*, the hermeneutics of factical life provides the framework for Heidegger's reading of Aristotle in *Plato's Sophist*.[2] Now, in the hermeneutics of factical life, as presented in the *Phänomenologische Interpretationen zu Aristoteles*, (Heideggerian) philosophy is the articulated self-grasp of existence, a difficult 'counter-ruinant motility' [*gegenruinante Bewegtheit*] (Heidegger, *Phänomenologische Interpretationen zu Aristoteles*, 1985, 153), while in the *Plato's Sophist* volume, (Aristotelian) *sophia* appears as a difficult 'counter-movement' [*Gegenbewegung*] (98/68) to the movement of worldly concern. As *sophia*, and as articulated self-grasping existence, philosophy is a difficult counter-movement.

Let us not minimize the differences between these two philosophic counter-movements. No small part of Heidegger's brilliance lies in his own analysis of hylomorphic metaphysics; his temporal interpretation of the Greek sense of being in *Basic Problems of Phenomenology* isolates a specific feature of Greek hylomorphic production, i.e. the vision of the architect to the form (*eidos*) as driving beyond the flow of nows to the constantly present appearance (Heidegger, *The Basic Problems of Phenomenology*, 1982, 149–58/106–12). The notorious 'metaphysics of presence' thence arises through the unthematized transfer of this sense of being to all regions of beings, including Dasein. Now although Heidegger thematizes hylomorphism in his critique of metaphysics, his interest lies in revealing the allegiance to presence hidden in the privilege of the architect's vision, not in analyzing the social conditions that produce such a privilege, nor in overturning the privilege of form over matter and proposing another theory of production. Thus while Heidegger can critique metaphysics as bound to presence due to its being based on a hylomorphic theory of production, in the name of his notion of a fundamental ontology that brings to bear a temporal/ontological difference, he can't critique hylomorphism *per se* in the name of another, artisanal/machinic, notion of production. As we will see, Heidegger is locked into thinking that hylomorphic production is production *per se* because he cannot see artisanal sensitivity, due to his ontologizing of somatic aesthetics and to his political prejudices against the work activities of 'the many', the *polloi*, which he in turn ontologizes as 'immediate and natural Dasein'.

We will draw these consequences in detail below. For now we must note that for Heidegger the unthematized Greek sense of being as presence explains why Aristotle privileges *sophia* (tarrying with the constantly present principles (*archai*)) over *phronēsis* (self-related, self-revealing insight into the concrete changeable situation, an insight conditioned by the prior goodness of the prudent man). This Aristotelian hierarchy is overturned in *Being and Time*, where anticipatory resoluteness as Dasein's self-related and self-revelatory insight, which allows self-grasping existence to articulate itself as fundamental ontology, is privileged over any 'intuition' of the constantly present, so that the question of being is now to be pursued by the heir to *phronēsis*, not the heir to *sophia*.[3]

Despite these differences, though, philosophy as counter-movement, either as *sophia* or as the articulated self-grasp of existence, is born from the struggle of movements, movements which, with the bracketing of locomotion as a merely ontic form of motion, are better seen as modes of the temporalizing of Dasein. To use terms finally codified in *Being and Time*, Dasein's temporality is a motility, *Bewegtheit*, not a motion, *Bewegung*. The Heideggerian difficulty of philosophy is thus the difficult struggle to give oneself the proper temporality, to wrench oneself from a fallen and turbulent preoccupation with beings to face one's own Being in the stillness of a moment of decision.

For Aristotle, on the other hand, one of the difficulties of philosophy is winning its place in the body politic, which is not a pure temporality, but a time/space where force works on bodies other than those of the philosophers, forcing them into the production of surplus time necessary for philosophizing. In thinking surplus time with Aristotle we will find the resources to think the political difference of architect and artisan, the political physics of hylomorphism.[4] This free time, which one cannot give to oneself, but which has to be given by others, was so obviously the *sine qua non* of *sophia* for the Greeks that the tradition has blended their word for such free time produced and given within the eco-civic body politic – *scholē*, leisure – with the very activity we philosophers carry on today: 'scholarship'.[5] This link is so firmly embedded in our academic culture that we even go so far as to call the financial package that provides the necessary leisure for young philosophers 'a scholarship'. Scholarly leisure, then, is the difficulty of philosophy faced by the Egyptian priests Aristotle refers to in the beginning of the *Metaphysica*. There he tells us that, after those arts related to the necessities of life, non-useful studies, e.g. mathematics, were first developed where leisure was allowed (*ekei gar apheithēscholazein*; Aristotle *Metaphysica*, 1957, 1.1.981b25; cf. 1.2.982b23), that is, among the priestly class in Egypt.

Philosophical difficulty for Aristotle consists in part then in the problem of leisure faced by the Egyptian priests, that is, negotiating the eco-civic body politic to be in position to receive the gift of time free from the worry for the care of the somatic body – the procurement of food, shelter and clothing, as we enumerate them. For Heidegger, in contrast, the difficulty of philosophy lies in developing and preserving the proper temporal orientation, that is, in giving oneself a motility precisely counter to the ruining motility generated by concern for the 'necessities' of life, necessities that in the body politic are met by the forced production and preservation of leisurely bodies, but that for Heidegger are ontologized beyond such ontic class differences into a mere structure of Dasein.

This chapter thus addresses forceful bodies politic – the leisured architectural or labouring artisanal bodies we find behind temporality-centred accounts of Dasein that guide Heidegger's reading of Aristotle.[6] I propose two guiding threads, which can be awkwardly and provisionally labelled the political and ontological consequences of the economy of exteriority in Heidegger's texts. By 'economy of exteriority' I mean the relations between different registers of exteriority. Although the high point of the Marburg period is the discussion in *Being and Time* of ecstatic temporality, Heidegger's reduction of locomotion in the texts of the mid-twenties reveals his desire to shelter authentic, ontological exteriority from the 'vulgar' space of the body moving to redress hunger. The political consequence of this decisive intervention in the economy of exteriority is the effacement of the body politic: by bracketing locomotion, Heidegger cannot address the movements of the enslaved, proletarianized, and feminized – forced – bodies whose labour in the form of muscle power or artisanal skill provided the free time – the leisured body – of the Greek architectonic philosopher. The ontological consequence of the bracketing of locomotion is the neglect of an 'eco-ontological chiasm of substance' Heidegger himself thematizes but does not pursue.

The key to our reading is the 1928 *Metaphysical Foundations of Logic*, in which Heidegger acknowledges the necessity of supplementing ontology with metontology, the analysis of the ontic 'presupposition' of ontology: 'the possibility that being is there in the understanding presupposes the factical existence of Dasein and this in turn presupposes the factical extantness [*Vorhandensein*] of nature' (Heidegger, *Metaphysical Foundations of Logic*, 1984 199/156). Exploring the presupposition of the factical *Vorhandensein* of nature would allow us to think through the relation of Dasein to human being simultaneously announced and postponed in the dual gesture of destroying the history of ontology and bracketing philosophical anthropology. Thinking through this relation would presumably lead one to the labour on this *vorhanden* nature, to the political economy implicit in the metontological supplement, to the *Arbeit* presupposed in the *Werk* of ontology and its philosophical articulation. The clue here in unravelling the 'ontic presupposition' is the eco-ontological chiasm of substance, the fact that the originally economic sense of substance as property supplements the ontological sense of substance as presence. Read backward from this point, the effacement of bodily space/time in the *Plato's Sophist* volume – and the consequent effacement of the forceful eco-civic body politic of forced and leisured somatic bodies – indicates a tension in the Heideggerian economy of exteriority that ultimately leads to the abandonment of a pure project of fundamental ontology, which was to have been the isolation, through the investigation of ecstatic temporality, of time alone as the transcendental horizon for the question of the sense of being.

HEIDEGGER'S EFFACEMENT OF THE BODY POLITIC

To follow the trail of the bracketing of locomotion in tracking the body-political consequences of Heidegger's decisions about space and time, let us first briefly touch on the methodology of the hermeneutics of factical life, that is, formal indication, the raising to the level of outline of different modes of temporalizing in Dasein. In other words, the ways of being of Dasein, 'how' it is motile, are the issue in formal indication, not the determinate movements of the factical social and political conditions of historical Dasein, the 'matter' the ontologist examines in order to discover therein formal structures. There is of course here an implicit methodological hylomorphism it would not be uninteresting to explore, though we cannot do so here.

Formal indication is put to work in developing a hermeneutics of facticity in the *Phänomenologische Interpretationen zu Aristoteles*, where the struggle for philosophy is to counter the flight into security away from questionability. The relational sense of life is care, and the character of the world in care is significance. In explicating significance, Heidegger tells us that to live in care for X sets up a system of references, a series of 'in order to . . .' relations. Thus life in its widest-grasped relational sense cares about our 'daily bread' (Heidegger, *Phänomenologische Interpretationen zu Aristoteles*, 1985, 90). Note that 'daily bread' is placed in scare quotes by Heidegger not only to acknowledge the scriptural allusion, but also to indicate a 'formal-indicative' ontologizing of bodily need. *Darbung* is ontologized need; as the ontological non-self-identity of Dasein it provokes a motility, not a movement – the movement of animals, say, to which somatic need, by necessity, gives rise in Aristotle's *De Motu Animalium*. The ontologizing force of formal indication, necessary to reach structures of Dasein, is here not merely a de-animalization, but also a de-somaticization, perhaps even a spiritualization.

To follow this lead which pushes Dasein from the body to the soul, we now move to consider Heidegger's reading of Aristotle in the *Plato's Sophist* volume, where we focus on Heidegger's discussion of Dasein as *psuchē*. We can see the bracketing of locomotion in his definition of *psuchē* as *metabolē* as an ontologizing de-somaticization. For Aristotle, *psuchē* is the principle of a living body (Aristotle, *De Anima*, 1956, 2.1.412a16–21); *psuchē* and *sôma* form the composite, the *suntheton*, from which *psuchē* can be isolated in analysis. In Heidgger the relation of *psuchē* to body, of Dasein to body, is left inarticulate. In discussing truth as a mode of being of Dasein, Heidegger tells us that the 'ontological definition' of *psuchē* entails that life – not the living body, but simply 'life' – is motion, *Bewegung*, a motion that is not locomotion, *Ortsbewegung*, but *metabolē*, the 'presence of change [*Anwesendsein des Umschlagens*]' (Heidegger, *Plato's Sophist*, 1997, 18/13; translation modified).[7] Now the interpretation of *metabolē* Heidegger gives here accords with a certain level of Aristotle's text, for he tells us in *Physica* 5.1 that change, *metabolē*, is the genus within which we find motion, *kinēsis*, one of whose species is *phora*, locomotion (225a35-b9). Further, Aristotle also tells us in *Physica* 4.13 that all change is ecstatic (222b16); as the genre of all motion, *metabolē*, as change is a pure ecstasis which is thus ontologically prior to the ontic space of locomotion. Heidegger's reading of *psuchē* as *metabolē* and the equation of Dasein and *psuchē* means that Dasein is ontologically ecstatic, then – motile, but not locomotive.

However, in this instance, and in the extended treatment of Aristotle in *Basic Problems of Phenomenology*, Heidegger ignores the researches of *Physica* 8 that purport to establish the ontic priority of locomotion not only to all other motions, but to all changes as well. Without locomotion, no change at all, and hence no pure ecstasis as the ontological sense of change: if one prefers, without extant, *vorhanden* locomotion, no extant changes, and hence no occasion for the discovery of the concept of ecstasis, or in Heideggerian terms, no access to the being of change. In other words, no ontology without metontology means no *Sein* without the *Existenz* of Dasein,[8] but also no *Existenz* of Dasein without the *Vorhandsein* of nature, and so finally no philosophy without the body politic.

Let us test how these later Heideggerian insights play out in the 1924–5 *Sophist* lectures. Here we see that Heidegger ignores Aristotle's presentation of an ontic phenomenon – the factical *Vorhandensein* of locomotion – conditioning the access to its ontological ground – pure ecstasis. For Aristotle, ontological ecstasis must be thought in relation to, not isolation from, locomotion, for *psuchē* and *sôma* are interwoven in the composite (which is furthermore explicitly thought as a body politic). For Aristotle, the soul is the principle of energetic unity in living creatures, although somatic fatigue prevents it from being pure activity. Rather, soul is *hexis*, the capability of a body to perform its characteristic functions (Aristotle, *De Anima*, 1956, 2.1.412a27). Under the rule of the soul, the body becomes unified, a single organ serving the soul (*panta yar ta physika sōmata tēs psychēs organa*; 2.4.415b18). Any formation of a unity is always that of ruler/ruled, Aristotle insists, and the unification of the animal body as organism under the rule of the soul is masterly rather than political (Aristotle, *Politics*, 1.5.1254a30). Thus psychic organ-ization entails somatic enslavement in the Aristotelian body politic. With this in mind we can see that the Heideggerian classification of *psuchē* as *metabolē* rather than as the organ-izing and masterly factor of the corporeal body politic intervenes in Aristotle's text to bracket locomotion in 'vulgar' space in favour of motility as ontologized ecstasis. Heidegger thus divorces *psuchē* from *sôma* and covers over the organic corporeal body politic of psychic mastery and somatic enslavement. Dasein is thereby divorced from the somatic bodies of all human beings, and thus from the forceful civic body politic, the forced bodies of labourers and artisans and the leisured bodies of architects and philosophers.

To see the link of this effacement of the body politic and our theme of the denigration of artisanal/aesthetic sensitivity, let us now discuss Heidegger's account in the *Plato's Sophist* volume of the 'genesis of sophia within the natural Dasein of the Greeks'.[9] Heidegger begins section 10 by considering *Metaphysica* 1.1, which is presented in terms of an intellectual ladder, an ordering according to which 'stages of understanding' are considered 'more wise' than the preceding. The fourth stage, according to Heidegger, is the architect (*architectôn*) as opposed to the artisan (*technités*), the *Handwerker*, he who possesses *technē*, the third stage (Heidegger, *Plato's Sophist*, 1997, 67/46). This is an extremely odd claim on Heidegger's part, especially with regard to his analysis in *Plato's Sophist* section 7b of *Nicomachean Ethics* 6.4 and *Metaphysica* 7.7, where he presupposes what Aristotle's text plainly says, namely that the handworker precisely does not have *technē*, but works without knowledge, as do inanimate forces like fire, although not through a natural tendency, but through habit (Aristotle, *Metaphysica*, 1957, 981b2—5).

This is an important point. Aristotle assigns *technē* to the architect and consigns the handworker to the non-technical levels of *aisthēsis*, experience and habit. Heidegger however breaks the list of comportments (*aisthēsis, empeiria, technē*) to insert as the fourth stage the name of an occupation, 'the architect', thereby imply that architecture is superior to mere handworking *technē*. Here he seems perhaps to open the door for acknowledging a technical artisanship which would be distinct from architectonic vision, but he fails to fulfill this tentative promise. Indeed, in his detailed account of *technē* in section 13 he repeats Aristotle's identification of the architect as the possessor of *technē* pure and simple, as the one who 'knows the causes' (Heidegger, *Plato's Sophist*, 1997, 91/63; cf. Aristotle, *Metaphysica*, 1957, 981b1). One reason for this invisibility of artisanal sensitivity is Heidegger's tendency to ontologize aesthetic, somatic, vision. I have explored this issue in detail in 'The "Sense" of "Sight"', so I will here only indicate a few points. In *Being and Time*, Heidegger's claiming of an ontological sense for 'sight' is possible only at the cost of a 'formalization' that cuts off the sensible body from the temporality of Dasein:

> But from the beginning onwards the tradition of philosophy has been oriented primarily toward 'seeing' as a way of access to entities *and to Being*. To keep the connection with this tradition, we may formalize 'sight' and 'seeing' enough to obtain therewith a universal term for characterizing any access to entities or to being, as access in general. (Heidegger, *Being and Time*, 1962, 147/187; Heidegger's italics)

This formalization of the received term 'sight' saves the relation to the tradition, but cuts off the sensible body. At least twice in *Being and Time* Heidegger insists 'seeing' has nothing to do with the perception of 'bodily eyes [*leiblichen Augen*]' (Heidegger, *Being and Time*, 1962, 147/187; 346/397). Here we see an ontologization of somatic vision that prevents Heidegger from the exploration of the aesthetic dimension of artisanal sensitivity.

When we return to the *Plato's Sophist* text and the treatment of *technē* therein, we see a unthematized double sense of the term 'handworker'. Aristotle uses 'handworker' in the *Metaphysica* text to refer to unskilled day-labourers or slaves, purveyors of mere muscle power, while Heidegger reads it as referring instead to skilled artisans.[10] The important point for us is to note the invisibility of artisanal sensitivity on either account. If artisans have *technē* for Heidegger, it resides not in the somatic skill and artisanal sensitivity we saw Deleuze and Guattari, following Simondon, thematize, but in the vision of the *eidos*, although presumably to a lesser degree than the architect. Thus in effect Heidegger elides the specific difference between artisanal sensitivity and architectonic eidetic vision, substituting instead a quantitative difference. But in so doing he creates a non-Aristotelian extra step to the ladder of comportments, crediting *technē* to the handworker. For Aristotle, the handworker is a mere possessor of muscle power to be directed by the architect, nothing but a forceful body. Indeed, the so-called efficient cause in Aristotle, as Heidegger notes, is not the action of hammer on stone, but is precisely the direction afforded by the architect in following his vision of the form of the object to be constructed by either the muscle power of labourers or by the unacknowledged somatic skill of artisans. Only in this way is the architect the source of the action (*archē tēs kinēseôs*), the commanding original principle of the change (Heidegger, *Plato's Sophist*, 1997, 43/30).

Doubly odd, then that Heidegger should first credit the handworker with *technē* in *Plato's Sophist* section 10, claiming the handworker possesses *technē*, and then not mention at all in his extended comments in section 13 Aristotle's degradation of handwork to the level of inanimate force. But perhaps this interpolation by Heidegger, his treating *technē* as the already-accomplished possession of the handworker, is motivated by his desire to avoid considering, in the context of the ladder of understanding, Aristotle's 'sign' of *technē*, that its possessor can teach (Aristotle, *Metaphysica*, 1957, 981b7–10), even though he did discuss the teachability of *epistēmē* in the context of *Nicomachean Ethics* 6.3 earlier in his commentary (Heidegger, *Plato's Sophist*, 1997, 35/25). In the context of the *Metaphysics*, the mention of teaching brings us to the eco-civic body politic and challenges the interpretation of the movement from *aisthēsis* through *sophia* as a homogenous ladder of intellectual aptitudes or revelatory temporalities, the ascension of which is open to those with more wisdom, or, in Heidegger's terms, those willing to face the difficult task of changing one's temporality.

We investigated in Chapter 5 Plato's link of teaching (viewed as masterly command) and *technē*. Whatever the body politic inherent in the Greek mode of teaching, the very activity of teaching refers us to the distribution of access to training in technical skill – the opening to *sophia* – and its connection to the rest of the system of the forced production of leisured bodies. Being able to be taught a *technē* presupposes a certain relatively privileged position in the household and civic bodies politic, for the slaves and day labourers to whom Aristotle refers as being without *technē* were severely disadvantaged on the labour market by being able to offer only muscle power. Keeping these workers unskilled and keeping the supply of skilled labour small was thus in the economic interest of the artisan class, although they would remain dependent on their patrons. Thus while free artisans did not face the brute force of the overseer as did their enslaved collaborators, they did face the threat of proletarianization, the reduction to the status of day-labourer. And in this way the artisan who is politically free in a democracy is still forced to work by market forces; such an unleisured and dependent economic position led Plato and Aristotle to argue against their enfranchisement (Plato, *Laws*, 846d; *Politics*, 1278a5–12). The teaching of *technē* (either artisanal sensitivity or architectonic vision) to only a few, in other words, installs an eco-political break in the supposedly homogenous intellectual or temporal ladder. This break is not merely a rupture though, for it forms the condition for further progress for those who are taught. A conditioning break then, perhaps even a 'supplement' in the Derridean sense: added on later, it becomes essential, for without teaching the form would die along with its first discoverer.

With this political supplement, this conditioning break between *empeiria* and *technē*, we come to an inversion of the power/knowledge scheme Aristotle sets up and Heidegger implicitly endorses. As someone fortunate enough to have been taught his *technē* by someone else, the architect is not put in a position of authority because he is able to see the form, as Aristotle would have it in justifying power by knowledge; rather, power enables knowledge, for only because of a certain power position in the eco-civic body politic is the architect able to learn how to see the form. Further, one could argue, power does not just enable knowledge by allowing learning, the acquisition of knowledge, but also by underlying the very production of knowledge. The chronologically first discovery of the form, through which teaching is possible, is open to the architect only because his eco-political position gives him the time to consider the form rather than be fixated on the properties of the object under consideration. The form is revealed only in given time, time free from the temporal demands put upon the handworker, whose somatic survival, due to his position in the eco-civic body politic, depends upon the completion of tasks which demand strict attention to the particular properties of the bodies being acted upon. The fundamental issue here is thus induction (*epagogē*). The 'vulgar' sense of induction derided by Heidegger is that knowledge comes only to those in power who have been given the time to compare the results of trial and error experiments and are hence able to achieve insight and pass it on in teaching. This notion of induction, focusing on the order of discovery, is opposed by Heidegger to the ontological sense of induction, in which in the order of being there must be a prior 'simple insight [*schlichtes Hinsehen*]' (Heidegger, *Plato's Sophist*, 1997, 36/25) to the form.

Let me leave this topic open for further research, though, having at least established the political supplement of teaching for the survival and transmission of *technē*, if not for its very constitution, and move on to explore a second political supplement to the ladder: leisure intervening between *technē* and *epistēmē/sophia*. There is, according to Heidegger, a 'tendency' in *epistēmē* to free itself from 'management [*Hantierung*]' and become independent (Heidegger, *Plato's Sophist*, 1997, 92–3/64). Now despite its revelatory character, Heidegger continues in citing Aristotle, no one calls *aisthēsis* a *sophia*, because of its being confined to picking out the particular, and thus its connection with *praxis* and *phronēsis* (Aristotle, *Metaphysica*, 1957, 981b10–11). The road to *sophia* goes through *epistēmē*, however, since the tendency to independent knowing lying in *technē* is marked for Aristotle by the possibility of 'wonder' (*thaumazesthai*; Aristotle, *Metaphysica*, 1957, 981b14–15), which for Heidegger 'demonstrates that in Dasein itself there lives a special appreciation of dis-covering' (Heidegger, *Plato's Sophist*, 1997, 93/64). According to Heidegger, Dasein has itself this tendency to move beyond utility, a tendency to change temporalities from the successive referrals of experience to pure tarrying. This wonder is a distancing from the body politic: the less the knowing is directed to the necessities of life and amusements, the more wise its possessor seems (Heidegger, *Plato's Sophist*, 1997, 93/64). 'Thus the first sciences, e.g. mathematics, developed in Egypt, since the priests were given time [*weil den Priestern Zeit gegeben war*] to do nothing other than merely observe' (94/65; translation modified; cf. Aristotle, *Metaphysica*, 1957, 981b23–5). The condition for *epistēmē* is thus the gift of time. Given time supplements the ladder of temporalities, allowing the move from *technē* to *epistēmē*.

But who gives this time? What sort of time can be given? What is the ontology and metontology of surplus time? Or perhaps the same question, what is the body politic implied in the political physics of surplus time? Why does Heidegger, the scholar of time, let slip such a provocative concept, 'given time', without comment? At the end of his career *es gibt Zeit* will be a key phrase. Here, Heidegger tells us only that bare disclosure, independent of utility, toward which there is a 'tendency' in Dasein, is 'authentically possible' only where 'Dasein is free from assignment to care for *anagkaia* [the necessities of life]' (Heidegger, *Plato's Sophist*, 1997, 94/65). Here at least one finds a reference to the body politic, but this linking of philosophy to the relief from necessities in leisure is left unexplored by Heidegger.

Leisured bodies are free from having their time soaked up by providing the 'necessities of life'. But let's not forget that *anagkaia* was for the Greeks a far more terrible word, more blood-soaked, than our 'necessities' of life, as they also heard in it the disciplinary and terroristic force applied to labouring – enslaved, proletarianized and feminized – bodies, to forced bodies, for *anagkē* could even in the extreme case mean 'torture'. *anagkē*: let's call it 'the social force of necessity'. Clinging to the supplemental gift of surplus time, the social force of necessity breaks the homogeneity of the ladder of temporalities by rooting philosophy and its temporal difficulties firmly in the forceful body politic, the time/space of political power working on forced bodies. What renders philosophy possible, but difficult, then, in the eco-civic body politic, has nothing to do with the resolute self-grasp of existence, but with positions in bodies politic, nothing to do with the purely temporal orientation of one's motility, but with the political physics of the forced time/space of bodily labour. What was necessary, but blocked to Heidegger because of his bracketing of locomotion – his skewed economy of exteriority – was an exploration of the relation between the body-political, hence spatial, condition of philosophy's 'authentic possibility' in the given time of leisure and the caricatural glorification of philosophy in the rest of the *Plato's Sophist* volume, as for instance, 'one of the extreme possibilities' of Dasein (Heidegger, *Plato's Sophist*, 1997, 12/8), open to those willing to face resolutely the difficulty of changing temporalities.

To continue with Heidegger's narrative, the second moment of *sophia* is that the wise one knows what is difficult to uncover, what will not yield itself to *aisthēsis*. Here, however, Heidegger's own politics gives itself away. After he excises the body politic, it slips back in with a particular ideological inflection. Aristotle writes that *aisthēsis* is common to all (*pantôn koinon*; Aristotle, *Metaphysica*, 1957, 982a12), but Heidegger refers to the predilection of the *polloi*, the many, for *aisthēsis* (Heidegger, *Plato's Sophist*, 1997, 95/66; 98/67). Here we see the most retrograde Platonic politics, with a particular ontological twist, inserting itself in Heidegger's Aristotle interpretation. Heidegger ontologizes '*polloi*', the marker of the most vicious and violent Greek class warfare, into 'immediate and natural Dasein'. Thus for Heidegger, the difficulty of *sophia* lies not in the activity of thinking principles, but in Dasein, in its peculiar mode of being, the proximate: having its presence in the now, in the world, Dasein has the tendency to close itself off in the proximate, as shown by the love of *aisthēsis*. This is an 'easy and self-evident self-moving in what appears to the eyes [*Sichbewegen im Augenschein*]' (Heidegger, *Plato's Sophist*, 1997, 98/67; translation modified). Against this easy self-movement, sophia counterposes a 'counter-movement' (*Gegenbewegung*) (98/68) to *aisthēsis*, which is not to be excluded, but used as a ground for further disclosure. With the 'counter-movement' of the independent tarrying with principles characteristic of *sophia* posed against vulgar aesthetic entrapment in the mere succession of nows we see clearly Heidegger's conception of *Metaphysics* 1.1 as a homogenous ladder of temporalities. Ascending this ladder, philosophy is the difficult struggle of temporalities, or more precisely the struggle of the philosophical few to ascend to the difficult temporality of *sophia* over against the easy, or even 'lazy' [*bequemerweise*] (95/66), temporality of the 'immediate and natural' many who love *aisthēsis*.

Now among the many inversions Heidegger has given us over the years, this is surely one the most remarkable. For Heidegger, in the looking glass, the lazy many are the ones who have it easy, while resolute philosophers struggle with difficulty. Such a thesis is only possible after an effacement of the body politic; with a notion of the body politic restored, it's clear that the alleged 'bewitchment' of Greek artisans by the world – what we have called 'artisanal sensitivity' in the previous chapter – was not due to some fantasized 'laziness' in their love of a certain temporality. Rather than such a temporality-inertia that confined them to the lower, easier stages of a homogeneous ladder otherwise open to their ascension, we see that sensitivity is the preferred mode of artisans not only because of its productivity, but because their life and that of their families depended on securing access not to principles, but to bodies their masters could have used or traded in their search for leisure. Heidegger himself tells us that 'one deals with bodies [*man hantiert mit dem* Körper]' (Heidegger, *Plato's Sophist*, 1997, 87/60; translation modified; Heidegger's italics), and the senses, Heidegger himself reminds us, are for Aristotle *kuriôtatai* ('most authoritative'), with regard to the particulars of bodies (92/64; cf. Aristotle, *Metaphysica*, 1957, 981b11). Further, we are also reminded by Heidegger that those with *empeiria* are often more successful than inexperienced holders of *logos* in matters of practice and generation, because of this access to the particular (Heidegger, *Plato's Sophist*, 1997, 75/52; cf. Aristotle, *Metaphysica*, 1957, 981a17). *Aisthēsis* and *empeiria* are the disclosive modes of handworkers, then, not because 'the many' lack intelligence, or are striken with spiritual cowardice, or even ontological laziness in confronting the difficulty of *sophia*, but because *aisthēsis* and *empeiria* are called for by the tasks assigned them, assignments made under the threat of force to be applied to their bodies in the eco-civic body politic. Since they must – by social force of necessity – aesthetically and experientially handle bodies, they cannot – by social force of necessity – become free of utility-ordered handling, and the most authoritative modes for these tasks: precisely *aisthēsis* and *empeiria*, which they are then scorned for adopting. The merely forceful body of the handworker, or even the skilled body of the artisan, working at the direction of the architect master in the phantasm of hylomorphic production, is a forced body. The social force of necessity, in other words, by a political supplement, ruptures the homogeneity of the ladder of intellectual aptitudes or revelatory temporalities and forbids any too-easy philosophic self-congratulation on being more wise or more resolute in the face of difficulty than 'the many'.

THE ECO-ONTOLOGICAL CHIASM OF SUBSTANCE

Let's shift gears to discuss the ontological consequences of the effacement of the body politic in Heidegger's economy of exteriority. The key here lies in Heidegger's resolution of the contest between *sophia* and *phronēsis* as the highest comportment of Dasein. The fifth criterion of happiness in *Nicomachean Ethics* 10.7 is one of political physics: *nous* is marked by self-rule, *autarkeia*. Famously, Aristotle demands that we recognize that like other men, the philosopher needs the necessities of life at his disposal (Aristotle, *Metaphysica*, 1957, 1177a30). Aristotle is clear that *phronēsis* includes politics and house-hold management; qua man, the philosopher needs such *phronēsis* to meet the condition of philosophizing in leisure (1178b7). However, he is free from needing other men while philosophizing, while the other virtues (e.g. justice, courage) require other people (1177a31). The question now about the self-rule of *sophia*: why is this a virtue for the Greeks, even if complete self-sufficiency or constant maintenance of *sophia* is forbidden us? I only note here that Heidegger's attribution of this failing – the 'impossibility' of *sophia* – to Dasein's 'mortality' (Heidegger, *Plato's Sophist*, 1997, 171/118) or 'mode of temporal being [*Art des Zeitlichseins*]' (134/92) calls for an analysis of the somatic body to which Aristotle attributes the intermittent nature of human access to *sophia* in *Nicomachean Ethics* 10.8: 'his nature is not self-sufficient [*ou gar autarkēs*] for study, but he needs a healthy body, and needs to have food and the other services provided' (Aristotle, *Metaphysica*, 1957, 1178b35). Nevertheless, despite or because of their inability to attain it completely, self-rule remained a virtue for Greek philosophers, and to explain this I propose that self-rule is the anxious negative image of the other-directedness of forced bodies,[11] the enslaved, proletarianized and feminized bodies whose muscle power or artisanal skill produces the necessities for the leisured body that allows for training in self-rule. Finding a determinate political interest at the basis of an ethical virtue is a classic move of ideology critique or one of its more sophisticated cousins, let's say genealogy, deconstruction or historical–libidinal materialism. But let us not remain content with these seemingly external approaches, but confront Heidegger on his own terms in the *Plato's Sophist* volume.

For Heidegger, the key to understanding the self-rule characteristic of those possessing *sophia* is not the body politic, but a matter of temporality, its character of tarrying, that is, keeping and preserving the principles rather than following the reference networks of the flow of appearances in *aisthēsis* or their progressive taming in *empeiria* and *technē*. Ontology is prior to ethics, Heidegger holds, so to follow the temporal clue he commands us to look to the Greek sense of being, for Greek ethical thought, he tells us, is oriented to presence (Heidegger, *Plato's Sophist*, 1997, 178/122). Thus, he continues in explicating the Greeks, since *nous* as the exercise of theory in *sophia* satisfies the criterion of presence, as such it is flourishing, in which consists the authenticity of the being of human life (179/123). Heidegger, though, has also taught us, in *Basic Problems of Phenomenology*, to look to Greek hylomorphic production and its reliance on the vision of the architect of the form as the clue to the sense of being that explains Greek ethics. Thus the key is to investigate the ontic roots of ancient ontology, to find a worldly time marking a particular inflection of the temporality of Dasein at the root of the temporal determination of being.

But why this particular feature of Greek production, the architect's vision? Why not the analysis of matter, the other key element of hylomorphism? Heidegger himself points the way to exploring the eco-civic body politic at the very heart of ontology. Let us return to some tantalizing hints dropped by Heidegger throughout the lectures of the 1920s about the original sense of substance (*ousia*). This economic sense – in the literal sense of the law of the household, the *nomos* of *oikos* – reveals *ousia* as property [*Besitz, Hausstand*][12] and thereby sets up the ontic supplement of the ontological Heidegger will come to recognize as necessary in 1928, but that is undeveloped here. Presence, the temporal sense of being, determines the ontological sense of *ousia* which, in Heidegger's interpretation of Greek philosophy, gives the palm to *sophia* as theoretical tarrying over *phronēsis*, the consideration of the contingencies of the eco-civic body politic. But *ousia* as property, acquired and preserved through the citizens' practical care of the time–space of the body politic granting leisure to some via the forced bodies of others, is the ontic condition of the allegedly ontologically pure temporality of the architect's vision of the form (that which determines *ousia* as presence). The eco-nomic body-political sense of *ousia* as property is then also the condition of the *sophia* which contemplates *ousia* and determines the sense of being as presence, and, I add, as conditioning necessary leisure is also the condition of Heidegger's philosophy, the successor who will come to thematize that very sense of being as presence in the history of Western metaphysics. Thus

Heidegger's slogan, 'no *Sein* without *Dasein*', ultimately entails that there is no (Greek) contemplation of being – or (Heideggerian) science of being – without leisure. So we see the extrinsic becomes essential. The (eco-civic body-political) ontic sense of *ousia* as property, first in the order of discovery but recalled only after the fact of its effacement in the history of Western metaphysics by Heidegger's *Destruktion* as historical evidence for the Greek failure at the ontological thematization of the operative sense of being, is revealed as a necessary condition for that thematization. The eco-ontic supplements the de-somaticized ontological.

On the basis of this eco-ontological chiasm of substance, then, I propose that Heidegger's text, properly read, allows us to think the political physics behind the Greek sense of being. On this reading, the Greek philosophical love of self-ruled corporeal bodies politic (the organism formed by psychic mastery and somatic enslavement) and the Greek philosophical predilection for self-immanent unchanging presence as the sense of being reflect an anxious negative image of the temporality inflicted upon the other-directed and threatened forced bodies politic of the slave, wage-worker, artisan and woman. The clue here is surplus time, given time. Surplus time is produced and given by the insertion of bodies into the field of a social force of necessity that denies any stability, any possibility of changing temporalities beyond the flow of nows, to the life of the slave, worker and woman. This forceful incarceration in *aisthēsis* and *empeiria* is then interpreted by Aristotle as the intellectual deficiency of the handworker or by Heidegger as the ontological laziness of the many.[13] Rather than simple intelligence or courage in facing the difficulty of philosophy, however, it is the political physics of surplus time, the attainment of a privileged position in the eco-civic body politic, which supplements the ladder of temporalities. A leisured somatic body allows for the ascension of that allegedly intellectual or temporal ladder: the progressive isolation of the form in *technē*, its handing on in teaching, and the further tarrying with the principles that is emblematic of *sophia* are all dependent on given time. Such surplus time (and behind it, threatened, forced, bodies), then, explains the Greek philosophical privilege of presence – and its eventual thematization by Heidegger.

In the register of temporalities, then, Heidegger reveals the ground of the metaphysical allegiance to presence as residing in the privilege of *technē*, but by not following the supplements to the ladder of temporalities, he doesn't place *technē* or *sophia* in the eco-civic body politic, the time–space organ-ized for the sake of the leisured somatic bodies of the citizens; he doesn't pursue the eco-ontological chiasm of substance and thereby trace the Greek ontological predilection for the temporality of immanent presence (the vision of the architect essential to hylomorphism) back to the vulgar time/space of insecure, threatened bodies, the forced bodies of the women, slaves and workers, either skilled artisans or mere providers of muscle power. The eco-ontological chiasm of substance can only be understood, however, on the basis of an economy of exteriority that articulates the relations between an ontologized ecstatic temporality and the space of an ontic and locomotive body politic. And it is precisely this understanding that is blocked for Heidegger by his bracketing of locomotion.

Heidegger's neglect of the locomotive, I would further argue, frustrates the Marburg transcendental project, as Heidegger himself recognized in 1928's *Metaphysical Foundations of Logic* in calling for a metontological 'overturning [*Umschlag*]' (Heidegger, *Metaphysical Foundations of Logic*, 1984, 199/157). Metontology was to have remedied the defective economy of exteriority of the Marburg project by a 'theological' supplement to ontology. Theology is to be understood here, of course, not in the Christian but in the Aristotelian sense, as the erotic spur of the mimetic locomotion of the cosmological and the mimetic generation of the biological. The irreducibility of Aristotelian theology to ontology, if explored fully, would have led Heidegger to the 'external' cause of generation, and thereby to the sun's locomotion and its effect on bodily generation.[14] And this exploration of the ontic supplement would have in turn necessitated a rethinking of the privilege of ontological ecstasis over locomotion in the economy of exteriority. In other words, if there is an eco-ontological chiasm of substance, if ontology has an ontic presupposition, if ontology needs a metontological supplement, and if a notion of the time–space of the eco-civic body politic is needed to understand metontology and the politic physics of surplus time at work therein, and if such a notion of time–space is blocked by a bracketing of locomotion, then not only Heidegger's politics but also his very ontological project is at stake here. The 1928 call for rethinking fundamental ontology, however, went unheeded, as Heidegger moved instead to the problematic of the metaphysics of Dasein. The subsequent neglect of the metontological supplement, in favour of the political disasters of the 1930s, strikes me as one of the most momentous 'roads not taken' of twentieth-century philosophy.

CONCLUSION

With this chapter we have seen how tenaciously deep-rooted are the philosophical prejudices of hylomorphism, the privilege of the archi-tect's vision and the invisibility or denigration of artisanal sensitivity. Although Heidegger thematizes hylomorphism in his critique of the metaphysics of presence, he has no resources for proposing an artisanal/machinic production, due to his ontologizing of aesthetic vision. And although he thematizes the eco-ontological chiasm of substance, he has no resources to explore the body politic, due to his ontologizing of bodily necessity. In the next and final chapter we will investigate the other side of hylomorphism to see how the notion of material self-ordering is thematized but finally rejected by Kant.

CHAPTER 7

Force, Violence and Authority in the Kantian Body Politic

[T]he analogy of these direct natural purposes can serve to elucidate a certain association, though one found more often as an idea than in actuality: in speaking of the complete transformation of a people into a state, which took place recently, the word *organization* was frequently and very aptly applied to the establishment of legal authorities, etc., and even to the entire body politic. (Kant, *Critique of Judgment*, 1987)

Introduction
Kant's Cognitive, Moral and Aesthetic Bodies Politic
Force, Coercion and Revolution
Revolution and the Force of Genius

INTRODUCTION

In this chapter we conclude our investigations of the implicit hylomorphism of the organized body politic by treating Kant, with a slight shift in focus and method from the previous two chapters. Rather than focusing on the privilege of the architect's vision and on the overlooking or denigration of aesthetic sensitivity, as we did in Chapters 5 and 6, here we focus on the force used in the transcendent organ-ization of the body politic, and on the concomitant rejection of the notion of material self-ordering that Kant himself thematizes at a crucial point in the *Critique of Judgment*. My method of reading in this chapter not only displays the Derridean 'formal' concern with close reading, but also, in our reading of the textual work performed by Kant's notion of 'coercion' as the organ-izing force of the contractual body politic, develops Derrida's 'substantive' concern with undecidability.

My guiding thread in reading Kant's representation of the body politic is the term *Gewalt*, which can be translated as 'force', 'violence', or 'authority'.[1] I prefer 'force' as a general term for *Gewalt* as the medium of the social contract, Kant's major concept in his political writing; the social contract is the regulation of force in the organ-ization of a body politic. State authority (*Staatsgewalt*) is to maintain a monopoly on the legitimate use of force; the private use of force is violence (the state of nature, besides being an anarchic chaos in need of being formed, is one in which the threat of violence (*Gewalttätigkeit*) is ever-present). The state forcibly deals with any usurpation of its privilege. The formula for the social contract could thus be: the chaotically violent are coerced to give up private force and submit to the public force of authority in an organ-ized body politic. There is thus a rationally configured economy of force, with violence and authority as its two poles. Once we accept the terms of the rationally configured economy of force, politics is the choice between violent anarchy and forceful state organ-ization. This forced alternative, how-ever, leaves us in the dark as to the source of the force coercively packaged and delegated to the state as authority.

Coercion is the key here to thinking the reservoir of force that the rationally configured economy of force – the social contract – tries to manage. The organ-ization of a contractual body politic relies upon a force Kant calls coercion, and coercion fits neither category of the restricted, dipolar, rational economy of force – it is neither violence nor authority. The undecidable factor in the institution of authority, the undecidable in the social contract, is coercion: as the force applied to bring about organ-ization, it cannot be legitimated in terms of the body politic it brings into being. Coercion taps into a reservoir of force that can be used to effect the social contract, but as a-legit-imate, undecidable, such force might be turned to creative, artistic/ vital dis-organ-ization and re-ordering into a non-organismic body politic; in other words, it might become 'revolution'. The source of force in organizing the body politic is, I'd like to suggest, borrowing from the Deleuzean-inspired writings of Negri and Hardt (*Labor of Dionysus* and *Empire*), the self-ordering potential of immanent democratic structuring. Although Kant cannot think this potential because of hylomorphic conceptual commitments that forbid any notion of material self-ordering, he comes close to it in describing 'life' or 'genius', for as we will see, the name for the channel of this life-force is genius.

This chapter then examines the way in which *Gewalt* – the rationally-configured economy of force – structures the entirety of Kant's writings on the 'social contract' for cognitive, moral, aesthetic and civic bodies politic. The ideal Kantian body politic is a commonwealth of reason, in which reason is itself brought to the proper political order, and the political order becomes rational. Thus while force is the medium of the body politic, reason is to be its organ-izer. But reason for Kant is dedicated to closure – the search for the completion of the series of syllogisms in theoretical reason and for the pure formal autonomy of practical reason. And this reason works in concert with an understanding that conceptually organ-izes a sensory, affective, aesthetic or political manifold, resulting in the formal reproducibility of bodies grasped in cognition, dealt with in practice, experienced as beautiful, or organ-ized politically. And it is this profoundly hylo-morphic notion of organ-ization as the result of a conceptual/formal determination of a chaotic sensuous/material manifold that keeps Kant from thematizing the source of force lying behind his rationally configured economy of force as the self-ordering potential of an immanent democratic structuring of a non-organismic body politic.

Briefly put, Kant is anxious about the undecidable force of coercion necessary to effect the organ-ization of an authoritative body politic, for the social contract is an important structure for the architectonic of each of the major fields of the critical philosophy. In the cognitive, theoretically knowing, body politic, understanding is to order the manifold of sensation (here the 'consitution of an object' would be equivalent to the 'organ-ization of a body [that could be experienced]'. In the moral body politic, the domain of the faculty of desire, pure practical reason is to have *Gewalt* over sensibility. The organization of the aesthetic body politic is more complicated, as beauty is announced in the reflection on the free play of imagination and understanding, while the sublime is announced through the violent imposition of reason's demands on the imagination. Thus the body capable of judging beauty would seem to be the free body, one that avoids stilling the play of the manifold by a conceptual ordering, and thus avoids *Gewalt*. But the free body open to the aesthetic judgment of taste and the announcement of beauty is only possible through the organization of a commonwealth of taste that takes the logical possibility, open to all, of distinguishing pure spiritual free play from agreeable somatic vibration and assigns that to a probabilistic distribution among cultured and vulgar bodies politic, a distribution in which *Gewalt* plays a major role.[2]

KANT'S COGNITIVE, MORAL AND AESTHETIC BODIES POLITIC

Let us recall the cognitive body politic sketched out in the Preface to the First Edition of *Critique of Pure Reason*. In an unforgettable phrase, Kant names metaphysics a 'battle-field' (Kant, *Critique of Pure Reason*, 1965, A viii). But in the very next sentence he shifts from this polemical description to a regal one by recalling the time when metaphysics was the queen of the sciences, whose government moved from barbarism to the despotism of the dogmatists to the anarchy in which nomadic sceptics broke up civil society. After repelling the attempt by Locke to demonstrate her vulgar, 'physiological' heritage, Queen Metaphysics now suffers the fate of being wearily ignored by those grown indifferent to her claims (Kant, *Critique of Pure Reason*, 1965, A viii–x). But this indifferentism is but the prelude to Kant's attempt at restoring a cognitive body politic as a commonwealth of critical reason in which the queen would at last receive her due, albeit as a constitutional and no longer absolute monarch.

Much later in the book, after all his immense critical labours, Kant returns to an intensive discussion of critique as the organ-ization of a body politic. Although he has used the judicial metaphor of the tribunal of pure reason throughout – perhaps most famously in the use of the term 'deduction', which he tells us answers the question of right (*quid juris*) (Kant, *Critique of Pure Reason*, 1965, B 116)[3] – he brings all the metaphors together in the section entitled 'The discipline of pure reason in respect of its polemical employment' (B 766–97). We should hear the war (*polemos*) in 'polemical', for this section caps the violent 'politics of metaphysics' by showing the social contract as the key to organ-izing the cognitive body politic. Kant writes, 'Reason depends on this freedom [of self-critique] for its very existence. For reason has no dictatorial authority [*Ansehen*]; its verdict is always simply the agreement of free citizens . . .' (B 766). This citizenship of reason is achieved only by coercing violence-prone individuals to accept a common authority. The polemical use of reason is the defence against dogmatic claims that would silence an opposing spokesperson: we could say it is the warring defence of the right of free speech for reason. When both sides have their say, we have antinomy, speculative stalemate. Now, the spectators to this combat are to *learn* from watching the speculative war that is antinomy; disinterested obser-vation of antinomy is to liberate practical interest. In Kant's terms, we are to gain from our spectatorship by trading in theoretical knowledge to make room for the discourse describing the arena for the exercise of practical reason:

> Instead, therefore, of rushing into the fight, sword in hand, we should rather play the part of the peaceable onlooker, from the safe seat of the critic. The struggle is indeed toilsome to the combatants, but for us can be entertaining; and its outcome – certain to be quite bloodless – must be of advantage as contributing to our theoretical insight. (Kant, *Critique of Pure Reason*, 1965, B 775)

Such battles, if fairly fought, would have worked to the maturity of reason. (We should note here that Kant's philosophy of history is the struggle to maintain the possibility of hope that real war will also turn a similar pedagogic profit).[4] But Kant bemoans the presence of 'deceit, hypocrisy and fraud' (Kant, *Critique of Pure Reason*, 1965, B 778) in the waging of speculative war. Sincerity here would force us to admit that there *should* in fact be no polemic of reason, since the very conditions of metaphysical assertion unavoidably expose weaknesses in a position that the other side can exploit, turning the supposed battle into the sham the critical spectators know it to be (B 778–9). Indeed the very uselessness of the fight is the lesson to be learned.

What then is to be done with this lesson? We must acknowledge the critique of pure reason as 'the tribunal for all disputes of pure reason', establishing 'the rights of reason in general' (Kant, *Critique of Pure Reason*, 1965, B 779). In the absence of this critique, Kant continues, reason is in the state of nature, and thus war. Explicitly naming Hobbes at this point, Kant claims that the state of nature (of pre-critical metaphysics)

> is a state of injustice [*Unrechts*] and violence [*Gewaltätigkeit*], and we have no option save to abandon it and submit ourselves to the constraint of law [*gesetzlichen Zwange*], which limits our freedom solely in order that it may be consistent with the freedom of others and with the common good of all. (Kant, *Critique of Pure Reason*, 1965, B 780)

So here we have a social contract for speculative reason, the coerced abandonment of speculative violence for the protection of the authority of critical reason in an organ-ized cognitive body politic.

Now in what does the violence of speculative reason's state of nature consist? A disorder among the faculties, the transcendent use of reason. Reason, the syllogistic faculty, demands totality by completing the series of judgments, and so drives on, *transcending* experience, yet calling on the categories of understanding, which are fit only to *produce* experience by allowing judgments about empirical intuition. Reason forces the understanding to make claims about the unity, substantiality and so on, of reason's objects, the pure ideas of God, soul and world. Reason should have been content to remain regulative, serving the understanding in guiding its empirical use by *Ideals*, but turned constitutive, forcing understanding to apply its categories to mere *Ideas* of reason. Reason usurps the leading role of the understanding, leading to a violent anarchy all the more insidious for its speculatively rational character. Metaphysical systems can quite easily be constructed, but they have no authority, no legitimacy in defending their claims. Metaphysics thus degenerates into a series of *coups d'etat*, and to establish the peaceful commonwealth of reason the cycle of revolution must broken, the combatants coerced to submit to the central judicial authority of critical reason. Speculative war must be turned into an edifying spectacle; in this economy of bloodless violence the untram-meled violent freedom of speculation is traded in to provide the discursive space, under the protection of critical reason, in which alone the description of practical reason can flourish.

With the commonwealth of critical reason established by the founding of the tribunal of critical reason, we can now turn to the ethical body politic, the commonwealth of practical reason, which operates in the space cleared by the reining in of the claims of speculative reason. *Gewalt* appears only in a few relatively inconsequential passages in the *Critique of Practical Reason* and the *Grounding for the Metaphysics of Morals*; in almost all these cases, which concern the capabilities of the willing subject to effect action in the world, the standard translation by 'power' produces relatively little disturbance in the economy of force we search to articulate here, and so I will not analyse them in this chapter. However, the alternative between heteronomous and autonomous principles controlling a person's actions is described in body-political terms close to those of the economy of *Gewalt*. For example, we might find something forceful in the painful establishment of the moral law as the ground of action in a person; such establishment, as the *Critique of Practical Reason* puts it, 'by thwarting all our inclinations, must produce a feeling which can be called pain' (Kant, *Critique of Practical Reason*, 1983, 73/75).[5] We might also examine the way the moral law, as positive in itself, commands respect in 'striking down, i.e., humiliating, self-conceit' (74/76). In organ-izing the body politic of the ethical self, Kant objects to the propensity to make our subjective grounds of choice into an objective determining ground of the will, self-love, a propensity that can even attempt to make our self-love into law, the condition Kant calls self-conceit. Thus respect for the moral law is no bully in humiliating self-conceit, but is merely reasserting the proper role of the rational moral law as sole legislator of the commonwealth of practical reason. Respect for the moral law is a palace guard, a counter-revolutionary.

The ethical body politic is even more clearly established in *Religion within the Limits of Reason Alone*. In the section entitled 'Man is by nature evil' Kant writes that man does not rebel against the moral law in the sense of renouncing obedience to it (Kant, *Religion within the Limits*, 1960 36/31). The moral law does not accept direct contravention: it is irresistible, and without other incentives man would

inevitably be good. Despite this irresistibility, there remains a pre-
tender to the throne, another set of incentives: those of self-love (36/
31). Now the difference between good and evil in man lies in the
relative roles of these two incentives, their subordination one to the
other. Evil would consist in the reversal of the proper order, the
making of inclination into the condition of fulfilling the moral law (36/
31). In other words, doing one's duty would be okay, if it didn't
interfere with the satisfaction of desire. Let us not forget at this point
that Kant is a demanding taskmaster: the desire to be satisfied might
merely be the desire to survive, to subsist on the meanest level. But
even these minimal desires must be subordinated to the moral law.
Survival must be moral survival.

The propensity to reverse the proper order between morality and
inclination, the propensity to such a *coup d'état* in the ethical body
politic, is 'radical evil' (Kant, *Religion within the Limits*, 1960, 37/32).
Such evil, Kant makes clear, is 'perversity [*Verkehrtheit*]', not 'wickedness [*Bosheit*]', which would consist in contradicting the moral law, not
merely in subordinating it to another principle (37/32). The perverted
coup that is radical evil in man means that the satisfaction of desire for
the existence of objects takes precedence over the form of the maxim
as the determining ground of the will. Now Kant makes it clear over
and over that he has nothing against happiness *per se*, nothing against
the satisfaction of desires.[6] If they could be satisfied in a way that
accords with the three formulations of the categorical imperative, that
is, if the maxim of the action by which our desires are satisfied were
universalizable, if it treated humanity as an end in itself, if it treated
all wills as universally legislative in a kingdom of ends, then happiness
is a good. Far from the private and empty formalism generations of
scholars have foisted upon him, Kant's ethics teaches us that *each* one
of us is morally obligated to struggle to lessen the conditions that
might tempt *any* one of us to reverse the proper order of incentives.
Merely condemning the succumbing to temptation is empty moralizing.
Moral action, Kant tells us, is working to improve social conditions so
that, with guaranteed access to the society's best means of securing
physical and emotional health, no one would ever again be put in the
terrible position of even being tempted to place the existence of
objects like food, shelter, clothing and the esteem of others over the

moral law. In other words, a properly organ-ized eco-civic body politic is the goal to which we strive because its establishment would help eliminate much of the temptation to a disordered ethical body politic forced on those with threatened somatic bodies.

In these struggles in the ethical body politic, the forceful struggle within the soul for the legislative authority that would control action in the world, we find a painful, humiliating struggle between respect for the law and self-love, a struggle which offers at least the hope of payoff. Although not named as such, we can see the outlines of an economy of *Gewalt* in which the violent anarchy within the subject that results from the heteronomous 'rule' of inclinations would be coerced by pain and humiliation to accept the moral law as the only proper authority. And so, when in a footnote in *Religion within the Limits* replying to Schiller, Kant writes that the moral law provokes respect, 'as of a subject toward his ruler', and hence 'awakens a sense of the sublimity of our own destiny' (Kant, *Religion within the Limits*, 1960, 23n/19n), we can understand his explicitly body-political language.

With this link of respect and the sublime, we now turn to the *Critique of Judgment*, where we find in the aesthetic body politic another economy of intra-subjective *Gewalt*. The Analytic of Aesthetic Judgment pivots from the Analytic of the Beautiful to the Analytic of the Sublime. In section 23, Kant smooths the transition by a series of comparisons and contrasts between the beautiful and the sublime. Both are reflective judgments we like for their own sake because of the harmonizing of the imagination with understanding or reason (Kant, *Critique of Judgment*, 1987, 244/97). The contrasts are more interesting, however. The naturally beautiful is judged as that whose bounded form instigates a harmonious interplay of imagination and understanding in the presentation of quality, bringing a direct pleasure, a feeling of increase in the life force. As such, independent natural beauty seems strangely purposive, strangely predisposed to our subjective makeup (244–5/98–9). On the other hand, the judgment of the sublime is provoked by a formless unboundedness, the presentation of whose quantity brings only an indirect pleasure via the release of previously inhibited vital forces. As such, that which arouses in us a feeling of the sublime appears 'contrapurposive for our power of judgment, incommensurate with our power of exhibition, and as it were violent [*gewalttätig*] to our imagination' (245/99). Yet this very violence is what constitutes its sublimity, Kant concludes. What is the violence of the sublime? How does it lead us to recognize the authority of reason? What is the constitution of the aesthetic body politic?

In his treatment, Kant distinguishes the mathematical and dynamic sublime. He begins his account of the mathematical sublime in section 25 by telling us the sublime is what is 'absolutely large', 'large beyond all comparison' (Kant, *Critique of Judgment*, 1987, 248/103). Sensory objects cannot thus be sublime, but can merely serve as provocations to a feeling of the sublime, which occurs when the imagination strives to progress to infinity by the demand of reason for totality in completing the series of judgments (250/106). Now imagination will always be inadequate to that task, even though it strives mightily at it. Why? Kant explains in section 26 that imagination apprehends progressively, while reason demands the exhibition of its idea in an intuition to be comprehended, that is, grasped all at once (255/112). The natural thing provoking this effort at overcoming a necessary inadequation seems, in Kant's phrase in section 27, to be like 'an abyss in which the imagination is afraid to lose itself' (258/115).

How exactly is the abyssal inadequation violent? The aesthetic judgment of the sublime judges the purposiveness of the conflict of imagination and reason. The conflict arises from the effort to comprehend in one instant that which is apprehended successively. This effort does violence to the inner sense, time.[7] Ap-prehending is a progression, a taking up and running through, one by one, of a multitude, an operation conditioned by time as the form of inner sense. On the other hand, com-prehending a multitude in a unity, that is, instantaneous comprehension of that which was apprehended successively, is a re-gression that cancels [*aufhebt*] time. Kant says that this cancellation is a violence [*Gewalt*] done by imagination to inner sense. 'And yet', Kant continues, 'this same violence that the imagination inflicts on the subject is still judged purposive *for the whole vocation* of the mind' (Kant, *Critique of Judgment*, 1987, 258/116). Here we see an economy of violence in the aesthetic body politic, in which imagination's being unable to exhibit that which is demanded of it by reason is a violence nonetheless judged purposive, because it reveals – as a complement to the inadequacy of the imagination – the unlimited power of reason.

The economy of the sublime is then a trading of initial displeasure at a violence done to the imagination for the later, greater, pleasure of realizing a higher calling in the infinite power of reason. As in the case of the critical spectator of antinomy, an investment in bloodless violence turns a pedagogic profit. We do not fall into the sublime abyss, but teeter on the edge and learn from the experience.

We are not yet done with *Gewalt* and the sublime, however, as we shift from violence to authority in the economy of *Gewalt* that structures the aesthetic body politic. Kant begins the treatment of the dynamic sublime in section 28 by defining *Macht* [might] as 'an ability that is superior to great obstacles'. *Gewalt*, Kant continues, is a might 'superior even to the resistance of something that itself possesses might' (Kant, *Critique of Judgment*, 1987, 260/119). Now the dynamic sublime is an aesthetic judgment that nature is a might with no *Gewalt* over us, a power with no authority over us (261–2/121). How can this be? Natural forces can easily crush us. Indeed they can, Kant notes, and as such are fearful. But in judging the sublime as fearful, we cannot be afraid of these natural forces. And we are not afraid of the fearful overwhelming might of nature, Kant tells us, when we realize that in reason we have a supersensible standard that shows our superiority to nature. Now this superiority is a superiority of our humanity to nature, even though as a human being – that is, a natural creature – we must bow to the *Gewalt* of nature. So, Kant continues, while properly speaking only humanity's supersensible determination is sublime, we can stretch the point and call nature 'sublime' in so far as it summons forth our non-natural 'strength [*Kraft*]' to regard our concerns for property, health and life – the conditions of our natural life – as small, and to hence consider our personality as not under the *Gewalt* of nature (262/121).

The aesthetic body politic thus turns on our not acknowledging the authority of nature, and thereby restoring reason to its properly legislative role. No mention was made, one should notice, of a legitimation of the *Gewalt* of nature: it is defined solely in terms of *Macht*, not of *Recht* – power, not right. Right is reserved for reason; the only true authority in the commonwealth of reason is to be one of rational right, guaranteeing an escape from violence in a seamless transition within the economy of *Gewalt*. However, when we turn from inner rule to outer rule, from the intra-subjective bodies politic of the cognitive, ethical and aesthetic selves to the embodied, inter-subjective eco-civic body politic, we encounter a violence without pedagogic profit, an abyss from which we learn nothing.

FORCE, COERCION AND REVOLUTION

As we have seen, force organ-izes the cognitive, moral and aesthetic bodies politic that are to be the components of the commonwealth of reason. But Kant's anxiety about this force is clearly revealed by his treatment of the formal regicide, the act of a revolutionary justice. Kant's abhorrence of formal regicide betrays his anxiety about the undecidable reservoir of force upon which the coercive organization of a body politic relies, but into which a revolutionary dis-organ-ization and re-organ-ization might dip. In the *Metaphysical Elements of Justice* the social contract is an escape from the anarchic violence (*Gewalttätigkeit*) of the state of nature. The actual violence needs to cease, of course, but more importantly, the natural rights to the private use of force need to be packaged and delegated to the highest state authority (*die oberste Gewalt*), which is to sanction the use of public force. This packaging and delegating is the function of coercion, *Zwang*, the forced removal of the right of recourse to private force.[8]

As Kant states it, the original contract demands, in exchange for the monopoly on force, that the sovereign ask whether each proposed legislation be possibly consistent with the greatest possible freedom of all, willed by all; only such agreement with the general will renders legislation *de jure* legitimate, not just *de facto* legal. As opposed to Rousseau's insistence that the people be in fact consulted regularly on legislation, Kant's relegation of the original contract to an idea of reason allows the possibility of an autocratic approximation to the ideal republic. In section 51, Kant tells us that autocracy is the most efficient, yet most dangerous form of government, since autocracy is easily converted to despotism, in which the legislator and executive are one (*Metaphysical Elements of Justice*, 1965, 339/110). As section 49 states, the danger of despotism consists in its reliance on the subjection of the executive to the law given by the legislator (316–17/82). When legislator and executive are one, the people must trust in the morality and intelligence of the despot, that is, they must hope that the despot will give himself⁹ the law (339/111). The autocrat, instead of being a sovereign that represents the general will by consulting the test of the original contract, can become a tyrant by consulting his private will. This reversal of general and private will is akin to the radical evil one finds in the politics of the ethical self discussed in *Religion within the Limits of Reason Alone*, in that the tyrant's inclinations that desire the existence of objects become the condition for universal legislation. In making this reversal, tyranny thus perverts rightful state authority, the people's being able to consent to legislation.

To find an explicitly political account linking the possibility of tyranny to the very workings of finite subjectivity, let us turn to 'The idea for a universal history from a cosmopolitan point of view' (in *Kant's Political Writings*, 1991). In this essay Kant writes that to read history philosophically we must assume that nature guides humanity in so arranging events that progress is guaranteed toward realizing our *telos*, the free use of reason, a freedom guaranteed by the laws of a free republic in a confederation of free republics. The role of human nature in such progress is made explicit in the fourth proposition of the 'Idea', where Kant describes an irreducible tension in society rooted in a tension in human nature. In all humans there is a pull to society constantly resisted by a pull to isolation, a thoroughgoing resistance that constantly threatens to disrupt the society. What is this resistance? It is nothing less than a will proper to each man to direct everything according to his own *Sinn*, that is, his own meaning or direction. The fourth proposition of 'Idea' continues by naming this inherent pull to individual dominance a *felix culpa*, an 'unsocial sociability' (Kant, *Kant's Political Writings*, 1991, 201/44); the expectation of similar resistance among his fellows awakens man's powers, driving him to seek honour, power or property. These desires are the steps from barbarism to culture, the transformation from pathologically enforced social union to a moral whole.

Now, the continued perfection of this move out of barbarism is the most difficult problem facing man, Kant writes in the sixth proposition of 'Idea'. The difficulty arises in the necessity for man to be mastered, while the master remains a man himself in need of mastery – in other words, the problem of tyranny. Kant develops this point by writing that, in society, man is an animal who needs a master. In what does this animality consist? In man's abuse of his freedom, which takes the shape of an attempt to exempt himself from the legislation he would impose on others. Kant writes:

> And even although, as a rational creature, he desires a law to impose limits on the freedom of all, he is still misled by his self-seeking animal inclinations [*seine selbstsüchtige tierische Neigung*] into exempting himself from the [limit-imposing] law where he can. (Kant, *Kant's Political Writings*, 1991, 23/46)

This tendency to self-exemption is a necessary structure of human subjectivity, the civic body-political version of 'radical evil'. As in the case of the pedagogic violence of metaphysical antinomy and aesthetic sublimity, we should emphasize that Kant writes of civic body-political radical evil as a *felix culpa*, for without the resistance to society that is the tyrannical urge, men would stay in a stultifying Eden, and the *telos* of reason would go unfulfilled. The realization of such a *telos* in a free society presupposes, however, the taming, the 'packaging' of rights to violence, the private use of force, so it can be delegated to legitimate state authority in an organ-ized body politic.

The question now becomes, why is it that the people cannot be trusted with knowledge of their role in the origin of state authority as a safeguard against tyranny? In other words, why is tyranny preferable to rebellion for Kant? In one of his more submissive moods, Kant writes: 'It is the people's duty to endure even the most intolerable abuse of supreme authority' (*Metaphysical Elements of Justice*, 1965, 320/86). Rebellion, the overturning of the proper relations between sovereign and subject, becomes more likely when people recognize that they are the ground of the rightful state authority. Tyranny is preferable to rebellion for Kant, since rebellion would completely subvert the very meaning of law, would land us in a violence without pedagogical payoff. Rebellion would be no mere reversal of principles, like tyranny, no substitution of private for general, but an attack on principle itself.

To avoid rebellion, state authority sets a limit to reason. Kant writes in section 49A of the *Metaphysical Elements of Justice* that the origin of authority must remain off-limits to the use of reason: 'The origin of the supreme authority [*obersten Gewalt*] is, from the practical point of view, not open to scrutiny by the people who are subject to it; that is, the subject should not be overly curious about its origin . . .' (Kant, *Metaphysical Elements of Justice*, 1965, 318/84). Later, in section 52, Kant writes that 'it would be a crime to conduct such an inquiry with the intention of changing the present existing constitution by force [*mit der Gewalt*]' (339–40/111). The people must not look into the origin of state authority because their own united will is itself the origin of that authority, and recognizing this fact may tempt them to rebellion.

What then about rebellion, that most popular of topics for scholars of Kant's political writings?[10] Kant devotes a stunning note to the matter in *Metaphysical Elements of Justice* section 49A. In most cases, Kant says, the criminal merely exempts himself from the law he would otherwise have universally enforced (Kant, *Metaphysical Elements of Justice*, 1965, 321n/87n). This is analogous to radical evil as the perverse, but not wicked, *coup d'etat* in the ethical body politic. Such would be the case with the murder of a monarch out of fear of his restoration; this fear might provide an 'excuse [*Vorwand*]' for the people (321n/87n). However, the notion of willing that violence be universalizable, is, Kant says, a contradiction to reason, not a mere exemption from its decrees. This is the notion of 'wickedness' that Kant says is impossible to man *qua* rational being. But that which is impossible to man *qua* rational is possible to man *qua* natural. Its possibility is horrific, but it must be thought and find a place in the system:

> Thus it is clear to us that to commit a crime of such formal (completely useless) malevolence is impossible for any man and cannot be introduced into a system of morality (except as the pure Idea of extreme evil) [*Äusserst-Bösen*]. (Kant, *Metaphysical Elements of Justice*, 1965, 322n/88n)[11]

Such would be the case with the formal regicide, the execution of the former king after a legal proceeding of the new regime. Formal regicide is putting a monarch to death not as a murder which might be excused but as a legal act. Such a use of force is unforgivably violent:

It is the formal execution of a monarch that fills the soul, conscious of the Ideas of human justice, with horror, and this horror returns whenever one thinks of scenes like those in which the fate of Charles I or Louis XVI was sealed. How can this feeling be explained? It is not an aesthetic feeling . . . but a moral feeling arising from the complete subversion of every conception of justice. (Kant, *Metaphysical Elements of Justice*, 1965, 321n/87n)

This negative moral feeling accompanying the downward flight of the guillotine's blade should be compared with the positive 'sympathy which borders on enthusiasm' of the spectators for the French Revolution in Kant's essay, 'Is the Human Race Constantly Progressing?' In this excerpt from *The Conflict of the Faculties* (the analysis of the academic body politic) Kant points to such a disinterested enthusiasm as proof of a moral disposition of humanity.

In the treatment of the Revolution in the *Metaphysical Elements of Justice*, however, the focus is not on the ideal principles of liberty, equality and fraternity, but on revolutionary justice, which seems to plunge the nascent body politic into an abyss. But this time, it is a violence without pedagogic profit. Instead of teetering on the edge and learning from the experience, instead of the pedagogic vertigo of the sublime, the violence of the formal regicide is outside any edifying economy of spirit. No supersensible vocation is discovered. Unlike Hegel then, Kant finds that no learning, no spiritual pedagogy, is possible from the Reign of Terror:

Accordingly, the employment of violence is brazenly and deliberately placed above the holiest right and justice; as such it is like being swallowed up in an abyss from which there is no return, like the state's committing suicide, and so it appears to be a crime that is incapable of being expiated. (Kant, *Metaphysical Elements of Justice*, 1965, 322n/88n)

Why such extreme language at the notion of revolutionary justice? Surely outrage at *ex post facto* proceedings is too weak, a desire to placate the Prussian authorities too base a motive to ascribe to Kant.

What is the *systematic* significance of revolutionary justice? Let us attempt to answer this by investigating, finally, coercion.

Coercion is necessary to escape the violence of the state of nature and to organ-ize the body politic. Now there is no need to wait for actual incidents of violence to know the state of nature is violent, since the essential tendency of humans to violence can be seen by introspection, and it is this very certainty that men will attempt to play the master over others that authorizes the use of coercion (*Zwang*; to join a civil society). In section 42 of the *Metaphysical Elements of Justice* Kant writes that one can 'quite adequately observe within himself the inclination of mankind in general to play the master over others' (Kant, *Metaphysical Elements of Justice*, 1965, 307/71). Such violence is explained as always possible in section 44 because it is rooted in the 'right' of man in the state of nature to 'follow his own judgment'; this individualism excludes the dependence on others' intentions (312/76). Coercion to quit the state of nature is force applied in the name of authority, as we hear in the wording of the 'principle of strict justice', which in Section E of the Introduction states 'the possibility of the conjunction of universal reciprocal coercion with the freedom of everyone' (232/36). Coercion is force applied in the name of, and consistent with, universal lawful freedom adjudicated by legitimate authority, forcing violent individuals out of the state of nature and into a society which accepts a central authority, that is, an organ-ized body politic. Coercion relies on the co-operation of the many for its application to the recalcitrant few; it taps into a reservoir of force lying in immanent self-ordering that it directs toward state organ-ization, that which takes over the monopoly on force.

Now as we recall, Kant valorizes the republic because it recognizes that state authority rests on an original contract of the people. But in a move that Rawls echoes two centuries later, Kant writes in section 52 that the contract must be considered an idea of reason, rather than an historical fact, since it is probable, due to 'the very nature of uncivilized men', that the historical formation of civil society was in fact 'achieved through the use of force [*mit der Gewalt*]' (Kant, *Metaphysical Elements of Justice*, 1965, 339/111). As uncivilized, the force here seems violent, and so in the removal of the original contract from history to ideality, the shift from 'prior' to *a priori*, we can see

Kant's desire to protect state authority from its coercive historical origins. Why? What is it about coercion at the historical origin of the state? Now in section 44 Kant will legitimate the historical fact of the forceful, violent coercion of the beginning of society. He writes that 'everyone [*jeder*] may use force [*Gewalt*] to compel another to enter a juridical state of society' (Kant, *Metaphysical Elements of Justice*, 1965, 312/76–7).[12] Here we find a private use of force legitimated! It is done in the name of the state to come, to be sure, but as accomplished by 'anyone', prior to the formation of the state that wields public force, it is here private, and hence violent. Or perhaps it is better still to say that coercion is here undecidable with regard to its privacy or publicity, its violence or legitimacy, its irrationality or rationality. For without its complement, 'the public', 'the private' is an inapplicable category. But then, as undecidable, is coercion not irremediably, unforgivably haunted by a type of uncivilized privacy, a sort of violence? Coercion then is *somewhat violent*, a worrisome force that will not sit still, shaking the smooth, rational operation of the economy of *Gewalt*.

Let me then suggest here that it is this undecidable force of coercion, tapping into the reservoir of force that is the potential for self-ordering ('*everyone* may use force'), a somewhat violent force at the origin of authority, that is revealed by the uneconomic violence of revolutionary justice, and that is behind Kant's horror. If violence is force without legal justification, then there is an irreducible violence in any coercive founding of an institution, since the legal, rational, justification of original coercion is always *de facto* retrospective, always too late, since it relies on institutions of justice that were coercively formed.[13] And this temporal contortion, making the force at the historical origin of rational authority somewhat violent, obtains even in the ideal case of a state whose claims to *de jure* legitimacy via the original contract stand up to rational scrutiny and whose coercive historical origins can then be rationally legitimated. (And here let us recall, as 'What is enlightenment' (in *Kant's Political Writings*) would have it, that the *de facto* government must be obeyed for Kant, even if its failings when it comes to *de jure* legitimation licenses a critical, public use of reason in those enlightened states lucky enough to have freedom of the pen and a concerned reading public.) In other words, the move to the *a priori* in Kant's politics is necessitated and haunted by the somewhat violent character of the undecidable force of coercion prior to the state, the force of self-ordering channelled by the social contract in the direction of an organ-ized body politic.

But if justification is always retrospective, foundation is always prospective. Coercion is done in the name of the law it is to found that will then be able, retrospectively, to justify it. Thus the coercion of forcing others to join the state to be founded is always out of time, always too early for the justification that will come if the coercion is successful. Since justification is retrospectively too late, coercion is prospectively too early. In a sense, then, as dependent on a coerced foundation, undecidable as to its violence and authority, *all* justice is out of time, too late to justify its too early founding coercion. Can we say then that *all* justice is somewhat violently *ex post facto*, even that all justice is *revolutionary* justice? And that Kant pulled back before the abyss of that thought, before a force that would not fit the rationally regulated economy of *Gewalt*, and hence before a somewhat violent force he feared could never be made to turn a spiritually pedagogic profit, a somewhat violent force whose effects he would have to trace back through the entire commonwealth of reason in all its bodies politic: cognitive, moral and aesthetic as well as eco-civic?

REVOLUTION AND THE FORCE OF GENIUS

In shifting gears from the Derridean concern with undecidability of the previous section to the Deleuzean concern with material self-ordering, I want to suggest here that the 'reservoir of force' or the 'somewhat violent force' which Kant fears is the self-ordering potential of the people in immanent democratic structuring. Kant cannot see this because of the limits of his hylomorphic production model, which insists on dead, chaotic matter and a transcendent imposition of order from a spiritual source. In the register of the civic body politic, such hylomorphism yields the forced alternative of anarchic violence and state authority. In the *Critique of Judgment*, at the end of his critical project, Kant gets to the point where he could think the genius as the one who reads the approach of singularities that trigger new patterns and thus taps the potential force therein. But Kant cannot abide the consequences of such a new thought, and his genius-concept devolves from such artisanal sensitivity to a vampiric transcendent spiritual ordering of chaos (albeit as a practical supplement of hylomorphism, the thought of the architect God as 'moral author' of the world).

One of the places to read the desire for openness, for life, that Kant thematizes in the genius is Kant's declaration in *Critique of Judgment* section 65 that nature – and hence genius, which takes dictation from nature – is a self-formative force opened up by 'deviation' to change with changing circumstance.

> In considering nature and the ability it displays in organized products, we say far too little if we call this an *analogue of art*, for in that case we think of an artist (a rational being) apart from nature. Rather, nature organizes itself, and it does so within each species of its organized products; for though the pattern that nature follows is the same overall, that pattern also includes deviations useful for self-preservation as required by circumstances. We might be closer if we call this inscrutable property of nature an *analogue of life*. (Kant, *Critique of Judgment*, 1983, 374/253–4)

Now since genius does not produce by concepts (production by genius is not under the *Gewalt* of the artist: there is no unification of a manifold under a concept) its production is not the hylomorphic 'art' here denigrated in favour of natural self-ordering. Rather, as genius is the mouthpiece of nature, the one who breaks the rules and founds schools rather than follows their dictates, he [sic] is closer to being an 'analogue of life'.

But Kant cannot explain the genius, since he grants non-conceptual production to him, and hylomorphic conceptual production – the transcendent[al] organizing of a chaotic manifold – is the only production model open to him. However, such hylomorphic production cannot explicate natural self-organization: 'Strictly speaking, therefore, the organization of nature has nothing analogous to any causality known to us' (Kant, *Critique of Judgment*, 1987, 375/254). The alternative to hylomorphism, to acknowledge the self-ordering properties of matter, would be to commit the fallacy of 'hylozoism' – granting life to dead matter.[14] In effect, even though he cannot understand natural self-organization as hylomorphic production, Kant nonetheless accepts the hylomorphic outlawing of material self-ordering as the limits of intelligible thought itself: 'But in that case [natural self-organization as an "analogue of life"] we must . . . endow matter, as mere matter, with a property, hylozoism, that conflicts with its nature' (374/254)

This limitation of speculative thought, as we might have expected, is of course redeemed by a hylomorphic supplement for practical purposes: the thought of the architect God. The 'antinomy of teleological judgment' (Kant, *Critique of Judgment*, 1987, 386–8/266–8) states that we must think nature as mechanistic and yet as contingent in its particulars (there are no mechanistic laws of biology, no 'Newton of a blade of grass' (400/282)) and in relation to us. The solution is to determine the supersensible basis of nature's lawfulness (that which was precisely left indeterminate but thinkable by the *Critique of Pure Reason*) as the negative idea of a non-discursive intellect (410/294). But this is inscrutable, so we must have recourse to the idea of a moral architect God as the practical determination of the supersensible. Thus nature and freedom are finally related in the thought of a moral architect God who guarantees that nature must at least co-operate with our moral action (444/333).

Prior to working out the hylomorphic supplement, however, Kant appends a fascinating footnote that reveals where he might have gone but for his respect for the hylomorphic outlawing of material self-ordering:

> The analogy of these direct natural purposes can serve to elucidate a certain association, though one found more often as an idea than in actuality: in speaking of the complete transformation of a people into a state, which took place recently, the word *organization* was frequently and very aptly applied to the establishment of legal authorities, etc., and even to the entire body politic. For each member in such a whole should indeed be not merely a means, but also a purpose; and while each member contributes to making the whole possible, the idea of that whole should in turn determine the member's position and function. (Kant, *Critique of Judgment*, 1987, 375n/254n)

But Kant doesn't take up this notion of self-ordering,[15] but moves to positing, in the hylomorphic supplement, the notion of an intelligent cause to the world, as a way station to the notion of a moral author. Given Kant's refusal to think self-ordering, his sticking with production as the transcendent ordering of chaos as the only thought thinkable for a discursive understanding, the actual workings of nature remain opaque to us, open only to an understanding, an *intellectus archetypus*, we can only posit as not our own. The force of nature remains unthought.

In this revolutionary life-force of creative self-ordering – disorganization and re-ordering – with which genius is in touch, that genius reads and coaxes, we see the basis for Kant's fear of genius, his call for taste to 'clip its wings' (319/188). How can taste help Kant's desire for stability and assuage his anxiety about creative force? Taste, although aconceptual, is distributed in a commonwealth of taste that reproduces a split along cultured vs vulgar lines, according to an ability to distinguish pure mental motility from bodily vibrations of enjoyment (*Genuss*) or health-producing bodily motion, as in recovery from fear (274/134), and hence requires a leisured somatic–aesthetic body produced in a civic body politic subject to the same constraints on revolution we discussed above.

Perhaps, though, Kant's caution is not such a bad thing, or at least, is not *simply* a bad thing. For indeed, the force of creative nature, of immanent democratic structuring, is undecidable; not all revolutions are 'progressive'. We cannot forget the National Socialist desire to have Hitler be the genius state-builder who creates by a mimesis of a pattern of past glory, of pure life – a pattern whose purity is guaranteed in that it never existed – in order to ensure pure formal reproduction. Can one safeguard Kantian genius, the openness to chance within a self-formation that follows, while disrupting, patterns, from the fascistic turn to formal reproduction and suicide? Perhaps Kant was right after all to fear revolution, to see only anarchic violence as the opposing pole to state authority in a restricted economy of force. Perhaps. This is always the risk of politics.[16]

Our analysis of *Gewalt* in the Kantian body politic does not claim the state 'rests' on violence or that 'revolutionary force' means taking to the barricades in the pursuit of a state power that would in turn have its own simple replication as its *telos*. It's obviously well beyond the scope of a chapter to give a positive account of these matters, but if I could have recourse to a formula, I'd say we need to think democracy as permanent revolution, or less provocatively as immanent structuring, with an emphasis on the event of structuring – thus democracy as an instituting whose formal procedures are always open to change prompted by the 'event of the other': an structure institutionally open to dis-organ-ization and re-ordering when new circumstances arise, when new voices are heard. This institutional openness to the other, to change that accommodates new voices, distinguishes, I hope, this model from the permanent fashion revolution Jameson diagnoses as post-modernity, as the cultural logic of late capitalism, which always returns to the same, a temporal collapse brought about by ever-faster cycles.

If one could say anything here in favour of genius and life, the key would perhaps be the emphasis on what Deleuze called 'a life of pure immanence' vs the pure life to be safeguarded in the organ-ized body dedicated to formal reproduction and hence frozen in the paradoxical frenzy of a suicidal state.[17] Only a life of pure immanence (one dedicated to variation producing novelty and ethical selection for immanent relations producing 'joy') would live up to the potential of creative dis-organ-ization and re-ordering inherent in some 'revolutions'. One of the struggles of political physics then would be to keep immanent life anti-fascistic,[18] a revolutionary scrambling of the codes that allows events of dis-organ-ization and creative novelty in a new ordering, but one in turn open to its own dissolution in time. The question of a life of pure immanence is then not how to last for a thousand years but how to connect with a thousand plateaus, not how to organ-ize chaos but how to coax forth the self-ordering force of immanent democratic structuring.

Afterword

In this book I've focused on the political physics of hylomorphism, indicating its relation to Derrida's concern with the metaphysics of presence and identity and to the political problem of fascism. In saying this I am of course not proposing that Plato, Aristotle, Kant, Hegel, Husserl, Heidegger or any of the other philosophers mentioned herein have a simple and straightforward relation to fascism, but I am trying to indicate the need to investigate the philosophical predilection for self-ruling organ-ized bodies politic, a form of rule with a certain relation both to fascism as a twentieth century event, and to the 'micro-fascism' that invests bodies politic in the New World Order.

This perspective allows us to see a profound similarity in the projects of Deleuze and Derrida: the struggle against fascism conceived as the fatal desire for the forceful imposition of complete organ-ization in a body politic. A completely organ-ized body politic without chance, change, motion is death: strata without flow, repetition without difference – that is, no repetition at all but pure reproduction, the complete hylomorphic triumph of divine form over dead matter. Here is the clue to the Nazi state's murder–suicide program, the identity between formal reproduction and death, the identity-machine linking fascism, metaphysics and hylomorphism.

Now I hope that in the course of this book I have shown that the search for hylomorphism can provide an important new perspective on the history of Western philosophy. When it comes to contemporary politics, however, I have to admit that there's something a little old-fashioned about my concern with hylomorphism, fascism and identity. But not completely. Fascism has two forms in Deleuze and Guattari. In *Anti-Oedipus*, fascism is the contemporary political form paranoia takes in the schizophrenic capitalist age. Capitalism is deterritorialization and decoding, accompanied by only partial, axiomatic, reterritorialization and local recoding. As an axiomatic system bringing together undetermined flows of labour and capital, capitalism dispenses with the need for an overarching code (in its last gasp in Europe, the codes set by a despot ruling a nation) determining material flows by linking them with determinate meanings. Flows of material production can thus self-organize under capitalism without regard to national borders, while capitalist meaning is always a local tactic merely providing subjective motivation for producers and consumers. The sheer locality and tactical nature of capitalist meaning (the 'search for truth' motivating scientists, the 'impact on young lives' motivating teachers, the 'elegant lifestyle' motivating consumers, and so on) bring with it the threat of a cynical ennui. Fascism thus proposes a two fold solution to capitalism: in place of the global flow of labour and capital it promises an autonomous 'national' market, and in place of local and cynical meaning it promises total meaning and total sincerity. In *Anti-Oedipus*, then, fascism is the massive and total reterritorialization and recoding onto the state, people, master race, etc., of capitalist deterritorialization and decoding.

In *A Thousand Plateaus*, Deleuze and Guattari nuance this picture considerably. First of all, they bring us forward from disciplinary/ industrial capital to what Deleuze later called the 'society of control' (Deleuze, *Negotiations*, 1995, 177–182).[1] 'Control' here means continuous modulation based on continuous measurement and feedback. Modulated control is the hallmark of late, globalized capitalism, in which feedback loops link marketing to sales to production to (re)training to productivity rewards. The major form of capture is interest on finance and speculative capital rather than profit, while the state has become only the mode of realization of capital, providing the infrastructure necessary for the 'informatic' conjunction of flows of capital and labour.

On the basis of this analysis of late capitalism Deleuze and Guattari distinguish micro-fascism, suicidal state fascism, and totalitarianism in *A Thousand Plateaus*, thus displacing the paranoia = fascism and schizophrenia = revolution model of *Anti-Oedipus*. Micro-fascism is the persistence of disciplinary subjectivity in a modulated control society: 'little command centres' proliferate everywhere, making coaches, teachers and cops all little Mussolinis (ATP, 279/228). Suicidal state fascism is distinguished from organic totalitarianism by its having made deterritorialization itself into its goal. Instead of a massive resonating state, a huge organ-ized totalitarian body politic, suicidal fascism is the appropriation of a state by a war-machine that has made war itself into its goal.[2] Thus the urge to pure formal reproduction, the pure hylomorphism of bodies politic, is not Deleuze and Guattari's final word on historical fascism, but is more the marker of totalitarianism. However, micro-fascist bodies politic still tend to represent themselves hylomorpically as the desire to have the will to 'whip your body into shape'; thus even with the modified analyses of ATP, investigating the hylomorphism/fascism connection retains its cogency and necessity, albeit more on the 'micro' rather than the 'macro' scale.

Indeed, although micro-fascism remains an ever-present 'micro-political' challenge, there seems no real threat of a suicidal state fascism for the foreseeable future, given the power of global capital to detect and crush, in the name of 'free trade', any attempt at an *Ersatz* home market, a necessary precondition for a fascist takeover of a state. However, vigilance against state fascism can never be relaxed if we follow Deleuze and Guattari in rejecting any notion of progress: the virtual singularity of state fascism could still be composed which would actualize a fascist suicidal state war machine. The question of totalitarianism (and of what Reagan-era hack Jeanne Kirkpatrick used to call 'authoritarian' regimes), merits similar concern.

Let's note here as well that the 'macro' and 'micro' forms of fascism are intertwined. The state does not simply rest on violence nor does revolutionary force mean taking to the barricades in the pursuit of a state power that would in turn have its own simple replication as its *telos*. Both Foucault and Deleuze and Guattari have shown that desires for state power are suspicious, to say the least, and that analyses of society that focus on state power need to be supplemented. The economy of *Gewalt* is complex and mediated; there's not always an iron fist in the velvet glove, or at least in the 'First World'. In fact I tend to believe Arendt that using force betrays the weakness of the state, which relies much more on consent than some might wish to believe. But I don't think 'consent' is so purely a matter of reason, as some others might wishfully believe. As Deleuze and Guattari suggest, via Spinoza and Reich, the desire for fascism is not just the desire of the few to give orders, but also the desire of the many to take orders, or better, the desire of all to live in a system run by orders. A much wider question then moves to the role of force in 'rational moral education' or the 'production of desire' (two equivalent phrases) in the body politic: both Plato and Aristotle say that laws are much better when they accord with custom, but that educating the young into the customs of the city (at least initially) relies on a carefully crafted regime of reward and punishment based on somatic pleasure and pain. Here we find a doctrine with which both Kant and Nietzsche's very different moral pedagogies would agree. What then is 'revolution' in such a context? The desire for party discipline to allow the efficient pursuit of state authority, the desire to rule the body politic, needs to be rethought, to say the least. But so equally does a simplistic celebration of difference: micro-fascism is a differential field of 'command centres'.

Now just as we cannot merely celebrate difference against identity, we cannot simply celebrate material self-ordering against hylomorphism. That self-ordering is no panacea should be clear from the celebration of capital as self-ordering by the likes of Kevin Kelly (*Out of Control*). What we need is not just self-ordering, but *democratic* self-ordering, as Michael Hardt and Antonio Negri make clear. Hardt and Negri's new work *Empire* provides an extraordinary analysis of differential globalization and the new juridical system it has brought with it. While Hardt and Negri are correct in showing the way a simple-minded post-modernist celebration of difference and flow plays directly into the hands of the new economy and its diversity managers (see especially chapter 2.4, 'Symptoms of passage'), a Derridean deconstruction of identity machines (which in highlighting *différance* is anything but a 'celebration of difference', as *différance* is precisely a way of thinking identity and difference) still finds a place in today's world. Contrary to an implicit epochalism in their work, I would insist that Hardt and Negri have identified not the complete triumph of global differentialism but the increasing tendency toward it in a world still rife with identity machines. These identity machines, even if they tend toward becoming more and more public relations on one level, nevertheless on another level remain key mechanisms in constructing the trigger points for homophobic, misogynist and racist rage (as shown in the work of Klaus Theweleit, *Male Fantasies*) – and thus remain irreducible targets for philosophical analysis and intervention, a key component of which is deconstruction.

Thus it seems to me that the 'targets' of deconstructions should be the claims to the naturality or simplicity of identities, not identities in themselves. ('Targets' should be in scare quotes, because deconstruction is immanent to the fields in which it works and so does not arbitrarily 'choose' its 'targets'; rather, deconstruction responds to the other – as Derrida says in 'Force of Law', 'deconstruction is the maximum intensification of a transformation in progress' (Derrida, 'Force of Law', 1990, 933).) According to this line of thought, deconstructive politics need not be seen as eviscerating any and all identity claims, for I take it as at least arguable that identity claims are necessary in producing improvements in the material life of those people occupying positions formerly denied the ability to participate in the formation of identities. Thus the recourse to nationalism in anti-colonial or anti-imperialist struggles, for instance; witness as well the hotly contested racial and sexual identities of African Americans and women – and African American women, to be sure. The key point to remember is that deconstruction's critical focus demands that identity claims be made in such a way as to highlight their provisional, constructed, and open-ended status.[3] This perspective resonates with Hardt and Negri, who insist that our contemporary task is to analyse and intervene in the system of differentialization and identification. As they put it with typical succinctness:

> It is not really a matter of either/or. Difference, hybridity, and mobility are not liberatory in themselves, but neither are truth, purity, and stasis. The real revolutionary practice refers to the level of *production*. Truth will not make us free, but taking control of the production of truth will. Mobility and hybridity are not liberatory, but taking control of the production of mobility and stasis, purities and mixtures is. (Hardt and Negri, *Empire*, 2000, 156)

In the terms of this book, then, such a productive politics is democracy as immanent structuring, with an emphasis on the event of structuring. Here democracy is an instituting whose formal procedures are always open to change prompted by the 'event of the other', an organ-ization institutionally open to dis-organ-ization and re-ordering when new circumstances arise, when new voices are heard. I believe that one can find here the outlines of a 'positive' notion of a 'progressive' body politic incorporating both Derridean and Deleuzean motifs.[4] However, while we have seen a common target of Derrida and Deleuze as the fascist or hylomorphic construction of organ-ized reproductive bodies politic I will conclude the book by focusing on their differing practices, for, while deconstruction and pragmatics are logically similar, they operate in different ontological registers.

Derridean deconstruction works by setting metaphysical oppositions back into the general text, an aconceptual field of force and signification from which philosophemes are drawn by the 'lifting' of allegedly pure conceptuality from irreducible force differences and are posited as oppositions in the book of nature, the metaphysical dream. The origin of metaphysical oppositions in the general text haunts them as the possibility of reinscription in a general economy. Deleuzean pragmatics, on the other hand, is the experimentation with real bodies produced by machinic assemblages that order the matter-energy flow on the geologic, organic, and 'alloplastic' (roughly speaking, the 'cultural') strata. The virtual is the field of material self-ordering potentials guiding the production of material systems, which tend to either limit of organism or BwO. The BwO thus haunts organ-ized bodies as the road not taken of non-organismic orderings.

Deconstruction must then be placed at the limit of the stratum of 'signifiance' Deleuze and Guattari locate on the alloplastic stratum. Deconstruction is the best antidote to the 'illusion of man' (ATP, 82/ 65) as self-enclosed pure signification; it shows the way that stratum's self-representation as rational self-ruling organism is inscribed in an encompassing field that defeats its pretensions. While deconstructive vigilance against such pretension is always necessary, the Derridean notion of a general text of force and signification cannot guide an empirical investigation of the construction of bodies politic, for such 'force' – like 'matter' for Derrida – is, while asignifying, still tied to signification as its limit; it is only a name for what can't be represented in the metaphysical book of pure significance.

Pragmatics, however, is the call to intervene and experiment on all the material strata of the world. Deleuze calls on us to propose research programmes by pragmatic experimentation, to determine the singularities of the body politic, its 'turning points and points of inflection; bottlenecks, knots, foyers and centres; points of fusion, condensation and boiling; points of tears and joy, sickness and health, hope and anxiety, 'sensitive' points' (*Logic of Sense*, 67/52). In other words, Deleuze bids us construct a political physics that considers in physiological detail the triggers for homophobic rage, for murderous frenzy, for totalitarian 'crystallization' (ATP, 279/228). Alternatively, we are to experiment with the 'construction of the plane of consistency' (ATP, 204/165), that is, the construction of a locus of immanent, horizontal, transverse communication allowing events of life, joy, love. It is this Deleuzean injunction to materialist experimentation that differentiates his project from the Derridean articulation of the logical and experiential aporias involved in welcoming, mourning, affirming 'the other'.

In this way Deleuze opens up what I believe to be the most promising avenue of contemporary thought: the articulation of post-structuralist historical–libidinal materialism with the research using complexity theory in biology, psychology, cognitive science, artificial intelligence and artificial life, especially as all these are interpreted by the school known as the 'embodied mind'. Deleuze bids us investigate how the material self-ordering potentials of the virtual realm are tapped into by machinic assemblages above and below the level of the 'individual'. In other words, he bids us investigate how material flows are ordered or organ-ized by the social machines of, say, democracy or fascism to produce the 'behaviour patterns' and 'problem-solving capacities' all too often reified as individual achievements by contemporary philosophers. The challenge posed by Deleuze's work is thus to replace the 'philosophy of mind' with the political physics of the body politic.

Notes

INTRODUCTION

1. This is not to say that no work has been done. See for instance Paul Patton, 'Strange Proximity' (1996); May, *Reconsidering Difference* (1997); and the essays in Patton and Protevi, eds, *Between Derrida and Deleuze* forthcoming.

2. I will define my sense of the term 'body politic' below. The term re-entered common academic usage with Ernst Kantorowitz, *The King's Two Bodies* (1957). Foucault cites Kantorowitz at *Discipline and Punish*, 1979, 37/28.

3. There is already a huge literature attempting to make accessible to a general audience the basics of complexity theory. Among others, see Prigogine and Stengers, *Order Out of Chaos* (1984), and Cohen and Stewart, *The Collapse of Chaos* (1994).

4. Derrida's work of the 1990s increasingly uses the figure of aporia. See among others the eponymous *Aporias* (1993).

5. In other words, Derrida's work can help in exposing the 'illusion constitutive of man' Deleuze and Guattari pinpoint at ATP, 82/63.

6. This movement from 'sign' to 'mark' renders utterly futile attempts to criticize Derrida's alleged 'semiological reductionism,' as in M.C. Dillon, *Semiological Reductionism* (1995).

7. Deleuze and Guattari have both an ultimate ontological sense of matter as 'Body without Organs' (BwO) or 'plane of consistency' (the quantum level): 'the unformed, unorganized, nonstratified or destratified body and all its flows: subatomic and submolecular particles, pure intensities, prevital and prephysical free singularities' (ATP, 58/43); 'nonstratified, unformed, intense matter, the matrix of intensity, intensity = 0; . . . Matter equals energy' (189/153), and a relative analytic sense as the input to a production process analysed without reference to a transcendent ordering agent (ontologically speaking, then, relatively stratified facing the BwO and relatively destratified facing the product). The resonance with the Aristotlean problematic of prime matter should be evident.

8. See the excellent discussion of Deleuze's notion of virtuality in Daniel W. Smith's 'Introduction' to his translation of Deleuze's *Critique et clinique*

(*Essays Clinical and Critical*, 1997). See also Boundas, 'Deleuze-Bergson: an Ontology of the Virtual,' (1996).

9. Deleuze's *Foucault* (1986) is both among the very best works written on Foucault and one of Deleuze's most intriguing books.

10. I hyphenate 'organ-ization' to draw attention to Deleuze and Guattari's concept of the forceful body as stretched along a continuum whose limit cases are the organism and the 'Body without Organs' (BwO), that is, a fixed, centralized body, transcendently formed by exclusive disjunctions, and a changeable body, immanently self-organized by inclusive disjunctions. While all bodies are ordered, not all tend toward the limit named 'organism'. See my 'The organism as judgment of god' (2001) for a detailed discussion of these terms.

11. Noteworthy recent philosophical discussions that interrogate the biological, political and legal notions of life include Keith Ansell Pearson's two works, *Viroid Life* (1997) and *Germinal Life* (1999); and Giorgio Agamben, *Homo Sacer* (1998). I reviewed *Viroid Life* in *Parallax*, 8.

12. For a noteworthy contribution to the already large literature on Derrida and politics, see Richard Beardsworth, *Derrida & the Political* (1996). I reviewed Beardsworth's book in *PLI*, 6.

13. By this I mean that Derrida himself does not dedicate his own work to the deconstruction of scientific texts; in particular, he does not address the epistemological or ontological presuppositions of contemporary complexity theory. This is not to say that a philosophy of science cannot be constructed using Derridean support (most notably, the notion of undecidability Derrida works out with reference with Gödel, and the work on idealization conducted in ITOG) as two recent texts demonstrate. Arkady Plotnitsky's *Complementarity* (1994) is a long and complex work detailing the 'analogies' (2), 'affinities' (3), and 'metaphoric parallels' (86) of Derrida's work with that of Niels Bohr, thereby showing a generalized 'anti-epistemological' effect of an ineluctable loss of meaning accompanying the necessary replacement of the restricted economy of classical physics and metaphysics by a general economy (1–2). Christopher Norris, on the other hand, enlists Derrida's aid in reining in Plotnitsky in support of a defence of some minimal commitment to ontological realism in science. (See especially Chapter 4, 'Quantum mechanics: a case for deconstruction' in Norris, *Against Relativism*, 1997.) Without claiming to decide the relative merits of the complex arguments of Plotnitsky and Norris, it seems to me that, even if one grants that Plotnitsky has proven his point, it should not be forgotten that for an anti-reductionist stance quantum effects are negligible in the 'mid-range' of material bodies – precisely those areas in which Deleuze can

help us see how complexity theory works in investigating bodies politic. See Prigogine's declaration of an 'end of universality' in science at 217–18 of *Order Out of Chaos* (1984); and Cohen and Stewart, *The Collapse of Chaos* 1994, 33–4 et passim; Deleuze and Guattari make the anti-reductionist point at 119 of *What is Philosophy?* (1994). In the biological context, Sarkar is very clear on this point: 'Whatever strong reduction in molecular biology is, it is not a reduction to the quantum level' (*Genetics and Reductionism*, 1998, 148).

In other words, granting Plotnitsky the point that Derrida's thought can be usefully articulated with Gödel's work on undecidability in mathematical systems (the 'highest' or signifying stratum of the material world) and to Bohr's work on complementarity in quantum mechanics (the 'lowest' or material/energetic stratum), it still has no purchase on the ontology needed for mid-range complexity theory work (the notions of phase space, attractors, bifurcators, emergent effects, and so on) that Deleuze's notion of the virtual enables us to think. The basic difference between Derrida and Deleuze relevant in this case is that between a post-phenomenology and a historical–libidinal materialism: the study of the breakdown of presence into *différance* and the study of the material production of bodies politic.

Several more or less unsatisfactory attempts have been made to link Derrida's thought to that of chaos theory, but none go beyond noting analogies at a very high level of abstraction. In descending order of rigor, see N. Katherine Hayles, *Chaos Bound* (1990), especially Chapter 7, 'Chaos and poststructuralism'; Laurie McRobert, 'On fractal thought' (1995); and Robert Smith, 'Short cuts to Derrida' (1996). Alexander Argyros' *A Blessed Rage for Order: Deconstruction, Evolution, and Chaos* (1991), while not uninteresting on the latter two topics of his subtitle, is sadly ill-informed and (hence) needlessly polemical on the first.

Derrida's relation to biology, cybernetics, and information theory is treated by Richard Doyle, *On Beyond Living* (1994), Chapter 5, 'Allergies of reading: DNA, language, and the problem of origins'; and Christopher Johnson, 'Derrida and science' (1998).

14. After being quite brutally and stupidly attacked in its first round. See Plotnitsky's devastating critique ' "But it is Above all Not True": Derrida, Relativity, and the "Science Wars"' (1997) of the serious reading and conceptual errors (and the lack of the merest professional courtesy, not to say ethics) in the attacks on Derrida by Gross and Levitt, *Higher Superstition* (1994) and by Alan Sokal in the *Social Text* (1996) and *Lingua Franca* (1996) articles in which he springs his now-famous 'hoax.' Plotnitsky adds a brief explanatory note in *Postmodern Culture* 7.3 (May 1997) and has a much longer

and more detailed exchange with a physicist who is critical but (unlike the others noted above) interested in a serious and respectful intellectual encounter in *Postmodern Culture* 8.2 (January 1998).

15. Alan Sokal and Jean Bricmont, *Fashionable Nonsense* (1998), 8. In general, Sokal and Bricmont's caveats about easy and exaggerated conclusions drawn by some minor authors about the so-called 'limits to science' or 'revolution against Newton' allegedly shown by the results of 'chaos theory' are extremely well-taken. See, for example, their very clear and useful Chapter 7, 'Intermezzo'. The reader will note the complete absence of such speculation in *Political Physics*, which deals exclusively with the implications of new scientific notions as reading grids for the history of philosophy. This consonance does not mean, however, I agree with their treatment of Deleuze and Guattari, although space does not permit a full examination of the remarkable chapter on Deleuze and Guattari in *Fashionable Nonsense*, in which extended quotation without context competes for space with out-of-hand dismissals without discussion.

16. One of Foucault's most noble late works is his wonderful critique of the polemical genre in 'Polemics, politics, and problematizations' (1984).

17. See notes 13 and 14 above.

18. About Manuel DeLanda's 'Non-organic life' (1992), which highlights the relation of Deleuze and complexity theory, no less severe critics than Gross and Levitt say in their *Higher Superstition* (1994), 267–8n17: '[although] there is some muddle . . . [it is] pretty clear and straightforward . . . a good and honest job, although one might wish for a more careful delineation of how much of this is really speculative'. As readers of *Higher Superstition* will attest, this is praise indeed from Gross and Levitt. Since DeLanda explicitly links his account with Deleuze and Guattari, and since Gross and Levitt somewhat approve of DeLanda – although admittedly without mentioning Deleuze and Guattari by name (they do contemptuously dismiss Deleuze's treatment of Riemann in his *Cinema* series, although they do not mention the similar treatment in ATP) – I assume the connection of Deleuze and Guattari and complexity theory is at least an avenue worth pursuing.

19. This is not to say Kant was at the forefront of his times, as was Deleuze. See Zammito, *The Genesis of Kant's Critique of Judgment* (1992), Chapters 8 and 9, for a critical assessment of Kant's relation to the science of his times, especially at 190: 'Kant's attitudes impeded his recognition of . . . recent developments in eighteenth-century science and left him sharply estranged from its most creative and effective currents'.

20. Throughout the *User's Guide* (1992) and in his otherwise splendid 'The Autonomy of Affect', (1996), Massumi makes the to my mind unfortunate assertion that quantum indeterminacy is 'fed forward' through all strata

(230). While the Deleuzean concept of virtual can be used to think the quantum level, as Massumi shows at 52–5 of *User's Guide*, identifying all indeterminacy, undecidability, physical free play, political resistance, economic crisis, and so on, with quantum indeterminacy is speculative overkill. Indeed Massumi himself seems a bit uneasy in wrestling with such identity and difference. He first writes that 'On each level, it [sc. quantum indeterminacy] appears in a unique mode adequate to that level', but then goes on to use scare quotes, which seem to indicate some hesitancy: 'Each individual and collective human level has its peculiar "quantum" mode . . .' See Cohen and Stewart's critique at 425–7 of *The Collapse of Chaos* (1994) of Penrose's analogous attempt to ground free will in quantum indeterminacy in *The Emperor's New Mind* (1991). For another take on Deleuze and quantum mechanics, this time from the perspective of the work of David Bohm, see Murphy, 'Quantum Ontology.'

21. See also the remarks on Deleuze and Guattari interspersed throughout DeLanda's *War in the Age of Intelligent Machines* (1991) and *A Thousand Years of Nonlinear History* (1998).

22. Deleuze and Guattari cite Simondon's major works, *L'individu et sa genèse physico-biologique* (1964) and *Du mode d'existence des objets techniques* (1969) at several crucial passages of the 'Nomadology' plateau of ATP, e.g. 457n28/ 555n33 and 508/408. Very little has been written about Simondon in English, although there is a translation of the Introduction to *L'individu* in Crary and Kwinter, eds., *Incorporations* (1992). For French literature, see the monograph by Gilbert Hottois, *Simondon et la philosophie de la culture technique* (1992), and the collection of essays published by the Collège International de Philosophie, *Gilbert Simondon: Une pensée de l'individuation et de la technique* (1994).

23. 'The' architect is only an ideal figure of hylomorphism, indicating the arrogation to the seer of form of the credit for an ordered product and the denigration of the corresponding figure of the 'artisan' who is allegedly responsible for the mere imposition of that form in a chaotic or passive matter. That a real person with the professional title 'architect' is aware of material limitations to the imposition of form is no escape from hylomorphism; what is needed is the 'artisanal' recognition of the ability to coax forth the positive contributions of material inputs to ordered products. I thus retain the reference to architecture more because of its links to the Greek *archē*, as we will see in Chapters 5 and 6, than to contemporary architectural practice, as analysed in a Deleuzean vein by John Rajchman, *Constructions* (1998).

24. Deleuze and Guattari's loose use of the term 'fascism' in *Anti-Oedipus* (1984), replicated here, is controversial. I detail ATP's rigorously materialist

sense of fascism in 'A Problem of Pure Matter'. For a view that upholds the *Anti-Oedipus* conception see Land, 'Making it with death' (1993). See the Afterword below for the important distinction between 'micro' and 'macro-fascism' that results from ATP's more nuanced stance regarding National Socialism as an historical event.

25. Deleuze and Guattari define coaxing as the work of the 'artisan'. 'We will therefore define the artisan as one who is determined in such a way as to follow a flow of matter, a *machinic phylum*. The artisan is *the itinerant, the ambulant*. To follow the flow of matter is to itinerate, to ambulate. It is intuition in action'. ATP, 509/409.

26. As developed in both *Labor of Dionysus* and *Empire*.

27. See the breathtaking naivety of Stuart Kauffman's *At Home in the Universe* (1995), or Kevin Kelly's *Out of Control* (1994). Gilles Châtelet critiques such identifications in 'Du chaos et de l'auto-organisation comme néo-conserva-tisme festif' (1995). See DeLanda, 'Non-organic life' (1992), 156, for the important qualifications to the assumptions held by mainstream economists necessary before 'the market' can be considered dynamically.

28. See Daniel Smith, 'The doctrine of univocity: Deleuze's ontology of immanence' (2001).

29. 'Crystallization' needs scare quotes as the self-ordering patterns of bodies politic are often far more complex than crystallization. It is, however, the basic example used by Simondon, on which Deleuze and Guattari rely. See note 23 above.

30. Deleuze, 6. Deleuze's work in the history of philosophy is the subject of Michael Hardt, *Gilles Deleuze: an Apprenticeship in Philosophy* (1993).

31. Deleuze and Guattari, *What is Philosophy?* (1994), 112/118.

CHAPTER 1

1. In the works examined in this chapter (*Speech and Phenomena*; 'Form and Meaning'), Derrida by and large focuses on those works of static phenome-nology (*Logical Investigations*; *Ideas I*) written prior to the development of genetic phenomenology, which, under the rubric of 'passive synthesis', opened up the intentionality of such factors as indication, motivation and association. 'Phenomenology . . . was very late in finding avenues to the exploration of association . . .' (Husserl, *Cartesian Meditations*, 1960, section 40). However, we should note that Derrida is thoroughly familiar with the question of the relation of static and genetic phenomenology, as his first major publication was the article '"Genesis and structure" in phenomenol-ogy' (reprinted in *Writing and Difference*, 1967) and his 1954 student *mémoire*, unpublished before 1990, is entitled *Le Problème de la genèse dans la philosophie*

de Husserl (1990). Now Derrida will sometimes make (admittedly nuanced) claims about the relation of static to genetic phenomenology that posit an inescapable relation to metaphysics in the entirety of Husserl's work, as in the following passage from *Speech and Phenomena*: '. . . we would perhaps have to conclude that, in spite of all the themes of receptive or intuitive intentionality and passive genesis, the concept of intentionality remains caught up in the tradition of voluntaristic metaphysics . . .' (Derrida, *Speech and Phenomena*, 1973, 37/34). Anthony Steinbock, in his important work, *Home and Beyond* (1995), criticizes Derrida's claim that for Husserl genetic phenomenology does not 'surpass' static phenomenology, but only 'deepens' its findings (264; Steinbock quotes from '"Genesis and structure" in phenomenology' at this point), while maintaining that his own approach – that genetic phenomenology does indeed 'surpass' static phenomenology (which is itself 'rattled' by the 'generative phenomenology' Steinbock reconstructs in his reading of Husserl's unpublished notebooks) – follows 'in the spirit of much of Derrida's work on Husserl' (265). In light of the complexity of the issues involved, and despite a certain violence toward Derrida – keeping in mind always the fact that for the most part he confines his analysis to Husserl's published works – the safest path is to bracket Derrida's claims about the relevance of his analyses to all of phenomenology, and to restrict ourselves to claiming that he shows the metaphysical entanglements of the static and Cartesian strands of Husserl's work, however those strands relate to other strands of phenomenology. This interpretative stance will enable us to highlight below the 'hylomorphic' element of static phenomenology without committing us to claims about the entirety of phenomenology. See also note 10 below.

2. On either of the two models of deconstruction (author's intention vs textual description or 'double reading'), Derrida never simply 'criticizes' a unitary subject named 'Husserl' for succumbing to metaphysics; rather, he shows the riches of the multiplicitous text signed 'Husserl', the way it includes both metaphysical and differantial strands.

3. Strictly speaking, for Derrida *différance* is neither central to any supposed Derridean 'system,' nor is it a 'concept' *per se*. However, the 'family resemblance' of other Derridean terms such as 'trace' to *différance* needs to be acknowledged. Much of the import of Gasché's *The Tain of the Mirror* (1986) lies in articulating these relations.

4. The inspiration for this phrase comes from Len Lawlor's forthcoming work, *The Basic Problem of Phenomenology*. I could cite this work, destined to become the standard reference on the Derrida/Husserl relation, on virtually every page of this chapter, so abundant are its insights. I will however restrict myself to noting only the most important connections. Both Lawlor's and

my phrase are of course plays on the title of Heidegger's 1927 lecture course, published as *The Basic Problems of Phenomenology*.

5. Left attacks on 'deconstruction[ism]' are legion, although often directed at 'post-modern literary criticism' or some such formulation. Geoffrey Bennington examines some of the more egregious examples in *Legislations*. Derrida's writing on Marx is largely restricted to *Specters of Marx* (1994).

6. Chapter 4 of Lawlor's *Basic Problem* analyses the roles of Tran Duc Thao and Cavaillès in *Le Problème*.

7. I work out these details in 'The economy of exteriority in Derrida's *Speech and Phenomena*' (1993).

8. Derrida's footnote at 32/30 is crucial to his claims about the significance of his analyses of the *Logical Investigations* for all of phenomenology. Here Derrida acknowledges that while Husserl reworked the theme of association in moving from the 'objectivist' *Investigations* to the later transcendental phenomenology, he 'never broached' the question of whether the essential distinction of indication and expression also needed to be reworked in moving to transcendental phenomenology.

9. Husserl, *Cartesian Meditations* (1960), 97. Although this phrase occurs in the context of a discussion of kinesthesia, the ruling-character of the 'I' survives the transcendental reduction and the investigations of passive synthesis – or at least, as we have seen Derrida note (*Speech and Phenomena*, 1973, 37/34), survives as far as the identity of expression and volition posited in *Ideas I* section 124 holds.

10. Here we see a point of articulation with a major theme of contemporary thought on the process of subjectification as the 'fold of the outside', as exemplified in Foucault's work on disciplinarity.

11. Here we see Derrida's theme of the limiting of sense to knowledge as object-presentation in the form of the living present, which he calls at *Speech and Phenomena*, (1973) 110/98 the 'weight' of Husserl's intuitionism upon his formalism.

12. In this instance I prefer the translation offered by David Allison of 'Form and Meaning', which is appended to his translation of *Speech and Phenomena*.

13. I consider this relation in two other phenomenologists in 'The "sense" of "sight": Heidegger and Merleau-Ponty on the meaning of bodily and existential sight' (1998).

14. Cf. 'The pit and the pyramid' in *Margins* (1982) for Derrida's reading of Hegel's semiology.

15. We will examine quasi-transcendentality in more detail in Chapter 3.

16. A lengthy analysis would have to be devoted to the use to which Derrida puts the notion of life and the living body (*Leib*) of language as he finds it in Husserl, especially in *Speech and Phenomena*, and how this might be related

to Deleuze's notion of life. The first line of attack in such a project would be to investigate the relation of Husserlian intentional 'animation' (a form-giving act rooted in the form of the living present) to hylomorphism

17. Respecting the specificity of Husserl's descriptions in *Ideas I*, Derrida does not identify the medium of expression with the voice in 'Form and meaning' as he does in *Speech and Phenomena*, which follows the *Logical Investigations*. We will soon call attention to the crossings between these texts, however.

18. Bass's mistranslation at this point is crucial: he inexplicably renders Derrida's 'cette originalité consist en effet à n'en pas avoir, à s'effacer comme une transparence improductive devant le passage du sens' as 'this originality consists in not having to erase itself . . .' Allison's translation is correct on this point.

19. See Derrida's footnote in ITOG to Hyppolite's expression, 'subjectless transcendental field', 88n. See also Deleuze, *Logic of Sense* (1990), 98.

20. Derrida: 'Elle [la reproduction] informe le sens dans le vouloir-dire'; Bass: 'It informs meaning with sense'; Allison: 'It forms the sense in the meaning'.

21. Eugen Fink, 'The phenomenological philosophy of Edmund Husserl and contemporary criticism' (1970). See Chapter 1 of Lawlor, *The Basic Problem of Phenomenology*, for an informative reading of the importance of Fink's essay for Derrida's interpretation of Husserl.

22. I use Kersten's translation of *Ideas I*. Bass and Allison use Gibson's slightly misleading translation, which nonetheless corresponds to Derrida's French: 'Expression is complete when the *stamp of conceptual meaning has been impressed (ausprägt) upon all the synthetic forms and matter (Materien) of the lower layer*' (Derrida, 'Form and meaning', 1982, 200/167).

23. Expressive hylomorphism is only one of a series of hylomorphisms found in Husserl. Expressive hylomorphism – the stamping of conceptual meaning on the forms and matters (*Materien*: the matter of an act is the mere presentation of the intentional object, accessible only as a moment abstracted from the full act, which also contains the 'quality' of the act) of the sense level – is different from perceptual hylomorphism, in which the *hylē* of sensuous data is animated (unified) by a perceptual act, and from the hylomorphism found in categorial intuition, in which categorial forms are distinguished from sensuous *Stoff*. See the sixth *Logical Investigation*, Chapter 6, for categorial intuition and section 85 of *Ideas I* for Husserl's classic statement of the doctrine of perceptual hylomorphism. Derrida discusses perceptual hylo-morphism at *Le Problème* (1990), 152ff. In his 'Husserl's genetic phenome-nology of perception' (1983), Donn Welton develops a non-hylomorphic doctrine of perception from Husserl's later work on passive synthesis. See also Welton's *The Origins of Meaning* (1983).

24. At this point one could analyse the relation of Husserl's notion of identity

as the simple identity of the species unifying a multiplicity of instances (*Logical Investigations* 1, Chapter 3, section 31) to what in Chapter 3 below I call the Derridean notion of differantial species-being.

25. This (ultimately Nietzschean) treatment of conceptuality (see 'On truth and lie' in particular) would no doubt be called that of 'understanding' by a Hegelian; we will consider Derrida's treatment of Hegel in the next chapter.

26. See Rotman, *Ad Infinitum* (1993), for an examination of the ontological presuppositions behind the allegedly non-material status of mathematical computation.

27. Allow me to repeat my disclaimer in note 1 above that I delimit the relevance of my analyses to the consequences able to be drawn from Derrida's focus on the static and Cartesian strands of Husserl's published writings. Steinbock's work in *Home and Beyond* (1995) on the social and political theory to be drawn from a study of Husserl's notebooks should be used as a supplement for a full picture of Husserl's thought on the body politic.

28. This doctrine of Husserl is Levinas' target in his 1930 *The Theory of Intuition in Husserl's Phenomenology* (1973), and remained his constant objection to phenomenology, and as the priority of the horizon of being to ethics, his objection to Western philosophy as a whole.

29. See the detailed examination of these questions in Chapter 7 of *Speech and Phenomena*.

CHAPTER 2

1. See the distinction between the thematic and methodological use of contradiction in Bole, 'Contradiction in Hegel's *Science of Logic*' (1987) and Chaffin, 'Hegel, Derrida and the sign' (1989).

2. On this point, see John Sallis, 'Hegel's concept of presentation', in *Delimitations* (1986). This section is indebted to Sallis' lectures at Loyola University Chicago in the years 1986–90.

3. See 'With what must the science begin', in *Hegel's Science of Logic* (1989).

4. See Kolb, *The Critique of Pure Modernity*, 1986, 45, where the *Science of Logic* is described as a series of 'ontologies with ever fuller conceptions of what it means to be'.

5. I discuss this issue in a Heideggerian context in *Time and Exteriority* (1994) and 'The "sense" of "sight" ' (1998); for a discussion in the Hegelian context, see Nancy, *Hegel* (1997), 69–81.

6. A Derridean 'philosophy of mind' might hold that the iteration of neural patterns is reinforced by a system of somatic and affective rewards and punishments. The utility of the Derridean categories of iteration and writing

in making sense of neuroscientific research seems relatively small, however, compared to the work possible with Deleuzean categories, as Massumi shows in his 'The autonomy of affect' (1996).

7. On this point see Honig, 'Declarations of independence' (1991).

8. See Beardsworth, *Derrida & the Political* (1996), and Critchley, *The Ethics of Deconstruction* (1992).

9. Kant is also hesitant to indicate a standard here. In the *Metaphysical Elements of Justice* (1965), at the point where the universal law and the singular case come into conflict, he calls equity 'a silent goddess who cannot be heard', 40.

10. The Kantian echo should be clear, as a moral act can never be shown to have occurred.

CHAPTER 3

1. Recent book-length works include Oliver, *Womanizing Nietzsche* (1994); Butler, *Bodies That Matter* (1993); and Chanter, *Ethics of Eros* (1995).

2. For commentary on the mother in *Glas*, see Bennington and Derrida, *Jacques Derrida* 1992, 204–8; Cornell, *Beyond Accommodation*, 1991, 89–92; and Cornell, *The Philosophy of the Limit*, 1992, 75–9.

3. Here a point of articulation with Agamben's challenging *Homo Sacer*.

4. Derrida's comments on biology and writing (*Of Grammatology*, 1975, 19/9) are shown by Doyle, *On Beyond Living*, 1994, 92–3, to entertain a certain indebtedness to the DNA-as-arche motif (for critical analysis of this trope, see Keller, *Refiguring Life*, 1995, 1–42). Though far beyond the scope of this book, an investigation of Deleuze's biological thinking would enable a critique of the hylomorphism of genetic determinism by calling attention to the material self-organizing processes of the embryo. For the distinction between genetic determinism and genetic reductionism, see Sarkar, *Genetics and Reductionism*, 1998, 9–13. See also the comments by Ansell Pearson (*Germinal Life*, 1999, 39–40) on the intersection of Bergson, Deleuze, embryology and complexity theory.

5. Maternal specifity without identification as woman's destiny is in Irigaray's words, a 'gift of [new] life'. She writes in 'The bodily encounter with the mother', in *The Irigaray Reader* (1991), 43: 'We have to be careful . . . we must not once more kill the mother who was sacrificed to the origins of our culture. We must give her new life, new life to that mother, to our mother within and between us'. This giving a new life to the mother is the thought of the mother as giving life: 'perhaps we might remind him [the Pope, the Father] that he would not be there if our body and our blood had not given him life, love, spirit' (45).

6. Derrida, *Otobiographies* (1984), 7. Cf. Aristotle's discussion of the impact of the fate of descendants on the happiness (*eudaimonia*) of the dead at *Nicomachean Ethics* 1.11.1100a10–1101b8.
7. *Philadelphia Inquirer*, 18 September 1993, B3.
8. The relation of mark to signifier and member to species is thought according to the relation of empirical instance to form: the same form must be able to be recognized across empirical differences of its instances. But for Derrida, following Husserl's dual critique of Platonism and psychologism in the 'Origin of geometry', form both guides and is constituted across its empirical instances; this generated structure and structured genesis sets up the investigation of the 'transcendental historicity' of form (ITOG 69/75) – a phrase that would no doubt shock and perhaps dismay Aristotle.
9. That is, beyond not only Aristotle's circle, but also the cyclical and monumental mythological times traditional given to women, as described in Kristeva's 'Women's time' (in *The Kristeva Reader*, 1986, 188–213). Beyond, no doubt, also the entry into linear historical time desired by the first generation of feminists of whom Kristeva writes in 'Women's time'. The space–time of generation beyond the circle would for Kristeva perhaps settle in the 'third generation' which is 'less a chronology than a *signifying space*, a both corporeal and desiring mental space' (209).
10. See, *inter alia*, *De Anima* 2.4; *De Generatione Animalium* 2.10. Pierre Aubenque, *Le problème de l'être chez Aristote* (1972), is an indispensable reference point here.
11. See Irigaray's attempts to think a feminine imaginary beyond the Aristotelian circle, using the thoughts of 'volume' in *Speculum of the Other Woman* (1985) and 'lips' in *This Sex Which is Not One* (1985). Whitford's commentary in her *Luce Irigaray: Philosophy in the Feminine* (1991), 53–74, mentions Irigaray's break with Aristotle's use of the Pythagorean table of opposites (59). See also Irigaray's 'The poverty of psychoanalysis', in *The Irigaray Reader* (1991), 97–8:

> An Aristotelian *model*? Or already a Parmenidian model? The circle of the same is postulated or presupposed. In the "at least two" lips, the process of becoming form – and circle – is not only never complete or completable; it takes place (no ek-sistance) thanks to this non-completion . . .

Further commentary on Irigaray and Aristotle can be found in Chanter, *Ethics of Eros* (1995), 151–9.
12. Irigaray writes: 'For man needs an instrument to touch himself: a hand, a woman, or some substitute' ('Volume without contours', *Irigaray Reader*, 1991, 58).

13. Michel Henry, *Marx: a Philosophy of Human Reality* (1983), 59. See also Derrida's critical remarks on Henry's simplified notion of pure life in *Specters of Marx*, (1993), 186n7.

14. We move very quickly here over ground that would require much careful work. Briefly, what Derrida shows in ITOG concerning Husserl's account of geometrical objects as 'free idealities' holds *a fortiori* for 'bound idealities' such as 'human being'. See especially ITOG 66–76.

15. This is a fairly common feminist typographic convention. See, for example, Garner, Kahane and Sprengnether, eds, *The (M)other Tongue* (1985).

16. 'Reproduction' here, by way of its classic Marxist echoes, indicates the point of articulation of this counter-reading with the counter-reading to 'family values' initiated by Engels in *The Origin of the Family, Private Property, and The State* (1985). And perhaps it is not by accident that Engels' account of origins also employs a 'zig-zag' method, as does, on Derrida's reading, Husserl's 'Origin of geometry'. One of Irigaray's abiding concerns is woman's role as the mother reproducing labour-power. For her critical comments on Engels, see 'The power of discourse and the subordination of the feminine', *The Irigaray Reader* (1991), 129. In the same collection, see 'The bodily encounter with the mother', *The Irigaray Reader* 1991), 35: 'What of that woman outside her social and material role as reproducer of children, as nurse, as reproducer of labor power?'

17. Derrida writes of this 'elementary kinship structure': 'In sum and in general, if one "sets aside all the facts", the logic can be found in all families' (17–18).

18. Irigaray discusses generation as the relation of woman to the pair mother–daughter in terms of a non-complete gift of space–time beyond the circle. See 'The limits of the transference', in *The Irigaray Reader* (1991), 109–10: 'Woman must . . . give birth within herself to mother and daughter in a never-completed progression'. This interior giving birth is 'a story to do with time and the way we measure it'. A new language could discuss this new imaginary: 'The *lips*? . . . The most subtle return . . . without closing the circle'. But, Irigaray concludes, the symbolic for this new imaginary is not yet in place for all to accept affirmatively this 'gift of space–time'. See also Chanter, *Ethics of Eros* (1995), 146–51.

19. Derrida goes on to refer to his reading of Blanchot's *The Madness of the Day* in 'Living on'. See also *The Gift of Death* (1995).

20. In the 'Avant-Propos' to his *Le problème de la genèse dans la philosophie de Husserl* (1990), Derrida cites the contamination of the transcendental–empirical distinction as an abiding concern of all his thought.

21. Gasché, *The Tain of the Mirror* (1986), 217–4; Bennington and Derrida, *Jacques Derrida* (1992), 267–84; Lawlor, *Imagination and Chance* (1992),

14–17, Thompson, 'Hegelian dialectic and the quasi-transcendental in Glas' (1998), 249–54.

22. Derrida, 'Force of Law' (1990), 971: 'Politicization, for example, is interminable, even if it cannot and should not ever be total'.

23. Derrida, 'The Politics of Friendship' (1988), 640–41:

> But the relation to the Other also passes through the universality of the law. This discourse about universality . . . always appeals to a third party, beyond the face-to-face of singularities. The third party is always witness to a law that comes along to interrupt the vertigo of singularity.

24. See on this point what Drucilla Cornell calls the analysis of 'phenomenological symmetry' in her *Philosophy of the Limit* (1992), 175.

25. For an excellent discussion of anti-abortion state intervention as forcing motherhood on women see Rubenfeld, 'The right of privacy' (1989).

26. Beardsworth provides an excellent reading of the relation of Derridean politics and Kant, focusing on aporia, in his *Derrida & the Political* (1996), 61–70.

27. Kant, *Critique of Practical Reason* (1983), 72.

28. See the admirably clear discussion in Lawlor's *Imagination and Chance* (1992), 103–5.

29. Cf. Kant, *Metaphysical Elements of Justice* (1965), 79, on the exclusion of apprentices, servants, minors and 'all women', from active citizenship.

30. Without this qualification, the gift of life would set up a Nietzschean bad conscience, as analysed in *On the Genealogy of Morals*, of debt to the ancestors. My thanks to Richard Findler for bringing this point to my attention.

CHAPTER 4

1. 'General population' is an obnoxious term, as it endorses the marginalization of PLWA (people living with AIDS), but I use it here to indicate those who have accepted the normalizing message about AIDS. For a discussion of AIDS vocabulary see Grover, 'AIDS: Keywords' (1988).

2. The scare quotes point to the insufficiency of a 'pure science' standpoint and to the necessity to conduct politico-economic analyses of the operation of science as it exists – as opposed to how some would like us to think it currently operates or how some might say it should operate were it reformed. 'Cynical' also then deserves scare quotes, since the assumption of the relevance of politico-economic analyses operates beyond a cynical vs naive opposition.

3. I adopt the terminology of restricted and general economies from Derrida's

essay, 'From restricted to general economy: a Hegelianism without reserve', in *Writing and Difference*.

4. 'It is not to be expected that kings will philosophize or that philosophers will become kings; nor is it to be desired, however, since the possession of power inevitably corrupts the free judgment of reason'. Kant, 'Perpetual peace' in *Kant's Political Writings* (191), 115; see also *The Conflict of the Faculties* (1979).

5. The term 'HIV' was only adopted in 1987 as a compromise name by a joint US–France political agreement, settling a suit over patent rights to the antibody test. Gallo had originally named his viral isolate HTLV–III, while Montagnier had named his LAV. See Gallo's self-presentation of the conflict in *Virus Hunting* (1991).

6. Thus avoiding the problems noted by Norris in *Against Relativism* (1997).

7. Despite Gallo's acknowledgement of co-factors to AIDS, he restricts them to influencing the course of the syndrome, for which 'HIV is the sole primary cause of the epidemic called AIDS'. *Virus Hunting* (1991), 283.

8. GRID: 'Gay Related Immune Deficiency'.

9. See Patton, *Inventing AIDS* (1990), 58–61 for a brief comparison of virological and immunological responses to AIDS.

10. Hughes, *The Virus* (1977), xi, dates the recognition of virology as an independent field to 1950.

11. Writing about the history of virology, Hughes quotes a 1966 retrospective on the superiority of bacteriophage (viruses feeding on bacteria) as an experimental object: '3. The investigator had nearly absolute control over the experimental environment'. Hughes, *The Virus* (1977), 90. On the next page she writes that bacteriophage work 'set a new standard for precise, quantitative results'.

12. Or 'magic cocktail', if one preferred a blend of drugs, as became a popular treatment modality in the late 1990s, when AIDS approached the status of a 'manageable disease' for a privileged few.

13. For AZT as a *pharmakon*, see Treichler, 'How to have theory in an epidemic' (1991), 57–106, especially 79–93.

14. Important struggles here include the women's health movement and the earlier struggle of the gay community with the psychiatric establishment.

15. See Radetsky's rather luridly titled *The Invisible Invaders* (1991), xii: 'Viruses are literally everywhere – inside us, outside us, constantly permeating the boundaries of self'. If such 'constant permeation' is indeed the case, then 'inside', 'outside', 'us', 'boundaries' and 'self' need to be rethought and thematically rewritten. Radetsky, caught in the restricted economy of the oppositional cultural imaginary, can only thematically stay with 'us' and 'self' even as his text performs a deconstruction of 'us' and 'self'.

16. 'Multifactorial is multi-ignorance'. Gallo, *Virus Hunting* (1991), 148.

17. For a discussion of the remark, see Derrida, 'The double session' in *La Dissémination* (1972). Commentary is available above in Chapter 3 (on 'quasi-transcendentality'), and in Gasché, Bennington and Derrida, and Lawlor (see note 21, Chapter 3).

18. The reliance of virology on a restricted economy of purely medical investigation is apparent when, amazingly enough, Gallo is able to attribute the 'near-eradication' of the 'American Indians' to their being 'microbially inexperienced', without bothering to mention the effects of the European military invasions and enslavements – cultural destruction, enforced labour, near-starvation, and so on – on the immunological resistance of these people. Similarly, the 1918–19 pandemic of influenza is attributed to the 'coming together of troops from several continents' with no mention of post-war psychic trauma, cold, hunger, etc. *Virus Hunting* (1991), 129–30.

19. This tendency is the most disappointing aspect of Root-Bernstein's *Rethinking AIDS* (1993).

20. Attacks on 'lifestyle' theories are too numerous to count. See Watney, *Policing Desire* (1989), for a good articulation of the political calculation backing the HIV model.

21. Duesberg, 'Human immunodeficiency virus and acquired immunodeficiency syndrome: correlation but not causation' (1991).

22. Sonnabend, 'AIDS: An explanation for its occurrence among homosexual men' (1989).

23. Callen, *Surviving AIDS* (1990).

24. For a discussion of AIDS panic, see Patton, *Sex and Germs* (1985).

25. For a sensitive discussion of this relation, see Critchley, *The Ethics of Deconstruction* (1992). In his latest work, however, Critchley notes that by 1999 'I am more doubtful about the persuasive force of Levinasian ethics in the way it was presented in *The Ethics of Deconstruction*' (*Ethics, Politics, Subjectivity*, 1999, ix). The entire issue of the Levinas/Derrida relation is too complex and difficult to be dealt with fully here. I should therefore reiterate that my reading of Derrida is based on the works of the 1960s through 1990's 'Force of Law'. It may very well be that the growing importance of Levinas in Derrida's thought in the 1990s indicates a move away from the primacy of the general text of force and signification to a primacy of aporia and religion. We could say this amounts to a turn from the breakdown of consciousness into the general text to a breakdown of consciousness into hospitality for the other. Or in other words, that Derrida shifts allies from Nietzsche to Levinas. With his exemplary rigour and insight, Lawlor investigates the Derridean 'turn' in terms of the relation to Nietzsche and Levinas in the Conclusion to his *The Basic Problem of*

Phenomenology, although he prefers to speak of the 'impossibility' of Derrida's 'strange amalgamation of Nietzsche and Levinas'. In any event, whether Derrida shifts allies or simply emphasizes another pole of his thought, it is the Nietzschean and not the Levinasian element in his thought that offers the closest articulation with Deleuzean materialism, which is why I emphasize it throughout Part I prior to these last few paragraphs.

CHAPTER 5

1. Vlastos, *Platonic Studies* (1981), 161. The present chapter can be considered a commentary on this brilliant article, first published in 1941. Although Vlastos came in later years to nuance his findings in this article (see the 'Postscript [1959]' in *Platonic Studies* 1981, 162–3; and *Plato's Universe*, 1975, xiii), I find it expresses the structure of the Platonic body politic with insight and clarity.

2. Although some sort of recognition of the Platonic body politic is quite unavoidable in reading Plato, it would perhaps be useful to list some proof texts for its widespread nature. For the translation of man to city, we have the notion of the unjust city as feverish (Plato, *Gorgias*, 518e; *Republic*, 372d, 405a, 409c, 425e, 444d, 556d), and conversely, the just city as healthy (*Republic*, 444d). For the translation of city to soul, we read of the appetites as the 'motley crowd' of the soul (*pollas kai pantodapas*, 431c; *to pleiston*, 442a; *dēmos te kai plēthos* (*Laws*, 689b)); for the translation of city to man, we read that the function of the soul is to 'rule and deliberate' (*archein kai boulesthai* (*Republic*, 353d)). For the translation of household to man, we see desires as mad masters (329d), and that the soul rules body as master (*Timaeus*, 34c). For the translation of city to cosmos we read of *nous* as 'king' of heaven and earth (*basileus* (*Philebus*, 28c)), and of the soul in cosmos governing (*Laws*, 896c) body. Finally, for the translation of man to cosmos, we see the Forms as father, receptacle as mother, and copy as child (*Timaeus*, 50d).

3. I use 'man' for *anthropos* even though the Greek term does not refer to the male sex (as does *anēr*) and thus could be translated as 'human being'. However, despite the complications brought about by the argument for the possibility of woman guardians in *Republic* 5, it is clear that the properties displayed by those who were masculinized in his time were the paradigmatic human virtues for Plato, and so the translation of *anthropos* by 'human being' in most Platonic contexts would cover over important historical evidence for patriarchal assumptions operating within the philosophical canon.

4. Almost every Plato commentator has noticed some aspect or other of this

isomorphism. Among the most insightful uses occur in Despland, 'The heterosexual body as metaphor in Plato's Religious City' (1991).

5. Because of the frequency with which I will use them, I will use both 'logos' and 'techne' as English markers for the Greek equivalents, with neither italics nor a diacritical mark for the final eta in techne.

6. The organism structure is recognized by Plato commentators of every stripe, hostile or sympathetic. Karl Popper writes: 'A closed society at its best can be justly compared to an organism', *The Open Society and its Enemies* (1963), 173; while Jonathan Lear writes in his 'Plato's politics of narcissism' (1994), 149n46: '[T]he primary sense of justice is a condition of organisms – city or individual – which holds if its parts are well functioning'.

7. See Parry, 'The intelligible world-animal in Plato's *Timaeus*' (1991).

8. See Lambert and Planeaux, 'Who's who in Plato's *Timaeus-Critias* and why' (1998).

9. I'm not concerned in this chapter with the so-called craft analogy for moral wisdom, well-summarized by Roochnik in *Of Art and Wisdom* (1999). Rather than the criterion for the possession of moral wisdom, I'm interested in the production of good character, good cities and households, and the good cosmos by the kingly techne demonstrated in deed in the *Republic* and *Timaeus* and theorized in the *Statesman*. Roochnik's work makes a good case that the early Socratic dialogues use the techne analogy to refute rival claims to moral wisdom or to exhort others to strive for philosophy. But as the Socratic dialogues dramatize the problems that philosophy faces in a complex multicultural, multiclass, city, they precisely demonstrate why a clean slate is needed for the work of the kingly techne, a clean slate that the construction of the city and the cosmos in logos in the *Republic* and the *Timaeus* provides.

10. The source of ordered motion is not the source of all motion, however, as Mohr points out at *The Platonic Cosmology* (1985), 22, in describing the action of the Demiurge.

11. For details on this view of Platonic technical production, see Roochnik, 'The goodness of *Arithmos*' (1994), and *Of Art and Wisdom* (1999).

12. For details on Deleuze and Guattari's sense of the organism, see my 'The organism as the judgment of God' (2001) and Ansell Pearson's *Germinal Life* (1999).

13. Roochnik often cites *Republic*, 522c, to the effect that each techne and episteme 'participates' in arithmetic and calculation. See *Of Art and Wisdom* (1999), 37, for his major discussion of this passage. See also *Statesman*, 285a: 'For all activities directed by arts involve measurement in some form or other'.

14. Roochnik, *On Art and Wisdom* (1999), 52 *et passim*.

15. In 'sensitivity' I would like to have heard both the Greek sense of somatic 'sensibility' (*aesthesis*) and the complexity theory sense of corporeal 'sensitivity' to slight changes in condition possible when systems are 'poised at the edge of chaos' (Kauffman, *At Home in the Universe*, 1995, 28–9).

16. The question of the existence of slaves as support for the citizens of the ideal city of the *Republic* is long and vexed, though there is no question of their existence as support for the citizens of the city of the *Laws*. For an argument affirming the existence of slaves as support for the city of the *Republic*, based in part on their being beneath notice, see Vlastos 'Does slavery exist in Plato's *Republic*', in *Platonic Studies* (1981), 140–46; for a critique of Vlastos and a denial of slavery as support for the ideal city, see Calvert, 'Slavery in Plato's *Republic* (1987). On slavery in the *Laws* see Morrow, 'Plato and Greek slavery' (1939).

17. I am bracketing for the moment the question of the possibility of training women guardians in the ideal city; it is clear from his remarks on women in degenerate cities that Plato regarded contemporary Athenian women as incapable of self-rule. Recall that the origin of the degeneration of the character of the timarch is in part the complaints of the mother to the son about the father (*Republic*, 549d). Note as well that the dictator 'takes refuge in his house and lives there for the most part like a woman . . .' (*Republic*, 579b).

18. Deleuze, 'The Simulacrum and Ancient Philosophy', in *The Logic of Sense* (1990).

19. See Varela, Thompson and Rosch, *The Embodied Mind* (1991); Clark, *Being There* (1997); and Lakoff and Johnson, *Philosophy in the Flesh* (1999). Precious little work has been done on a possible Deleuzean contribution to this area, other than Massumi, 'The autonomy of affect' (1991).

20. Lakoff and Johnson have recourse to the research into 'basic-level categories' by Elizabeth Rosch. In their formulation of Rosch, basic-level categories (e.g. 'bed' as opposed to 'furniture' or 'Queen Ann') have four criteria. They are: (a) the highest level at which a single mental image can represent the entire category; (b) the highest level at which category members have similarly perceived overall shapes; (c) the highest level at which a person uses similar motor actions for interacting with category members; and (d) the level at which most of our knowledge is organized (*Philosophy in the Flesh*, 1999, 27–8). Lakoff and Johnson go on to conclude that basic level categories are thus: (a) body-based; (b) provide optimal interactions; (c) explain the appeal of metaphysical realism; and (d) explain the stability of scientific knowledge by extending basic-level perception, imagination, intervention (28–9).

21. Socratic midwifery, the remembrance of embedded ideas, and the turning

of the soul, all famous Platonic conceptions of philosophic teaching, are irrelevant here in our investigation of technical teaching.

22. Perhaps the most radically anti-Platonic implication of the 'embodied mind' is that the 'body' – somatic skill – is 'smarter' than the 'mind' – rational inference, symbol manipulation, information processing and so on – for it is able to negotiate complex situations in a faster, more fine-grained way. Andy Clark writes that the embodied mind thesis necessitates 'a new vision of the nature of biological cognition: a vision that puts explicit data storage and logical manipulation in its place as, at most, a secondary adjunct to the kinds of dynamics and complex response loops that couple real brains, bodies and environments' (1–2).

23. See Hutchins, *Cognition in the Wild* (1996), for a description of distributed cognition on board contemporary ships as opposed to the arche-fantasy of Plato at *Theatetus*, 170a–b: 'When they are in distress . . . in a storm at sea, all men turn to their leaders [*archontas*] . . . as to God'.

24. See Laks, 'Legislation and demiurgy' (1990) for a detailed discussion of the Platonic notion of possibility in this context.

25. Morrow, 'The Demiurge in politics: the *Timaeus* and the *Laws*' (1954), 7. See also Laks, 'Legislation and demiurgy' (1990).

26. Murrow, *Plato's Cretan City* (1960). Stalley, *An Introduction to Plato's Laws* (1983).

27. Mohr, *The Platonic Cosmology*, (1985), 142.

28. Leucippus fragment 2 (Diels Kranz 67 B 2). For text and commentary, see Bailey, *The Greek Atomists and Epicurus* (1928), 85.

29. Cherniss, 'The sources of evil according to Plato' (1971).

30. Mohr, *The Platonic Cosmology* (1985).

31. Vlastos, 'The Disorderly Motion in the *Timaios*' (1939).

32. Lee Smolin writes in his *tour de force* of contemporary physics, *The Life of the Cosmos* (1997), 143:

> in this dialogue [the *Statesman*] we can see how Western cosmology and political theory arose together from the opposition of the spirit and the body, the eternal and the decaying, the externally imposed order and the internally generated chaos.

33. Major twentieth-century English-language interpretations of the dialogue as a whole include: Taylor, *A Commentary on Plato's Timaeus* (1928); Cornford, *Plato's Cosmology* (1937); and Sallis, *Chorology* (1999). I was first introduced to the *Timaeus* by Sallis' lectures at Loyola Chicago in 1987. Two noteworthy books on the cosmological issues concerning us here are Vlastos, *Plato's Universe* (1975) and Mohr, *The Platonic Cosmology* (1985).

34. Christopher Bobonich, in his 'Persuasion, compulsion and freedom in Plato's *Laws*' (1991), attempts to show that Plato allows a sense of persuasion as the winning of rational assent after argument in the *Laws*. That may be, but it does not concern us in the cosmological context of the Timaeus, as Bobonich himself implies at 388.

35. For the latest contribution, which provides a good though compressed overview of the controversy, see Pendrick, 'Plato, *Timaeus* 52c2–5' (1998).

36. For commentary on these issues see Annas, *Aristotle's Metaphysics M–N* (1976).

37. See Derrida, '*Khōra*' (1993), in *On the Name* (1995).

38. See Sallis, 'Daydream' (1998).

39. In their writings on the *Timaeus* cited above Vlastos and Mohr split company on the question of whether such material self-ordering is compatible with Demiurgic ordering, Vlastos taking the negative and Mohr the affirmative.

40. Deleuze and Guattari, ATP, 483–4/389:

> Arithmetic, the number, has always had a decisive role in the State apparatus. . . . This arithmetic element of the State found its specific power in the treatment of all kinds of matter: primary matters (raw materials), the secondary matter of wrought objects, or the ultimate matter constituted by the human population. Thus the number has always served to gain mastery over matter, to control its variations and movements . . .

CHAPTER 6

1. Fink's phrase, blessed by Husserl, in the former's 'The phenomenological philosophy of Edmund Husserl and contemporary criticism' (1970).

2. The investigations in the *Plato's Sophist* volume, Heidegger tells us, presuppose a phenomenology of Dasein (62/43).

3. This issue is treated exhaustively in McNeill, *The Glance of the Eye* (1999). Chapter 2 of this admirably careful and scholarly work is devoted to Heidegger's reading of Aristotle in the *Plato's Sophist* volume, without, however, thematizing the body politic.

4. For a magisterial treatment of the ancient Greek social context of all the issues treated in this chapter, see de Ste Croix, *The Class Struggle in the Ancient Greek World* (1989).

5. This is of course a fundamental concept for Arendt's *The Human Condition* (1958).

6. My focus on the body politic distinguishes this chapter from David Krell's analysis of the living body in his *Daimon Life* (1992) and John Caputo's plea for justice for the victimized body in *Demythologizing Heidegger* (1993).

7. *Psuchē* as *logos* in the text on Plato making up the greater part of the *Plato's Sophist* volume will be explicated as a *sumplokē*, an interweaving, of the five greatest kinds, but the relation of *psuchē* to *sôma* in the *suntheton* – the relation of temporality and bodily space–time (not Dasein's spatiality, derivative as it is from Dasein's temporality) in the Dasein/human being couplet – is left unexplored by Heidegger.

8. 'Sein gibt es nur, sofern Dasein existiert', *Metaphysical Foundations of Logic* (1984), 194/153.

9. I can only allude in this context to the theme David Krell explores in *Daimon Life* (1992), the problematic relation of animality and Dasein, by noting here that Heidegger does not address Aristotle's discourse on animals in the beginning passages of the *Metaphysics*. Suffice it to say a full exploration of this theme would focus on the body and the vulgar space in which it moves to meet the demands of the necessities through *aisthēsis* and, in some cases, memory. I also note here another point for further discussion of the body in Heidegger: his reading in the *Plato's Sophist* volume of *phronēsis* in *Nicomachean Ethics* 6.5 as the 'struggle [*Kampf*]' against the tendency to covering over in Dasein due to our susceptibility to 'pleasure and pain', which belong to the 'basic constitution of humans [*Grundbestimmung des Menschen*]' (52/36–7). See also Ansell Pearson's comments on Heidegger's relation to biology at *Viroid Life* (1997), 115–16.

10. Arendt follows the Heideggerian formulation of *Handwerker* as artisan at *The Human Condition* (1958), 80.

11. In this reading I follow Patterson's *Freedom* (1992).

12. *Phänomenologische Interpretationen zu Aristoteles* (1985), 92; *Plato's Sophist* (1997) 467/323; *Metaphysical Foundations of Logic* (1984) 183/145.

13. That artisans are 'incarcerated' in *aesthēsis* is a statement I make only from the perspective of the critique of the forceful body politic hidden behind Greek philosophy and Heidegger's reading of the same. As I discuss in Chapter 5, the rehabilitation of artisanal sensitivity, and of the somatic body in general, in the linked contexts of the critique of hylomorphism and the research conducted under the rubric of the 'embodied mind', is one of the most important tasks of contemporary philosophy.

14. I explore these issues in the Conclusion to *Time and Exteriority* (1994).

CHAPTER 7

1. Arendt distinguishes these terms, along with 'strength' and 'power', at *On Violence* (1970), 43–6, but does not mention the lexical/conceptual scope of *Gewalt*. Nor is that term used in her *Lectures on Kant's Political Philosophy* (1982).

2. On the distinction of the 'feeling of life' and merely bodily 'gratification' see *Critique of Judgment*, 1987 section 54. For an extended commentary on Kant's notion of life, see Makkreel, *Imagination and Interpretation in Kant* (1990), Chapter 5, 'The life of the imagination'.

3. David Lachterman provides a sustained interrogation of the juridical metaphor in his 'Kant: the faculty of desire' (1990), which also provides references for discussions of the medical and topological metaphorics in Kant.

4. Arendt develops this theme in her *Lectures on Kant's Political Philosophy* (1982).

5. For an uninhibited exploration of Kant's predilection for 'the fierce delights of martyrdom', see Land, 'Delighted to death' (1991).

6. My interpretation of Kant's moral politics on this and other points is influenced by van der Linden, *Kantian Ethics and Socialism* (1988).

7. The major recent 'continental' commentators mention the notion of 'violence' here, but none connect it to the overall economy of *Gewalt* in Kant. See Makkreel, *Imagination and Interpretation in Kant* (1990), 73; Lyotard, *Lessons* (1994), 143; Sallis, *Spacings* (1987), 117.

8. Although it does not thematize *Gewalt*, a useful treatment of the *Metaphysical Elements of Justice* (1965) can be found in Shell, *The Rights of Reason* (1980). Also available as English-language treatments are Murphy, *Kant: the Philosophy of Right* (1970) and Riley, *Kant's Political Philosophy* (1983). For a critique of the delegation model in the social contract as presupposing a levelling down to the 'average man', see Châtelet, 'Du chaos et de l'auto-organisation comme néo-conservatisme festif' (1995).

9. Here as elsewhere I replicate Kant's gender-specific language.

10. Hans Reiss' article 'Kant and the Right of Rebellion' (1956) is a classic of the post-World War II era. A special edition of *Journal of the History of Ideas*, 32 (1971), includes articles by Lewis White Beck and Sidney Axinn on this topic as well. See also van der Linden, *Kantian Ethics and Socialism* (1988), 165–94.

11. Translation modified. Ladd's translation of *Äusserst-Bösen* as 'extreme perversity' loses the distinction in *Religion* between 'perversity' and 'wickedness'. Kant is here describing the latter, so I chose 'extreme evil' as my translation.

12. Translation modified. Ladd's translation 'everyone may use violent means to compel another', precipitously decides the undecidability of *Gewalt* between force and violence in the context of the historical origin of the state.

13. See Chapter 2. My reading there is constructed in light of three essays by Derrida: 'Déclarations d'indépendence'; 'The Laws of Reflection: Nelson Mandela, In Admiration; and 'Force of Law'. For a comparison of Derrida and Arendt, see Honig, 'Declarations of Independence' (1991).

14. See Chapter 9 of Zammito, *The Genesis of Kant's Critique of Judgment* (1992), for a reconstruction of Kant's relation to contemporary natural science and his insistence on the utter passivity of matter. In avoiding both a mechanism and a metaphysical vitalism Kant was led to sacrifice any realist science of biology in outlawing determinate judgments about organic structure, life and nature. We should note here that the Deleuzean notion of material self-ordering drawn from complexity theory, as experimentally grounded, has nothing to do with the metaphysical speculations Kant derided as 'hylozoism'; another key difference is that between the unity of organic force in hylozoism and the differential materialism of Deleuze.

15. Arendt cites this passage at *Lectures on Kant's Political Philosophy* (1982), 16, but without mentioning the tension between self-organization and hylomorphism.

16. I treat these issues in my 'A problem of pure matter' (2000).

17. On the Deleuzean notion of a 'life of pure immanence' see Smith's Introduction to Deleuze's *Critique et clinique* in *Essays Critical and Clinical* (1997); and May, 'The politics of life in the thought of Gilles Deleuze' (1991). On 'pure life' see Agamben, *Homo Sacer* (1998).

18. A detailed analysis would be necessary to stage the confrontation of this conception of politics (immanence is non-fascism) with that of Phillipe Lacoue-Labarthe's *Heidegger, Art and Politics* (1990), where transcendence breaks open fascist immanence.

AFTERWORD

1. See the excellent article by Holland, 'From schizophrenia to social control' (1998).

2. A crucial mistranslation must be noted here. At ATP 231, the conclusion of the 'Micropolitics and segmentarity' plateau, the English version reads: 'A war machine that no longer had war as its object', instead of the correct 'A war machine that no longer had anything but war as its object'.

3. Deleuze and Guattari make a similar point at ATP, 579/463 in validating the 'struggle on the level of the axioms' (the demand for juridical recognition of 'minorities'). See Chapter 6 of Patton's *Deleuze & the Political* (2000) for a discussion in the Deleuzean terms of 'capture' and 'axiom' of the struggle for native/aboriginal land rights in Canada and Australia.

4. Paul Patton invokes the Deleuzean side of this project with his notion of philosophy as aiming at 'new and creative forms of the counter-actualization of the present' (*Deleuze & the Political*, 2000, 137).

Bibliography

Agamben, Giorgio. *Homo Sacer: Sovereign Power and Bare Life*. Stanford: Stanford University Press, 1998.

Annas, Julia. *Aristotle's Metaphysics M–N*, Oxford: Oxford University Press, 1976.

Ansell Pearson, Keith. *Germinal Life*. London: Routledge, 1999.

— *Viroid Life*. London: Routledge, 1997.

Arendt, Hannah, *The Human Condition*. Chicago: University of Chicago Press, 1958.

— *Lectures on Kant's Political Philosophy*, Chicago: University of Chicago Press, 1982.

— *On Violence*. New York: Harcourt Brace Jovanovich, 1970.

Argyros, Alexander. *A Blessed Rage for Order: Deconstruction, Evolution, and Chaos*. Ann Arbor: University of Michigan Press, 1991.

Aristotle. *The Complete Works of Aristotle*. 2 vols. Edited by Jonathan Barnes. Princeton: Princeton University Press, 1984.

— *De Anima*. Edited by David Ross. Oxford: Clarendon, 1956.

— *De Generatione Animalium*. Edited by H. J. D. Lulofs. Oxford: Clarendon, 1965.

— *Metaphysica*. Edited by Werner Jaeger. Oxford: Clarendon, 1957.

— *Physica*. Edited by David Ross. Oxford: Clarendon, 1950.

Attridge, Derek, ed. *Acts of Literature*. London: Routledge, 1992.

Aubenque, Pierre. *Le problème de l'être chez Aristote*. Paris: PUF, 1972.

Bailey, Cyril. *The Greek Atomists and Epicurus*. New York: Russell & Russell, 1928.

Beardsworth, Richard. *Derrida & the Political*. London: Routledge, 1996.

Bennington, Geoffrey. *Legislations: The Politics of Deconstruction*. London: Verso, 1994.

— and Jacques Derrida. *Jacques Derrida*. Chicago: University of Chicago Press, 1992.

Bobonich, Christopher. 'Persuasion, compulsion and freedom in Plato's *Laws*'. *Classical Quarterly* 41.2 (1991): 365–88.

Bole, Thomas. 'Contradiction in Hegel's *Science of Logic*'. *Review of Metaphysics* 40 (March 1987): 515–34.

Boundas, Constantin. 'Deleuze-Bergson: an ontology of the virtual'. In Patton, ed., *Deleuze: a Critical Reader*. Oxford: Blackwell, 1996.

Bryden, Mary, ed. *Deleuze and Religion*. London: Routledge, 2001.

Butler, Judith. *Bodies That Matter*. London: Routledge, 1993.

Callen, Michael. *Surviving AIDS*. New York: HarperCollins, 1990.

Calvert, Brian. 'Slavery in Plato's *Republic*'. *Classical Quarterly* 37.2 (1987): 367–72.

Caputo, John. *Demythologizing Heidegger*. Bloomington: Indiana University Press, 1993.

Chaffin, Deborah. 'Hegel, Derrida and the sign'. In *Derrida and Deconstruction*. Edited by Hugh Silverman. London: Routledge, 1989.

Chanter, Tina. *Ethics of Eros: Irigaray's Rewriting of the Philosophers*. London: Routledge, 1995.

Châtelet, Gilles. 'Du chaos et de l'auto-organisation comme néo-conservatisme festif'. *Les Temps Modernes* 581 (March–April 1995): 34–69.

Cherniss, Harold. 'The sources of evil according to Plato'. In *Plato: II Ethics, Politics and Philosophy of Art and Religion*. Edited by Gregory Vlastos. New York: Doubleday, 1971.

Clark, Andy. *Being There: Putting Brain, Body, and World Back Together Again*. Cambridge, MA: MIT Press, 1997.

Cohen, Jack and Ian Stewart. *The Collapse of Chaos*. New York: Penguin, 1994.

Collège International de Philosophie, ed. *Gilbert Simondon: Une pensée de l'individuation et de la technique*. Paris: Albin Michel, 1994.

Cornell, Drucilla. *Beyond Accommodation: Ethical Feminism, Deconstruction and the Law*. London: Routledge, 1991.

—— *The Philosophy of the Limit*. London: Routledge, 1992.

Cornford, F.M. *Plato's Cosmology*. London: Routledge & Kegan Paul, 1937.

Crary, Jonathan and Sanford Kwinter, eds. *Incorporations*. New York: Zone Books, 1992.

Critchley, Simon. *The Ethics of Deconstruction: Derrida and Levinas*. Oxford: Blackwell, 1992.

—— *Ethics, Politics, Subjectivity: Essays on Derrida, Levinas and Contemporary French Thought*. London: Verso, 1999.

DeLanda, Manuel. 'Non-organic life'. In *Incorporations*. Edited by Jonathan Crary and Sanford Kwinter. New York: Zone Books, 1992.

—— *A Thousand Years of Nonlinear History*. New York: Zone Books, 1998.

—— *War in the Age of Intelligent Machines*. Cambridge, MA: MIT Press, 1991.

Deleuze, Gilles. *Cinema 1: the Movement-Image*. Translated by Hugh Tomlinson and Barbara Habberjam. London: Athlone Press, 1992. (*Cinema-1: L'Image-mouvement*. Paris: Minuit, 1983.)

— *Cinema 2: the Time-Image*. Translated by Hugh Tomlinson and Robert Galeta. London: Athlone Press, 1994. (*Cinema-2: L'Image-temps*. Paris: Minuit, 1985.)

— *Essays Clinical and Critical*. Translated by Daniel W. Smith and Michael A. Greco. Minneapolis: University of Minnesota Press, 1997. (*Critique et Clinique*. Paris: Minuit, 1993.)

— *Foucault*. Translated by Seán Hand. Minneapolis: University of Minnesota Press, 1988. (*Foucault*. Paris: Minuit, 1986.)

— *The Logic of Sense*. Translated by Mark Lester with Charles Stivale. New York: Columbia University Press, 1990. (*Logique du sens*. Paris: Minuit, 1969.)

— *Negotiations 1972–1990*. Translated by Martin Joughin. New York: Columbia University Press, 1995. (*Pourparlers 1972–1990*, Paris: Minuit, 1990.)

— *Nietzsche and Philosophy*. Translated by Hugh Tomlinson. New York: Columbia University Press, 1983. (*Nietzsche et la philosophie*. Paris: PUF, 1962.)

— Deleuze, Gilles and Félix Guattari. *Anti-Oedipus*. Translated by Robert Hurley, Mark Seem and Helen R. Lane. London: Athlone, 1984. (*L'Anti-Oedipe*. Paris: Minuit, 1972.)

— *A Thousand Plateaus*. Translated by Brian Massumi. Minneapolis: University of Minnesota Press, 1987. (*Mille Plateaux*. Paris: Minuit, 1980.)

— *What is Philosophy?*. Translated by Hugh Tomlinson and Graham Burchell. New York: Columbia University Press, 1994. (*Qu'est-ce que la philosophie?*. Paris: Minuit, 1991.)

Derrida, Jacques. Afterword: toward an ethic of discussion'. In *Limited Inc*. Evanston: Northwestern University Press, 1988.

— *Aporias*. Stanford: Stanford University Press, 1993.

— 'Before the law'. Translated by Avital Ronnell and Christine Roulston. In Attridge, ed. *Acts of Literature*. London: Routledge, 1996. ('Préjugés: devant la loi'. In *La Faculté de Juger*. Paris: Minuit, 1985.)

— 'Declarations of Independence'. Translated by Tom Keenan and Tom Pepper. *New Political Science* 15 (1986): 7–15. ('Déclarations d'indépendence'. In *Otobiographies: l'enseignement de Nietzsche et la politique du nom propre*. Paris: Galilée, 1984.)

— *Dissemination*. Translated by Barbara Johnson. London: Athlone Press, 1981. (*La dissémination*. Paris: Seuil, 1972.

— *The Ear of the Other: Otobiography, Transference, Translation*. Partially translated by Peggy Kamuf. Lincoln: University of Nebraska Press, 1988. (*Otobiographies: l'enseignement de Nietzsche et la politique du nom propre*. Paris: Galilée, 1984.)

— *Edmund Husserl's 'Origin of Geometry': An Introduction*. Translated by John Leavey. Edited by David Allison. New York: Nicholas Hays, 1977. (*Traduction et Introduction à L'Origine de la Géometrie de Edmund Husserl*. Paris: PUF, 1962.

— *L'éthique du don: Jacques Derrida et la pensée du don*. Paris: Métailié-Transition, 1992.

— 'Force of law: the mystical foundation of authority'. Translated by Mary Quanitance. In *Cardozo Law Review* 11 (1990): 919–1045. ('Force de loi: Le "Fondement mystique de l'authorité"'.)

— 'Force and signification'. Translated by Alan Bass. In *Writing and Difference*. Chicago: University of Chicago Press, 1978. ('Force et signification'. In *L'écriture et la différence*. Paris: Seuil, 1967.)

— 'Form and meaning'. Translated by Alan Bass. In *Margins: of Philosophy*. Chicago: University of Chicago Press, 1982. ('La forme et la vouloir-dire: note sur la phénoménologie du language'. In *Marges: de la philosophie*. Paris: Minuit, 1972.)

— *The Gift of Death*. Translated by David Wills. Chicago: University of Chicago Press, 1995. (*Donner la mort*. In *L'éthique du don: Jacques Derrida et le pensée du don*. Paris: Métailié-Transition, 1992.)

— *Given Time: I. Counterfeit Money*. Translated by Peggy Kamuf. Chicago: University of Chicago Press, 1992. (*Donner le temps*. Paris: Galilée, 1991.)

— *Glas*. Translated by John Leavey and Richard Rand. Lincoln: University of Nebraska Press, 1986. (*Glas*. Paris: Galilée, 1974.)

— *Of Grammatology*. Translated by Gayatri Spivak. Baltimore: Johns Hopkins University Press, 1975. (*De la grammatologie*. Paris: Minuit, 1967.)

— *Khōra*. Translated by Ian McLeod. In *On the Name*. Edited by Thomas Dutoit. Stanford: Stanford University Press, 1995. (*Khōra*. Paris: Galilée, 1993.)

— 'The laws of reflection: Nelson Mandela, in Admiration'. Translated by Mary Ann Caws and Isabelle Lorenz. In *For Nelson Mandela*. Edited by Jacques Derrida and Mustapha Tlili. New York: Henry Holt, 1987. ('Admiration de Nelson Mandela ou les lois de réflexion'. In *Psyché. Inventions de l'autre*. Paris: Galilée, 1987.)

— *Limited Inc*. Evanston: Northwestern University Press, 1988.

— 'Living on. Border lines'. Translated by James Hulbert. In *Deconstruction and Criticism*. Edited by Harold Bloom *et al*. New York: Seabury Press, 1979. ('Survivre. Journal de bord'. In *Parages*. Paris: Galilée, 1986.)

— *Margins: of Philosophy*. Translated by Alan Bass. Chicago: University of Chicago Press, 1982. (*Marges: de la philosophie*. Paris: Minuit, 1972.)

— *Memoires – for Paul de Man*. Translated by Cecile Lindsay, Jonathan Culler, Eduardo Cadava and Peggy Kamuf. New York: Columbia University Press, 1989. (*Mémoires: pour Paul de Man*. Paris: Galilée, 1988.)

— *On the Name*. Edited by Thomas Dutoit. Stanford: Stanford University Press, 1995.

— *Parages*. Paris: Galilée, 1986.

— 'The politics of friendship'. Partially translated by Gabriel Motzkin. *The*

Journal of Philosophy 85.11 (1988): 632–45. (*Politiques de l'amitié*. Paris: Galilée, 1994.)

— *Positions*. Translated by Alan Bass. Chicago: University of Chicago Press, 1981. (*Positions*. Paris: Minuit, 1972.)

— *The Post Card: From Socrates to Freud and Beyond*. Translated by Alan Bass. Chicago: University of Chicago Press, 1987. (*La Carte postale: de Socrate à Freud et au-delà*. Paris: Aubier-Flammarion, 1980.)

— *Le Problème de la genèse dans la philosophie de Husserl*. Paris: PUF, 1990.

— *Psyché: inventions de l'autre*. Paris: Galilée, 1987.

— 'The *retrait* of metaphor'. Translated by F. Gasdner *et al*. *Enclitic*, 2.2 (Fall 1978): 5–33. ('Le retrait de la métaphore'. In *Psyché: inventions de l'autre*. Paris: Galilée, 1987.)

— 'Signature event context'. Translated by Alan Bass. In *Margins: of Philosophy*. Chicago: University of Chicago Press, 1982. ('Signature evenement contexte'. In *Marges: de la philosphie*. Paris: Minuit, 1972.)

— *Speech and Phenomena*. Translated by David Allison. Evanston: Northwestern University Press, 1973. (*La voix et le phénomène*. Paris: PUF, 1967.)

— *Specters of Marx*. Translated by Peggy Kamuf. London: Routledge, 1994. (*Spectres de Marx*. Paris: Galilée, 1993.)

— *Spurs: Nietzsche's Styles*. Translated by Barbara Harlow. Chicago: University of Chicago Press, 1976. (*Eperons: les Styles de Nietzsche*. Paris: Flammarion, 1978.)

— *Writing and Difference*. Translated by Alan Bass. Chicago: University of Chicago Press, 1978. (*L'écriture et la différence*. Paris: Seuil, 1967.)

Despland, Michel. 'The heterosexual body as metaphor in Plato's Religious City'. *Religion* 21 (1991): 31–50.

de Ste Croix, G.E.M. *The Class Struggle in the Ancient Greek World*. Ithaca: Cornell University Press, 1989.

Dillon, M.C. *Semiological Reductionism: a Critique of the Deconstructionist Movement in Postmodern Thought*. Albany: SUNY Press, 1995.

Doyle, Richard. *On Beyond Living*. Stanford: Stanford University Press, 1994.

Duesberg, Peter. 'Human immunodeficiency virus and acquired immunodeficiency syndrome: correlation but not causation'. In *The AIDS Reader: Social Political Ethical Issues*. Edited by Nancy F. McKenzie. New York: Penguin, 1991.

Engels, Friedrich. *The Origin of the Family, Private Property, and The State*. Translated by Alick West. Edited by Michèle Barrett. New York: Penguin, 1985.

Fink, Eugen. 'The phenomenological philosophy of Edmund Husserl and contemporary criticism'. In *The Phenomenology of Husserl: Selected Critical Readings*. Edited by R.O. Elveton. Chicago: Quadrangle Books, 1970.

Foucault, Michel. *Discipline and Punish: the Birth of the Prison.* Translated by Alan Sheridan. New York: Vintage, 1979. (*Surveiller et punir: Naissance de la prison.* Paris: Gallimard, 1975.)

— *The History of Sexuality. Volume I: an Introduction.* Translated by Robert Hurley. New York: Pantheon, 1978. (*Histoire de la sexualité I: La Volonté de savoir.* Paris: Gallimard, 1976.)

— 'Polemics, politics, and problematizations'. In *The Foucault Reader.* Edited by Paul Rabinow. New York: Pantheon, 1984.

Gallo, Robert. *Virus Hunting: AIDS, Cancer, and the Human Retrovirus: a Story of Scientific Discovery.* New York: Basic Books, 1991.

Garner, Shirley, Claire Kahane and Madelon Sprengnether, eds. *The (M)other Tongue: Essays in Feminist Psychoanalytic Interpretation.* Ithaca: Cornell University Press, 1985.

Gasché, Rodolphe. *The Tain of the Mirror.* Cambridge MA: Harvard University Press, 1986.

Gill, Mary Louise. 'Matter and flux in Plato's *Timaeus*'. *Phronesis* 32.1 (1987): 34–53.

Gross, Paul and Norman Levitt. *Higher Superstition: the Academic Left and its Quarrels with Science.* Baltimore: Johns Hopkins University Press, 1994.

Grover, Jan Zita. 'AIDS: keywords'. In *AIDS: Cultural Analysis/Cultural Activism.* Edited by Douglas Crimp. Cambridge, MA: MIT Press, 1988.

Haraway, Donna. 'The biopolitics of postmodern bodies: determinations of self in immune system discourse'. *Differences* 1.1 (1989): 3–43. Reprinted in *Simians, Cyborgs, and Women: The Reinvention of Nature.* London: Routledge, 1991.

Hardt, Michael. *Gilles Deleuze: an Apprenticeship in Philosophy.* Minneapolis: University of Minnesota Press, 1993.

— and Antonio Negri. *Empire.* Cambridge, MA: Harvard University Press, 2000.

Hayles, N. Katherine. *Chaos Bound: Orderly Disorder in Contemporary Literature and Science.* Ithaca: Cornell University Press, 1990.

Hegel, G.W.F. *Hegel's Logic.* Translated by William Wallace. Oxford: Oxford University Press, 1975. (*Werke in zwanzig Bänden (8): Enzyklopädie der philosophischen Wissenshaften (1830): Erster Teil: Die Wissenshaft der Logik.*)

— *Hegel's Science of Logic.* Translated by A.V. Miller. Atlantic Highlands: Humanities International Press, 1989. (*Werke in zwanzig Bänden (5–6): Wissenschaft der Logik.* Frankfurt: Surhkamp, 1969.)

— *Lectures on the Philosophy of World History: Introduction: Reason in History.* Translated by H.B. Nisbet. Cambridge: Cambridge University Press, 1975. (*Werke in zwanzig Bänden (12): Vorlesungen über die Philosophie der Geschichte.* Frankfurt: Suhrkamp, 1970.)

— *Phenomenology of Spirit.* Translated by A. V. Miller. Oxford: Oxford University Press, 1977. (*Werke in zwanzig Bänden (3): Phänomenologie des Geistes.* Frankfurt: Surkamp, 1970.)

Heidegger, Martin. *The Basic Problems of Phenomenology.* Translated by Albert Hofstadter. Bloomington: Indiana University Press, 1982. (*Die Grundprobleme der Phänomenologie.* Gesamtausgaße volume 24. Frankfurt: Klostermann, 1975.)

— *Being and Time.* Translated by John Macquarrie and Edward Robinson. New York: Harper & Row, 1962. (*Sein und Zeit.* Tübingen: Max Niemeyer Verlag, 1984.)

— *The Metaphysical Foundations of Logic.* Translated by Michael Heim. Bloomington: Indiana University Press, 1984. (*Metaphysische Anfangsgründe der Logik.* Gesamtausgaße volume 26. Frankfurt: Klostermann, 1978.)

— *Phänomenologische Interpretationen zu Aristoteles.* Gesamtausgaße volume 61. Frankfurt: Klostermann, 1985.

— *Plato's Sophist.* Translated by Richard Rojcewicz and André Schuwer. Bloomington: Indiana University Press, 1997. (*Platon: Sophistes.* Gesamtausgaße volume 19. Frankfurt: Klostermann, 1992.)

Henry, Michel. *Marx: a Philosophy of Human Reality.* Translated by Kathleen McLaughlin. Bloomington: Indiana University Press, 1983.

Holland, Eugene. *Deleuze and Guattari's* Anti-Oedipus: *Introduction to Schizoanalysis.* London: Routledge, 1999.

— 'From schizophrenia to social control'. In Kaufman and Heller, eds, *Deleuze and Guattari: New Mappings in Politics, Philosophy, and Culture.* Minneapolis: University of Minnesota Press, 1998.

Honig, Bonnie. 'Declarations of independence: Arendt and Derrida on the problem of founding a republic'. *American Political Science Review* 85.1 (March 1991): 97–113.

Hottois, Gilbert. *Simondon et la philosophie de la culture technique.* Brussels: De Boeck, 1992.

Hughes, Sally. *The Virus: a History of the Concept.* New York: Science History Publications, 1977.

Husserl, Edmund. *Cartesian Meditations.* Translated by Dorion Cairns. The Hague: Nijhoff, 1960. (*Cartesianische Meditationen und Pariser Vorträge.* Husserliana I. Edited by S. Strasser. The Hague: Nijhoff, 1950.)

— *Ideas Pertaining to a Pure Phenomenology and to a Phenomenological Philosophy. Book I: General Introduction to Pure Phenomenology.* Translated by Fred Kersten. The Hague: Nijhoff, 1982. (*Ideen zu einer reinen Phänomenologie und phänomenologischen Philosophie. Erstes Buch: Allgemeine Einführung in die reine Phänomenologie.* Husserliana III. Edited by Walter Biemel. The Hague: Nijhoff, 1950.)

— *Logical Investigations.* Translated by J. N. Findlay. 2 vols. London: Routledge

& Kegan Paul, 1970. (*Logische Untersuchungen.* 2 vols. Husserliana XVIII–XIX. Edited by Elmar Holenstein and Ursula Panzer. The Hague: Nijhoff, 1975–82.)

Hutchins, Edwin. *Cognition in the Wild.* Cambridge MA: MIT Press, 1996.

Irigaray, Luce. *The Irigaray Reader.* Edited by Margaret Whitford. Oxford: Blackwell, 1991.

— *Speculum of the Other Woman.* Translated by G.C. Gill. Ithaca: Cornell University Press, 1985.

— *This Sex Which is Not One.* Translated by C. Porter with C. Burke. Ithaca: Cornell University Press, 1985.

Johnson, Christopher. 'Derrida and science'. *Revue Internationale de Philosophie* 205 (1998): 477–93.

Kant, Immanuel. *The Conflict of the Faculties.* Translated by Mary J. Gregor. New York: Abaris, 1979.

— *Critique of Judgment.* Translated by Werner S. Pluhar. Indianapolis: Hackett, 1987.

— *Critique of Practical Reason.* Translated by Lewis White Beck. Indianapolis: Bobbs-Merrill, 1983.

— *Critique of Pure Reason.* Translated by Norman Kemp Smith. New York: St. Martin's Press, 1965.

— *Grounding for the Metaphysics of Morals.* Translated by James W. Ellington. Indianapolis: Hackett, 1983.

— *Kants gesammelte Schriften.* Berlin: Königlich Preussliche Akademie der Wissenschaften, 1902–.

— *Kant's Political Writings.* Edited by Hans Reiss. Cambridge: Cambridge University Press, 1991.

— *The Metaphysical Elements of Justice.* Translated by John Ladd. London: Macmillan, 1965.

— *Religion within the Limits of Reason Alone.* Translated by Theodore M. Greene and Hoyt H. Hudson. New York: Harper & Row, 1960.

Kantorowitz, Ernst. *The King's Two Bodies: an Essay in Mediaeval Political Theology.* Princeton: Princeton University Press, 1957.

Kauffman, Stuart. *At Home in the Universe.* Oxford: Oxford University Press, 1995.

Kaufman, Eleanor and Kevin Jon Heller, eds. *Deleuze and Guattari: New Mappings in Politics, Philosophy, and Culture.* Minneapolis: University of Minnesota Press, 1998.

Keller, Evelyn Fox. *Refiguring Life: Metaphors of Twentieth-Century Biology*. New York: Columbia University Press, 1995.

Kelly, Kevin. *Out of Control: the New Biology of Machines, Social Systems, and the Economic World*. Reading MA: Addison-Wesley, 1994.

Kolb, David. *The Critique of Pure Modernity: Hegel, Heidegger and After*. Chicago: University of Chicago Press, 1986.

Krell, David Farrell. *Daimon Life: Heidegger and Life-Philosophy*. Bloomington: Indiana University Press, 1992.

Kristeva, Julia. *The Kristeva Reader*. Edited by Toril Moi. New York: Columbia University Press, 1986.

Lachterman, David. 'Kant: the faculty of desire'. *Graduate Faculty Philosophy Journal* 13.2 (1990): 181–211.

Lacoue-Labarthe, Phillipe. *Heidegger, Art and Politics: The Fiction of the Political*. Translated by Chris Turner. Oxford: Blackwell, 1990.

Lakoff, George and Mark Johnson. *Philosophy in the Flesh: the Embodied Mind and its Challenge to Western Thought*. New York: Basic Books, 1999.

Laks, André. 'Legislation and demiurgy: on the relationship between Plato's *Republic* and *Laws*'. *Classical Antiquity* 9.2 (1990): 209–29.

Lambert, L. and C. Planeaux. 'Who's who in Plato's *Timaeus-Critias* and why'. *The Review of Metaphysics* 52.1 (1998): 87–125.

Land, Nick. 'Delighted to death'. *PLI: Warwick Journal of Philosophy*. 3.2 (1991): 76–88.

— 'Making it with death: remarks on Thanatos and desiring-production'. *Journal of the British Society for Phenomenology* 24.1 (January 1993): 66–76.

Lawlor, Leonard. *The Basic Problem of Phenomenology*. Bloomington: Indiana University Press, forthcoming.

— *Imagination and Chance*. Albany: SUNY Press, 1992.

Lear, Jonathan. 'Plato's politics of narcissism'. In *Virtue, Love and Form: Essays in Honor of Gregory Vlastos*. Edited by Terrence Irwin and Martha Nussbaum. Edmonton: Academic Press, 1994.

Levinas, Emmanuel. *The Theory of Intuition in Husserl's Phenomenology*. Evanston: Northwestern University Press, 1973.

— *Totality and Infinity*. Translated by Alphonso Lingis. Pittsburgh: Duquesne University Press, 1969. (*Totalité et Infini: essai sur l'extériorité*. The Hague: Nijhoff, 1971

Lyotard, Jean-François. *Lessons on the Analytic of the Sublime*. Translated by Elizabeth Rottenberg. Stanford: Stanford University Press, 1994.

McNeill, William. *The Glance of the Eye: Heidegger, Aristotle and the Ends of Theory*. Albany: SUNY Press, 1999.

McRobert, Laurie. 'On fractal thought: Derrida, Hegel, and chaos science'. *History of European Ideas* 20.4–6 (1995): 815–821.

Makkreel, Rudolph. *Imagination and Interpretation in Kant: the Hermeneutical Import of the Critique of Judgment*. Chicago: University of Chicago Press, 1990.

Marx, Karl. *Capital*. Volume 1. New York: International Publishers, 1967.

Massumi, Brian. 'The autonomy of affect'. In Patton, P., ed. *Deleuze: a Critical Reader*. Oxford: Blackwell, 1996.

— *A User's Guide to Capitalism and Schizophrenia: Deviations from Deleuze and Guattari*. Cambridge, MA: MIT Press, 1992.

May, Todd. 'The politics of life in the thought of Gilles Deleuze'. *SubStance* 20.3 no. 66 (Winter 1991): 24–35.

— *Reconsidering Difference: Nancy, Derrida, Levinas, Deleuze*. University Park: Pennsylvania State University Press, 1997.

Mohr, Richard. *The Platonic Cosmology*. Leiden: Brill, 1985.

Morrow, Glenn. 'The Demiurge in politics: the *Timaeus* and the *Laws*'. *Proceedings and Addresses of the American Philosophical Association* 27 (1954): 5–23.

— 'Plato and Greek slavery'. *Mind* 48 (1939): 186–201.

Murphy, Jeffrie G. *Kant: the Philosophy of Right*. London: Macmillan, 1970.

— *Plato's Cretan City: a Historical Interpretation of the Laws*. Princeton: Princeton University Press, 1960.

Murphy, Timothy. 'Quantum ontology: a virtual mechanics of becoming'. In Kaufman and Heller, eds, *Deleuze and Guattari: New Mappings in Politics, Philosophy, and Culture*. Minneapolis: University of Minnesota Press, 1998.

Nancy, Jean-Luc. *Hegel: L'inquiétude du négatif*. Paris: Hachette, 1997.

Negri, Antonio and Michael Hardt. *Labor of Dionysus: a Critique of the State Form*. Minneapolis: University of Minnesota Press, 1994.

Nietzsche, Friedrich. 'On truth and lies in an extra-moral sense'. In *Philosophy and Truth: Selections from Nietzsche's Notebooks of the Early 1870s*. Edited by Daniel Breazeale. Atlantic Highlands: Humanities Press, 1979.

— *La Volonté de Puissance*. Translated by G. Bianquis. Paris: NRF, 1935–37.

— *The Will to Power*. Translated by Walter Kaufman and R.J. Hollingdale. New York: Vintage, 1968.

Norris, Christopher. *Against Relativism: Philosophy of Science, Deconstruction and Critical Theory*. Oxford: Blackwell, 1997.

Oliver, Kelly. *Reading Kristeva: Unraveling the Double Bind*. Bloomington: Indiana University Press, 1993.

— *Womanizing Nietzsche*. London: Routledge, 1994.

Parry, R.D. 'The intelligible world-animal in Plato's *Timaeus*'. *Journal of the History of Philosophy* 29.1 (Jan 1991): 13–32.

Patterson, Orlando. *Freedom: Freedom in the Making of Western Culture*. Volume 1. New York: Basic Books, 1992.

Patton, Cindy. *Inventing AIDS*. London: Routledge, 1990.

— *Sex and Germs: the Politics of AIDS*. Boston: South End Press, 1985.

Patton, Paul, ed. *Deleuze: a Critical Reader*. Oxford: Blackwell, 1996.

— *Deleuze and the Political*. London: Routledge, 2000.

— 'Strange proximity: *Deleuze et Derrida dans les parages du concept*'. *Oxford Literary Review* 18.1–2 (1996): 117–33.

— and John Protevi, eds. *Between Derrida and Deleuze*. London: Athlone Press, forthcoming.

Pendrick, GJ. 'Plato, *Timaeus* 52c2–5'. *Classical Quarterly* 48.2 (1998): 556–9.

Penrose, Roger. *The Emperor's New Mind*. New York: Penguin, 1991.

Plato. *The Collected Dialogues of Plato*. Edited by Edith Hamilton and Huntington Cairns. Princeton: Princeton University Press, 1961.

— *Opera*. Edited by John Burnet. Oxford: Clarendon, 1905–13.

Plotnitsky, Arkady. '"But it is Above all Not True": Derrida, Relativity, and the "science wars"'. *Postmodern Culture* 7.2 (January 1997): 1–30.

— *Complementarity: Anti-Epistemology after Bohr and Derrida*. Durham: Duke University Press, 1994.

Popper, Karl. *The Open Society and its Enemies*. 2 volumes. Princeton: Princeton University Press, 1963.

Prigogine, Ilya and Isabelle Stengers. *Order Out of Chaos: Man's New Dialogue with Nature*. New York: Bantam, 1984.

Protevi, John. 'The economy of exteriority in Derrida's *Speech and Phenomena*'. *Man and World* 26.4 (1993): 373–88.

— 'The organism as the judgment of God: Aristotle, Kant and Deleuze on nature (that is, on biology, theology and politics)'. In Bryden, ed., *Deleuze and Religion*. London: Routledge, 2001.

— 'A problem of pure matter: Deleuze and Guattari's treatment of fascist nihilism in *A Thousand Plateaus*'. In *Nihilism Now!: 'Monsters of Energy'*. Edited by Keith Ansell Pearson and Diane Morgan. London: Macmillan, 2000.

— Review of Richard Beardsworth, *Derrida & the Political. PLI: Warwick Journal of Philosophy*, 6 (Summer 1997), 133–7.

— Review of Keith Ansell Pearson, *Viroid Life*. In *Parallax* 8 (1998), 156–8.

— 'The "sense" of "sight": Heidegger and Merleau-Ponty on the meaning of bodily and existential sight'. *Research in Phenomenology*, 28 (1998): 211–23.

— *Time and Exteriority: Aristotle, Heidegger, Derrida*. Lewisbug: Bucknell University Press, 1994.

Radetsky Peter. *The Invisible Invaders: the Story of the Emerging Age of Viruses*. Boston: Little, Brown, 1991.

Rajchman, John. *Constructions*. Cambridge, MA: MIT Press, 1998.

Reiss, Hans. 'Kant and the right of rebellion'. *Journal of the History of Ideas* 17 (1956): 179–92.

Ricoeur, Paul. *The Rule of Metaphor*. Translated by Robert Czerny with Kathleen McLauglin and John Costello. Toronto: University of Toronto Press, 1977.

Riley, Patrick. *Kant's Political Philosophy*. Totowa: Rowman & Littlefield, 1983.

Roochnik, David. 'The goodness of *Arithmos*'. *American Journal of Philology* 115 (1994): 543–63.

— *Of Art and Wisdom: Plato's Understanding of Techne*. University Park: The Pennsylvania State University Press, 1999.

Root-Bernstein, Robert. *Rethinking AIDS: the Tragic Cost of Premature Consensus*. New York: Free Press, 1993.

Rotman, Brian. *Ad Infinitum: the Ghost in Turing's Machine*. Stanford: Stanford University Press, 1993.

Rubenfeld, Jed. 'The right of privacy'. *Harvard Law Review* 102.1 (Feb 1989): 737–807.

Sallis, John. *Chorology: On Beginning in Plato's Timaeus*. Bloomington: Indiana University Press, 1999.

— 'Daydream'. *Revue Internationale de Philosophie* 52.3 (1998): 397–410.

— *Delimitations: Phenomenology and the End of Metaphysics*. Bloomington: Indiana University Press, 1986.

— *Spacings – of Reason and Imagination*. Chicago: University of Chicago Press, 1987.

Sarkar, Sahotra. *Genetics and Reductionism*. Cambridge: Cambridge University Press, 1998.

Shell, Susan Meld. *The Rights of Reason: a Study of Kant's Philosophy and Politics*. Toronto: University of Toronto Press, 1980.

Simondon, Gilbert. *L'individu et sa genèse physico-biologique*. Paris: PUF, 1964.

— *Du mode d'existence des objets techniques*. Paris: Aubier, 1969.

Smith, Daniel. 'The doctrine of univocity: Deleuze's ontology of immanence'. In Bryden, ed., *Deleuze and Religion*. London: Routledge, 2001.

— '"A life of pure immanence": Deleuze's "Critique et Clinique" project'. In Daniel W. Smith and Michael A. Greco, trans. *Essays Clinical and Critical*. Minneapolis: University of Minnesota Press, 1997.

Smith, Robert. 'Short cuts to Derrida'. *Oxford Literary Review*, 18.1–2 (1996): 135–44.

Smolin, Lee. *The Life of the Cosmos*. Oxford: Oxford University Press, 1997.

Sokal, Alan. 'A physicist experiments with cultural studies'. *Lingua Franca* 6.4 (1996): 62–4.

—— 'Transgressing the boundaries – towards a transformative hermeneutics of quantum gravity'. *Social Text* 46–47 (1996): 217–52.

—— and Jean Bricmont. *Fashionable Nonsense: Postmodern Intellectuals and the Abuse of Science*. New York: Picador, 1998.

Sonnabend, Joseph. 'AIDS: an explanation for its occurrence among homosexual men'. In *AIDS and Infections of Homosexual Men*, 2nd edition. Edited by P. Ma and D. Armstrong. Boston: Butterworth, 1989.

Stalley, R.F. *An Introduction to Plato's Laws*. Oxford: Blackwell, 1983.

Steinbock, Anthony. *Home and Beyond: Generative Phenomenology After Husserl*. Evanston: Northwestern University Press, 1995.

Taylor, A.E. *A Commentary on Plato's Timaeus*. Oxford: Oxford University Press, 1928.

Theweleit, Klaus. *Male Fantasies*. 2 vols. Minneapolis: University of Minnesota Press, 1987–9.

Thompson, Kevin. 'Hegelian dialectic and the quasi-transcendental in *Glas*'. In *Hegel after Derrida*. Edited by Stuart Barnett. London: Routledge, 1998.

Tran, Duc Thao. *Phenomenology and Dialectical Materialism*. Dordrecht: Reidel, 1986.

Treichler, Paula. 'How to have theory in an epidemic: the evolution of AIDS treatment activism'. In *Technoculture*. Edited by C. Penley and A. Ross. Minneapolis: University of Minnesota Press, 1991.

van der Linden, Harry. *Kantian Ethics and Socialism*. Indianapolis: Hackett, 1988.

Varela, Francisco, Evan Thompson and Eleanor Rosch. *The Embodied Mind: Cognitive Science and Human Experience*. Cambridge, MA: MIT Press, 1991.

Vlastos, Gregory. 'The disorderly motion in the *Timaios*'. *Classical Quarterly* 33.2 (April 1939): 71–83.

—— *Platonic Studies*. Princeton: Princeton University Press, 1981.

—— *Plato's Universe*. Seattle: University of Washington Press, 1975.

Watney, Simon. *Policing Desire: Pornography, AIDS, and the Media*, 2nd edition. Minneapolis: University of Minnesota Press, 1989.

Welton, Donn. 'Husserl's genetic phenomenology of perception'. In *Husserl and Contemporary Thought*. Edited by John Sallis. Atlantic Highlands: Humanities Press, 1983.

—— *The Origins of Meaning*. The Hague: Nijhoff, 1983.

Whitford, Margaret. *Luce Irigaray: Philosophy in the Feminine*. London: Routledge, 1991.

Zammito, John. *The Genesis of Kant's* Critique of Judgment. Chicago: University of Chicago Press, 1992.

Index

AIDS, 13, 92–105, 107–11,
214–16; and meaning, 107–10;
and scientific truth, 95–100; and
sexual identity, 104–107
alterity: of democratic justice, 71; of
force, 28, 30; of the gift of life,
88; of matter, 6, 19, 43–4; of
the mother, 81–2; of the re-
mark, 49; of woman, 73
Anima, De, 155, 156
'Aphorism Countertime', 78
Apology, 121, 132, 136
arche-thinking, 8–9, 11, 13, 33
architect: as figure of hylomorphic
production, 7–8, 14, 170, 205;
in Aristotle, 150–2, 157–60,
164; in Heidegger, 166, 168–9;
in Kant, 189–90; in Plato,
121–3, 128, 137, 143, 148. *See
also* hylomorphism; techne
Arendt, Hannah, 195
Aristotle: and *aisthesis*, 150, 157,
163, 167; and generation
('teleological semenology') 13,
67, 72, 78–81, 212; Heidegger's
reading of, 149–69; and justice,
70; and law, 196; and leisure,
165, 167; and mathematics, 146;
and motion, 155–6; and nous,
141, 165; and techne, 120, 122,
157–61
artisan(s), 8, 14, 206, 222; in

Aristotle, 150, 152, 157–60,
163–64, 167–9; in Plato, 117,
123–4, 127–8, 130–3, 135–7,
143, 145, 148. *See also*
hylomorphism
authority: and *différance*, 28, 91; in
Kant, 170–1, 174–91; 'mystical
force of,' 4, 46, 66; in Plato,
115; and revolution, 196

Bennington, Geoffrey, 86
Basic Problems of Phenomenology, 151,
156, 166
Being and Time, 150, 152, 158
biology: and AIDS, 97, 98, 102,
120; and Aristotle, 168; and
complexity, 203; in Deleuze, 7,
211; in Derrida, 211; and gift of
life, 84; in Kant, 7, 224; as
register of bodies politic, 3, 7, 62
bisexuality, 106
body politic: academic, 107–10;
aesthetic (Kantian), 178–81;
Aristotelian, 156; civic or eco-
civic, 89–91, 136–40, 160,
166–7, 191; cognitive (Kantian),
172–6; and complexity theory,
8, 11, 17; conscious or
phenomenological (Husserlian),
12, 18, 23–8, 38–40, 44, 210;
corporeal, 127, 130, 167;
cosmic, 140–8; ethical (Kantian),